Andrews University

Seventh-day Adventist Theological Seminary

TOWARDS A MISSIOLOGICAL MODEL FOR WORLDVIEW
TRANSFORMATION AMONG ADHERENTS TO
AFRICAN TRADITIONAL RELIGION
IN YORUBALAND

A Dissertation

Presented in Partial Fulfillment

of the Requirements for the Degree

Doctor of Philosophy

by

Kelvin Okey Onongha

April 2014

© 2016 EMS Press
All rights reserved. No part of this work may be reproduced or transmitted in any form or by any means, electronics or mechanical, including photocopying and recording, without the prior permission of the publisher. The only exceptions are brief quotations in printed reviews.

Published by EMS Press
5511 SE Hawthorne Blvd., Portland, OR 97215
www.emsweb.org

Towards a Missiological Model for Worldview Transformation among Adherents to African Traditional Religion in Yorubaland
By Kelvin Okey Onongha

ISBN: 978-1-945607-02-8

ABSTRACT OF GRADUATE STUDENT RESEARCH

Dissertation

Andrews University

Seventh-day Adventist Theological Seminary

Title: TOWARDS A MISSIOLOGICAL MODEL FOR WORLDVIEW TRANSFORMATION AMONG ADHERENTS TO AFRICAN TRADITIONAL RELIGION IN YORUBALAND

Name of the researcher: Kelvin Okey Onongha

Name and degree of faculty adviser: Bruce L. Bauer, D.Miss.

Date completed: April 2014

Seventh-day Adventist missions in the western region of Nigeria are a century old, yet reversion to pre-Christian practices such as divination and sorcery are reported, especially during periods of personal crises. This study sought to understand the influence of the traditional worldview on the practices of divination and sorcery and to develop a model that would move the Yoruba Adventists from dependence on these practices to a biblically shaped faith and praxis.

A grounded theory approach was adopted for conducting this qualitative research. Data were collected from two focus group discussions and from face-to-face interviews with five pastors, five diviners, and three members who had once consulted diviners.

Concepts that emerged from the analyzed data revealed the need for a theory of worldview transformation. This theory entailed having better biblical explanations to counter existing worldview assumptions, the exigency of encountering the power of the gospel in a power-oriented context, and the importance of experiential relationships with Christ to replace the role of diviners in that context.

The study culminated in a worldview transformation model that would lead Yoruba Adventists away from dependence upon pre-Christian customs to a biblically shaped worldview, and authentic faith and discipleship. Central to this worldview transformational paradigm is the Adventist doctrine of the Great Controversy.

Dedicated to the Lord, my Provider, Inspiration, and Strength

TABLE OF CONTENTS

ACKNOWLEDGMENTS vi

Chapter
1. INTRODUCTION 1

    Background of Study 1
    Statement of Problem 5
    Statement of Purpose 5
    Research Questions 6
    Theoretical Framework 6
    Methodology 7
    Scope/Delimitations 8
    Limitations 9
    Justification 9
    Validity 10
    Assumptions and Presuppositions 11
    Chapter Outline 11

2. CULTURE AND RELIGION OR THE YORUBA PEOPLE 13

    Yoruba History 13
    Social Context 16
    Cultural Context 22
        Affective Facets of Yoruba Culture 22
        Cognitive Facets of Yoruba Culture 26
        Evaluative Facets of Yoruba Culture 29
    Religious Context 31
        Yoruba Cosmology 40
            Olorun 41
            Orisa 43
                Obatala (Orisa nla) 45
                Orunmila (Ifa) 45
                Ogun 45
                Esu 45
                Sango 46
                Osun 46
            Ancestors 47
        Islam in Yorubaland 51
        Yoruba Christianity 54
        Aladura 56

3. CONVERSION AND WORLDVIEW TRANSFORMATION 60

    Introduction 60
    Conversion 61
    Definition 62
    Nature of Conversion 65
    Factors Affecting Conversion 67
    Stages of Conversion 68
    Psychological Paradigm 70
    Sociological Paradigm of Conversion 72
    Educational Paradigm of Conversion 74
    Anthropological Paradigms of Conversion 76
    The Biblical Paradigm: Conversion in Acts 82
        Simon Magus 83
            Context 83
            Convert 84
            Community 84
            Crisis 84
            Change 84
            Consequence 85
        Ethiopian Eunuch 87
            Context 87
            Convert 88
            Community 88
            Crisis 89
            Change 89
            Consequence 89
        Paul of Tarsus 91
            Context 91
            Convert 91
            Community 92
            Crisis 92
            Change 93
            Consequence 93
        Peter and Cornelius 94
            Converts 94
            Community 95
            Crisis 95
            Change 96
            Consequence 96
        Bar-Jesus 97
            Context 97
            Convert 97
            Community 98
            Crisis 98

Change	98
Consequence	98
Lydia	99
Context	99
Convert	100
Community	100
Crisis	100
Change	101
Consequence	101
Slave Diviner	101
Context	101
Convert	102
Community	102
Crisis	102
Change	103
Consequence	103
Conversion in the Yoruba Context	104
Missiological Implications	108
4. FIELD ANALYSIS ON DIVINATION AND SORCERY AMONG ADVENTISTS IN YORUBALAND	111
Introduction	111
Description of the Research Context	112
Field Research Design	114
Grounded Theory	114
Researcher's Background and Limitations	116
Purposive Sampling	118
Human Subject Protection	118
Data Collection Procedures	120
Interviewing Process	120
Focus Groups	121
Examples of Interview Questions	123
Sample of Questions to Members	123
Sample of Questions to Pastors	125
Sample of Questions to Diviners	126
Sample of Questions to Focus Groups	127
Research Analysis	127
Computer Software	128
Constant Comparative Analysis	129
Coding and Categorization	130
Memoing	132
Rigor of the Qualitative Process	132
Findings	135
Worldview Transformation by Explanation, Encounter, and Experience	136
Explanation	136

        Causation 137
            Parental and Societal Influence 138
            Currency and Frequency 139
            Insignificant Influences 141
            Orality 145
        Encounter 146
            Quest for Power 147
            Rapid Response 147
            Needs and Fears 148
        Experience 154
            Spiritual Leadership 154
            Trusting God 155
            Personal Testimonies 157

5. TOWARDS A TRANSFROMATIONAL MODEL 159

    Introduction 159
    Context 160
        Divination and Sorcery in ATR 162
        Divination in the Old Testament 166
            Among the Nations 166
            Among the Israelites 167
        In the New Testament 168
        Sorcery in the Old Testament 171
        Sorcery in the New Testament 173
    Causation 177
        Ever-Presence of God 182
        The Ministry of Angels 183
        New Focus 186
        Supernaturalistic Worldview 187
    Curriculum 189
        Orality 190
        Storytelling 191
        Contextualization 194
        Functional Substitutes 197
        Discipleship 197
    Conflict 198
        The Great Controversy 199
        Power Encounter 199
        Prayer and Boldness 203
    Crisis 204
    Community 206
        Fellowship 207
        Joy 208
        Reconciliation 210
    Change Agent 213

	Self-Examination	213
	Relationships	215
	Mentorship	216
6.	SUMMARY, RECOMMENDATIONS, AND CONCLUSION	218

    Introduction 218
    Summary 219
        Yoruba Culture and Religion 219
        Conversion in Social Science and Scripture 220
        Research on Divination and Sorcery 221
        Significance of Worldview 222
    Misssiological Model for Worldview Transformation 222
    Recommendations 223
    Conclusion 225

BIBLIOGRAPHY 226

ACKNOWLEDGMENTS

Besides the Lord who opened up doors and provided the mentors and sponsors that made this dissertation possible, there are a number of persons who need to be recognized and appreciated.

Through stressful moments and tension-filled occasions my beautiful wife Juliet was an unflagging support. My children, Michel and Rachel, also showed mature understanding and accommodation when they were "abandoned" by their father, while immersed in the task to be accomplished.

Mentors are rare to find, and sometimes not fully appreciated. In this rank I would like to recognize my advisor and chair, without whom this dream would probably never have seen the light of day. Turn-around time for returning corrected manuscripts by Prof. Bauer was simply record-breaking. Bruce and Linda's contribution to my family's well-being and stay in Andrews has been monumental—they totally went above and beyond the call of duty. Another unforgettable mentor has been Prof. Chiemela Ikonne who believed in and supported this dream. And another who might not realize the impact he has had on this project is the gentle and amiable Prof. John Matthews.

In chasing the goal of graduating within a period I had been told would need a miracle to accomplish, the assistance of others, such as my methodologist Dr. Shirley Freed and committee member Dr. Teresa Reeve, was invaluable. They are greatly appreciated. On the aspect of financial and moral support here in Andrews University, Drs. Niels-Erik Andreasen, Christon Arthur, and Tom Shepherd are deserving of great commendation. I would be remiss if I forgot to mention dissertation secretary Bonnie Proctor for her speed, accuracy, and support.

On the home front, the commitment of Dr. Deji Adeleke and the assistance of Prof. James Makinde launched this dream and provided the foundation for the accomplishment of this dissertation. Many others prayed and supported in various other ways; may the Lord reward you all richly and abundantly.

CHAPTER I

INTRODUCTION

Background of Study

Across the continent of Africa the most significant and persistent missiological challenges arise from the fact that, although a change of religion and behavior has occurred in converts from African Traditional Religion (ATR) practices, many times the worldview has remained resolute. During periods of crises, cases of reversion to traditional remedies are well known.[1] Incidents of converts resorting to sorcery and divination give rise to the conviction that, although the external elements of the culture of the African people has changed, the worldview too often remains the same.

This study focused on the Yoruba who are one of the most researched and written about tribal groups on the continent of Africa.[2] They are found across the southwestern region of Nigeria, in sub-Saharan West Africa; they are a group whose spread traverses several other countries in the region, and whose reign once extended into other parts of Nigeria. The Yoruba are also an influential, educated, and migrant group whose

---

[1]David Tonghou Ngong, "Salvation and Materialism in African Theology," *Studies in World Christianity* 15, no. 1 (April 2009): 11.

[2]Stephen A. Akintoye, "From Early Times to the 20th Century," in *Understanding Yoruba Life and Culture*, ed. Nike S. Lawal, Matthew Sadiku, and P. Ade Dopamu (Trenton, NJ: Africa World Press, 2004), 3; Noel Q. King, *African Cosmos: An Introduction to Religion in Africa* (Belmont, CA: Wadsworth, 1986), 6.

footprints can be found in Europe and the Americas.[3] They comprise about one-fifth[4] of the over 162.5 million inhabitants of Nigeria.[5] Nigeria accounts for a sixth of the total Africans in the world,[6] a little more than 16 percent of the African population.

Significantly, in the modern Christian revival emanating from what is presently referred to as the "majority world,"[7] some of the largest migrant churches in Europe and America have Nigerians as their founders and leaders.[8] Sunday Adelaja's Embassy of God Church in the Ukraine boasts 100,000 members, largely comprising indigenes of Kiev, Ukraine.[9] In the United Kingdom, Matthew Ashimolowo's Kingsway International

---

[3]King, *African Cosmos*, 6; S. A. Thorpe, *African Traditional Religions: An Introduction* (Pretoria, South Africa: University of South Africa, 1991), 85; Thomas Lawson, *Religions of Africa: Traditions in Transformation* (San Francisco: Harper and Row, 1984), 51.

[4]*CIA World Fact Book*, "Nigeria," reports that the Yoruba ethnic group makes up 21% of the country's total population, https://www.cia.gov/library/publications/the-world-factbook-geos/ni.html (accessed November 7, 2011).

[5]UN Population Fund, "The State of World Population 2011" (New York: UNFPA, 2011), 119.

[6]UN Habitat, "The State of African Cities, 2010," reports that the total population for Africa just exceeded the one billion mark in 2009, http://www.unhabitat.org/documents/SOAC10/SOAC-PR1-en.pdf (accessed November 7, 2011).

[7]Craig Ott, Stephen J. Strauss, and Timothy C. Tennent, *Encountering Theology of Mission: Biblical Foundations, Historical Developments, and Contemporary Issues* (Grand Rapids, MI: Baker Academic, 2010), xvii.

[8]Kwabena J. Asamoah-Gaydu, "Spirit, Mission and Transnational Influence: Nigerian-led Pentecostalism in Eastern Europe," *PentecoStudies* 9, no. 1 (2010): 77.

[9]Ibid., 81.

Christian Church is known to have the largest congregation.[10] Studies also reveal that some of the largest churches in East, West, and Southern Africa are led by Nigerians.[11] The Redeemed Christian Church of God, one of the largest denominations in Nigeria with reportedly 5 million members, has in recent years opened up several branches in America. Its membership in the U.S. is estimated at 15,000. A large property in Texas was purchased in 2007 to serve as the headquarters for its mission to America.[12] What is noteworthy about this phenomenon, now referred to as reverse missions, is that Nigerians[13] (especially Yoruba clergymen) play key roles in this movement.[14]

These local and international African-initiated or African-led churches portray a

---

[10]Ayuk Ayuk, "Portrait of a Nigerian Missionary," *Asian Journal of Pentecostal Studies* 8, no. 1 (2005): 127.

[11]Ibid., 128; Asonzeh Ukah, "African Christianities: Features, Promises and Problems,"18, www.ifeas.uni-mainz.de/workingpapers/AP79.pdf (accessed November 2, 2008).

[12]Andrew Rice, "Mission from Africa," *New York Times*, 8 April 2009, http://www.nytimes.com/ 2009/04/12/magazine/12churches-t.html?pagewanted=all (accessed March 3, 2011).

[13]Asamoah-Gyadu, "Spirit, Mission and Transnational Influence," 77.

[14]Reverse mission is an expression used in mission circles to describe a recent trend in which countries which once were at the receiving end of missionaries sent to them, are now the ones taking the gospel message to secular nations of the Western world. Simeon O. Ilesanmi, "From Periphery to Center: Pentecostalism Is Transforming the Secular State in Africa," *Harvard Divinity School* 35, no. 4 (2007), http:www.hds. harvard.edu/news/bulletin_mag/ articles/35.4_ilesanmi.html (accessed December 1, 2010); Afe Adogame, "Reverse Mission: Europe a Prodigal Continent?" http://www .edinburgh2010.org/fileadmin /files /edinburgh2010/files/News/Afe_ Reverse%20 mission_edited.pdf (accessed October 7, 2011).

strain of Christianity heavily tinged with the African traditional religious worldview.[15] Consequently, elements of syncretism are clearly visible in the ministries and methods employed by these churches.[16] It also appears that the clergymen have replaced the roles traditional religious priests and healers played in the social structure of the community.

Some Mission churches, such as the Adventist Church, with strong influences from their Western home bases, have not demonstrated similar growth patterns to indigenous churches.[17] In sharp contrast, local Pentecostal congregations have blossomed and dot the religious landscape. Demonstrating a keen perception of the fears and needs of the people, these churches display syncretistic ministry models that often further affirm local witchcraft beliefs and the ubiquitous presence of evil spirits. As a result, worldview continuity is witnessed, rather than the discontinuity and transformation that the Christian faith demands of certain pre-Christian practices.[18]

This turn of events has at times given rise to manipulative Christians who, rather than submitting to the will of God, seek every conceivable means to force the hand of

---

[15]Elizabeth Isichei, *A History of Christianity in Africa: From Antiquity to the Present* (Grand Rapids, MI: Eerdemans, 1995), 278.

[16]Cyril C. Okorocha, "Religious Conversion in Africa: Its Missiological Implications," *Mission Studies* 9, no. 2 (1992): 179.

[17]Between 1914 (when the Adventist message came to west Nigeria) and 2009, records show that membership has reached 59,529. General Conference Office of Archives and Statistics, "West Nigeria Conference: 1914-2009," http://www.adventiststatistics.org/view_Summary.asp? FieldInstID=1696061 (accessed 5 October 2011).

[18]The continuous practice of sorcery and divination even after profession of Christianity is referred to here. Such practices are expected to be discontinued, however, they continue to be reported among some Christians.

God, even if this entails the use of sorcery and divination. Therefore, this study examined the factors that lead to full conversion and mature discipleship among the Yoruba.

Statement of Problem

Over a century ago Africans massively adopted the new religion brought by Christian missionaries. Presently, however, in contrast to their professed beliefs, practices such as sorcery and divination have led to witchcraft accusations,[19] dual allegiance, and syncretism, which are reportedly widespread and persistent. These are evidences of an incomplete worldview transformational model. Therefore, a better, biblical, contextual model needed to be developed in order to lead to a more authentic Christian worldview[20] transformation and discipleship among the Yoruba.

Statement of Purpose

The purpose of this study was to develop a transformational model that is biblically consistent, which takes into account sociological, cultural, and missional factors, with the goal to move Yoruba believers from syncretistic primal religious practices to practices based on a biblically shaped worldview.

---

[19]Distinction is made between witchcraft belief and accusations in the book edited by Gerrie ter Haar, *Imagining Evil: Witchcraft Beliefs and Accusations in Contemporary Africa* (Trenton, NJ: Africa World Press, 2007).

[20]Kraft defines worldview as "the totality of the culturally structured images and assumptions (including value and commitment or allegiance assumptions) in terms of which a people both perceive and respond to reality." Charles H. Kraft, *Worldview for Christian Witness* (Pasadena, CA: William Carey Library, 2008), 12.

Research Questions

This project was undertaken to respond to two research questions: (1) How can transformation from the traditional Yoruba worldview be achieved? and, (2) What can the Seventh-day Adventist Church do in response to the needs and fears that induce dual allegiance?

Theoretical Framework

The theoretical framework used in this research was an adaptation of the model developed by Charles Kraft, a foremost Christian anthropologist who served for many years as a missionary in Nigeria. Kraft asserts that worldview change can be achieved when a person or group undergoes a crisis (experience) that leads to a revision of old paradigms. Another factor that he believes can lead to change is when exposure to new experiences leads to a search for new answers (explanations), thereby resulting in change.[21]

Lewis Rambo's sequential stage model was another approach that was significant to this study.[22] He developed a multi-disciplinary model entailing seven stages in the process of conversion, drawing insights from psychology, sociology, anthropology, theology, and missiology. Other models that were considered included that of anthropologist Paul Hiebert, whose holistic theology model addresses the three dimensions of worldview—cognitive, affective, and evaluative—with three levels of

---

[21] Charles H. Kraft, *Anthropology for Christian Witness* (Maryknoll, NY: Orbis Books, 1996), 56-57.

[22] Lewis R. Rambo, *Understanding Religious Conversion* (New Haven, CT: Yale University Press, 1993), 17.

encounter: truth encounter, power encounter, and empirical encounter.[23] Hans Kasdorf also examined the issue of conversion from missiological, theological, and anthropological perspectives, so his approach merited consideration.[24]

These were some of the models that were examined, although other methods for achieving behavioral change can be found in the realms of business, education, sociology, and psychology. While the social sciences provide understanding of human nature and how change may occur, it is only through the process of heart conversion that lasting transformation can be effected. Consequently, a transformational model with scriptural undergirding was designed reflecting the Great Controversy doctrine of the Seventh-day Adventist Church.

Methodology

Library research in the social sciences and missiology was carried out to facilitate understanding of existing models of worldview transformation. Models of change by foremost scholars such as Kraft and Hiebert were examined, including other authorities on the subject. Recognizing the limitations of human models, no matter how good, and the primacy of Scripture in life-transformation, the next step was biblical exegesis of relevant scriptural passages.

---

[23]Paul G. Hiebert, "The Flaw of the Excluded Middle," in *Perspectives: On the World Christian Movement*, ed. Ralph D. Winter and Steven C. Hawthorne, 4th ed. (Pasadena, CA: William Carey Library, 2009), 412-414.

[24]Hans Kasdorf, *Christian Conversion in Context* (Scottdale, PA: Herald Press, 1980), 20.

Exegetical studies of selected biblical passages focused on conversion narratives in the book of Acts in order to gain insights on the process and nature of biblical transformation. These passages were studied with a view to applying their implications in developing biblically appropriate responses to the needs and fears of Yoruba people, which trigger reversion to pre-Christian practices during times of crises.

Qualitative field research was conducted employing purposeful sampling of selected persons knowledgeable and experienced in the subject of divination and sorcery. This grounded theory research entailed face-to-face interviews with key informants and others conversant with this issue. Data were handwritten and recorded with a digital recorder. Among those interviewed were: (1) five diviners, to provide insight as to why they are patronized by church members, (2) five pastors with experience in such matters who provided a rich source of data and insight into the practices, and (3) three church members who had employed the services of a diviner in the past but had discontinued the practice. Two focus group interviews were also carried out among groups of men and women in two selected churches where Yoruba members were prevalent to provide additional information on the subject.

Scope/Delimitations

Yoruba history dates back several centuries, and its cultural heritage is rich and diverse. However, in discussing this people group and their worldview, attention was focused on the present state of affairs and those aspects of their experience that have a bearing on their conversion. Additionally, because the Christian population of the Yoruba is quite large and the churches in the region are widespread and varied, research activities were undertaken only among two selected congregations of the Seventh-day Adventist

Church in southwest Nigeria, one in a rural area and the other in an urban setting. The rural church was Ilishan Number 1 Church, whereas Orile Iganmu Church was the church in the urban context.

Limitations

A main limitation of this research was my inexperience in employing grounded theory methodology. In addition, this was also the first time of using the software program Dedoose in project analysis. It can only be expected that the research process would have been enhanced had I been more experienced with the methodology and the software employed for data analysis.

Justification

Although more than half of the Yoruba population consider themselves Christian, it is evident that some of the religious practices among this people group raise questions about their conversion experience and issues of syncretism. Against this backdrop of dual allegiance and syncretism, there is a massive wave of global Christian growth spearheaded by churches from this region. In another vein, during the last three decades there has been remarkable growth of the Yoruba tradition among Black populations in Brazil, the United Kingdom, and the United States.[25] It was imperative, therefore, that missiologists and church leaders understand the implications of this growing worldwide phenomenon and this people group whose influence is trans-national.

---

[25]M. Darrol Bryant and Christopher Lamb, "Introduction: Conversion—Contours of Controversy and Commitment in a Plural World, in *Religious Conversions: Contemporary Practices and Controversies*, ed. Christopher Lamb and M. Darrol Bryant (London: Cassell, 1999), 4.

Furthermore, reports of lifestyle habits that are incongruent with Christian standards are indications of worldview continuity. It was incumbent on this research to examine past witnessing and nurture processes in order to ascertain whatever inadequacies existed and to design a better model that would be contextually relevant and biblically faithful. While this study was focused on the Yoruba, it should also be of some value to the entire church in Africa and beyond where Christians are confronted with similar challenges and where others are seeking to lead church members to experience worldview transformation.

Validity

Project validity was sought by a number of factors that served to keep the dissertation focused. The focus group interview questions and other semi-structured interview questions were validated by the dissertation committee, a research methodologist, and the Andrews University's Institutional Review Board (IRB) prior to implementation and analysis.

Interviews were recorded and transcribed while notes are taken. Responses were coded and documented for proper analysis to establish relevant patterns. Data obtained from all the interviews were securely stored and backed up for safety.

Reliability of the study was enhanced by research triangulation, checking for consistency in the responses given by the subjects interviewed, and from other data collected during the interviews, including the testing of concepts and ideas obtained from prior interviews from other subjects. Findings from these interviews were then analyzed and charted to obtain conclusions and recommendations.

Assumptions and Presuppositions

This research is premised on the importance of a double exegesis of the cultural context and the scriptural text to produce holistic worldview transformation. The social sciences provide valid sources of truth for understanding the local culture and processes of conversion. However, a major assumption of this project is that the Scriptures are the authoritative, revealed will of God which supersede all sources of truth and serve as a guide for critiquing and evaluating all truth.

Chapter Outline

The research project is presented in six chapters. Chapter 1 presented the background and rationale for this study, and discussed the methodology employed in carrying out this research. It also highlighted the local and global significance of this study to the church in general.

Chapter 2 dwells on the cultural and religious context of the Yoruba people. It provides an understanding of the background of the people and the cultural and worldview influences that shaped the beliefs and practices of Christians in Yorubaland.

In chapter 3 the issues of conversion and worldview transformation are examined. The need for worldview transformation rather than the prevailing practice of simply making converts is discussed. The subject of conversion is explored from the perspectives of the social sciences and the Scriptures. In addition, conversion to Christianity in the Yoruba context is evaluated to discover insights and lessons from the past.

The findings from the qualitative grounded theory research are presented in chapter 4. In this chapter the nature, reason, and purpose of this particular research methodology are explained. The chapter also features the findings from the interviews and focus group discussions, and an analysis of the data, culminating in a suggested theory for worldview transformation.

A recommended missiological model for holistic worldview transformation[26] Among Christians in Yorubaland is the focus of chapter 5, which was the product of this study. In it is explained the core concepts imperative for worldview transformation among the Yoruba people from pre-Christian habits to biblically-shaped praxis.

Chapter 6 presents the summary, conclusion, and recommendations of this grounded theory research. It reviews what needs to be done by the Seventh-day Adventist Church to make its members immune to the temptation to revert to pre-Christian practices, and how they can be discipled to acquire authentic Christian faith and spirituality.

---

[26]Scott Moreau explains the difficulty of arriving at a precise definition of worldview in his article, "Paul G. Hiebert's Legacy of Worldview," *Trinity Journal* 30, no. 2 (Fall 2009): 223.

CHAPTER II

CULTURE AND RELIGION OF THE YORUBA PEOPLE

Yoruba History

The earliest historical source of the origins of the Yoruba can be traced to one of the first indigenous ministers, Reverend Samuel Johnson, who unfortunately died before he saw his magisterial epic published. An edited volume was later compiled and published by his brother from surviving notes, after a publisher in England had callously misplaced the original manuscript of the book.[1]

Curiously, the name for this group was not derived from the people themselves but finds its origins in records of the Hausa and Fulani names used for the country and capital in West Africa, east of Dahomey, with a population of 2 million, and whose capital was Katunga. Thus the name Yoruba, from *Yarriba*, came to represent the people of the ancient Oyo empire.[2] Hausa sources trace the origin of the name to Islamic records found with the Sultan of Sokoto where the name is derived from *Yarub*, an illustrious personage from early Arab genealogies; from there, the name was passed down to travellers and diplomats.[3] Reverend Johnson similarly acknowledges that the Yorubas

---

[1] J. D. Y. Peel, *Religious Encounter and the Making of the Yoruba* (Bloomington, IN: Indiana University Press, 2000), 308.

[2] Obadiah Johnson, *The History of the Yorubas* (London: Routledge and Kegan Paul, 1921), xix; Robert Smith, *Kingdoms of the Yoruba* (London: Methuen, 1969), 16.

[3] Peel, *Religious Encounter*, 283.

descended from Lamurudu, one of the kings of Mecca, whose son was Oduduwa, the ancestor of the Yorubas.[4] Yoruba mythology in contrast contends that Oduduwa's ancestry is traceable to the Olodumare, the Supreme God who let him down from heaven on a chain to create earth, and the spot he first landed was Ile Ife, birthplace of Yoruba civilization.[5] Despite the disputed origins of the Yoruba race, it is accepted that Oduduwa, the ancestor of the nation, established his palace in Ile Ife, which became the nerve center of the political life of the Yoruba people.[6] Yoruba country is said to have extended from the Volta basin in the west to the Niger valley in the east, with Ile Ife as the center for the spreading of the *Ifa* and *Ogun* cults.[7]

While it cannot be disputed that the Yoruba people arrived at their present location as a result of migration, the manner and origins of such migrations remain contentious. One such plausible linkage is found with the Bini people whose *oba's* rule is

---

[4]Johnson, *The History of the Yorubas*, 3; Smith, *Kingdoms of the Yoruba*, 11. Johnson claims that Lamurudu is the biblical character Nimrod. The major premise of Olumide Lucas is to establish the connection between the Yoruba people and the Egyptian civilization. See J. Olumide Lucas, *The Religion of the Yorubas: Being an Account of the Religious Beliefs and Practices of the Yoruba Peoples of Southern Nigeria, Especially in Relation to the Religion of Ancient Egypt* (Lagos, Nigeria: C.M.S. Bookshop, 1948). Note the book's subtitle.

[5]Robin C. C. Law, "Traditional History," in *Sources of Yoruba History*, ed. Saburu O. Biobaku (Oxford: Clarendon Press, 1973), 30.

[6]Stephen A. Akintoye, "From Early Times to the 20th Century," in *Understanding Yoruba Life and Culture*, ed. Nike S. Lawal, Matthew N. O. Sadiku, and P. Ade Dopamu (Trenton, NJ: Africa World Press, 2004), 5.

[7]Peel, *Religious Encounter*, 28.

considered to have once extended into Eastern Yoruba land.[8] Also, the present dynasty of Lagos *obas* further suggests to the Bini origins, including the fact that the first three obas of Lagos, Asipa, Ado, and Gabaro had Benin connections.[9] Conversely, Yoruba traditions list the *oba* of Benin as one of the earliest princes of Ife who left to found kingdoms of his own, one of which was the Benin kingdom that was notable for its bronze, metal works, and ivory.[10]

Acceptance of the appellation, Yoruba, for this large people group was not universal at the beginning. The Yoruba were previously referred to as the Eyo or Aku, until the publication by Samuel Ajai Crowther of his *Vocabulary of the Yoruba Language* in 1843, after which they were never called by any other name.[11] Crowther was also instrumental in the translation of the Yoruba Bible—the first Bible in any African language.[12] The standard definition of who was a Yoruba person was attributed to (1) a common language and (2) a common origin that was traceable to Ile Ife as the cradle of the race.[13]

---

[8]Law, "Traditional History," 34-36. In his later volume on the history of the Oyo kingdom, Law, however, endorses the position that Oduduwa was the progenitor of the founder of Benin. See, Robin Law, *The Oyo Empire: c. 1600-c. 1836—A West African Imperialism in the Era of the Atlantic Slave Trade* (Oxford: Clarendon Press, 1977), 27.

[9]Law, "Traditional History," 39.

[10]Akintoye, "From Early Times to the Twentieth Century," 6.

[11]Peel, *Religious Encounter*, 284; Law, *The Oyo Empire*, 5. The name Yoruba was never used to designate the people prior to the nineteenth century.

[12]Andrew F. Walls, *The Cross-Cultural Process in Christian History* (Maryknoll, NY: Orbis Books, 2002), 160.

[13]Peel, *Religious Encounter*, 286; Smith, *Kingdoms of the Yoruba*, 10-11.

Social Context

A notable feature of the Yoruba is their love for ceremonies. They are a people known to celebrate life to the fullest. Each achievement or attainment in life was a reason to party, besides annual community festivals and other rites of passages. The life rituals that were cause for rejoicing and festivities included child-naming, marriage, installation, initiation, and burial rites.[14] None of these festivities or celebrations could be divorced from the religious function in the traditional worldview of the people.[15] This is quite understandable when it is realized that "no major achievement in the life of an individual, a group, or a community is considered possible without the active support of the supernatural."[16]

Yoruba societies, like most in Africa, are strongly communal in nature, with group interests considered superior to those of the individual.[17] Yoruba life however reflected a paradoxical tension where, on the one hand, individual desires were subjugated to those of the community while, on the other hand, individual worth and

---

[14]Oyin Ogunba, "Ceremonies," in *Sources of Yoruba History*, ed. Saburi O. Biobaku (Oxford: Calrendon Press, 1973), 87.

[15]P. A. Dopamu, "Traditional Festivals," in *Understanding Yoruba Life and Culture*, ed. Nike S. Lawal, Matthew N. O. Sadiku, and P. Ade Dopamu (Trenton, NJ: Africa World Press, 2004), 651.

[16]Ogunba, "Ceremonies," 87.

[17]Emmanuel Babatunde, "Traditional Marriage and Family," in *Understanding Yoruba Life and Culture*, ed. Nike S. Lawal, Matthew N. O. Sadiku, and P. Ade Dopamu (Trenton, NJ: Africa World Press, 2004), 218; Peel, *Religious Encounter*, 53.

creativity were constantly recognized and celebrated.[18]

Urban life has always been an essential aspect of Yoruba communities, with each *ilu* (town or community) comprised of nucleated settlements.[19] In the political design of each *ilu*, or community, the *oba* (king) played a pivotal function, as "the symbol and possessor of the town."[20] Such a hierarchical society had the *oba* sitting at the top of the pyramid of power, followed by the high chief and other chiefs, then followed by honorary chiefs, elders, and the generality of men and women, with the children coming at the bottom.[21] Only in rare or truly special circumstances could the *oba* be approached directly without first going through the pecking order. The palace of the *oba* was situated in the center of the town, for the centrality of the *oba* in the community also had a cosmological function, because he was regarded as a quasi-divine personage who mediated with the deities for the well-being of the people.[22] Another appellation or designation for the *oba* was the concept of *kabiyesi* ("who should we ask or challenge?")

---

[18]Babatunde, "Traditional Marriage and Family," 219.

[19]Peel, *Religious Encounter*, 30. The Yoruba are regarded as "the most urban of all African peoples of comparable size." William Bascom, "Some Aspects of Yoruba Urbanism," in *Africa: Social Problems of Change and Conflict*, ed. Pierre L. Van Den Berghe (San Francisco, CA: Chandler Publishing Co., 1965), 369.

[20]Peel, *Religious Encounter*, 31.

[21]O. E. Alana, "Traditional Religion," in *Understanding Yoruba Life and Culture*, ed. Nike S. Lawal, Matthew N. O. Sadiku, and P. Ade Dopamu (Trenton, NJ: Africa World Press, 2004), 74.

[22]Peel, *Religious Encounter*, 31. The palace and the wealth of the *oba* were reflections of the prestige of the town among its neighbors; see P. C. Lloyd, "Sacred Kingship and Government among the Yoruba," in *Africa and Change*, ed. Colin M. Turnbull (New York: Alfred A. Knopf, 1973), 298.

whose authority could never be challenged by any of his subjects.[23] Johnson attests that the *oba* was more dreaded than even the gods.[24]

Besides being addressed as *Kabiyesi* ("he who no one dares query"), another appellation for the *oba*, denoting his veritable linkage between his people and the world of the gods and ancestors, was "*Alase ekeji orisa*" ("ruler, second only to the gods, or ruler, companion of the gods").[25] Among the Yoruba, sacred kingship was an ancient, established institution.[26]

Communities were composed of compounds usually populated by about fifty persons with the *baale*, who was the oldest person, as the head.[27] Compounds were grouped to form wards (*adugbo*). The *oba* ruled in conjunction with his Council of Chiefs (*Igbimo*), who were representatives from each ward; together they developed the laws that governed the lives of the community.[28] Despite the power of the *oba*, Yoruba

---

[23] Tunde Onadeko, "Yoruba Traditional Adjudicatory Systems," *African Study Monographs* 29, no. 1 (March 2008): 16, http://repository.kulib.kyoto-u.ac.jp/dspace/bitstream/2433/66225/1/ASM_29_15.pdf

[24] Johnson, *The History of the Yorubas*, 40.

[25] Richard A. Olaniyan, "Installation of Kings and Chiefs Past and Present," in *Understanding Yoruba Life and Culture*, ed. Nike S. Lawal, Matthew N. O. Sadiku, and P. Ade Dopamu (Trenton, NJ: Africa World Press, 2004), 276.

[26] Lloyd, "Sacred Kingship and Government among the Yoruba, 291.

[27] A. O. Y Raji and H. O. Danmole, "Traditional Government," in *Understanding Yoruba Life and Culture*, ed. Nike S. Lawal, Matthew N. O. Sadiku, and P. Ade Dopamu (Trenton, NJ: Africa World Press, 2004), 260.

[28] Onadeko, "Yoruba Traditional Adjudicatory Systems," 16.

society was democratic.[29] Directly below the *oba* and his Council were the *adugbo* (wards) led by the *Olori Adugbo* or *Olori Itun* (head of the community), whose appointment was ratified and approved by the *oba*. Following this was the *Ago Ile* (extended family) led by the *Olori Ebi*, and at the bottom was the nuclear family led by *Baba*, the father of the home.[30]

Traditional Yoruba society is highly stratified with age as the major determinant of status.[31] Another reflector of status was polygamy, or marriage to several wives. In this patrilocal system, the number of wives a man had was indicative of his wealth and status, for a person married as many as his wealth permitted.[32] In recent times, money has become the basis of the Yoruba status system, and education, the key to wealth and social advancement.[33]

The family is the basic unit of the Yoruba community. In the family, roles are clearly defined with the husband/father responsible for strenuous labor such as working on the farm, assisted by the children, while the role of the women was mainly domestic; trading or marketing commodities was also regarded as the duty of women.[34] Yoruba women were active in business, and because the welfare and education of their children

---

[29]Smith, *Kingdoms of the Yoruba*, 118.

[30]Onadeko, "Yoruba Traditional Adjudicatory Systems," 17.

[31]J. D. Y. Peel, *Aladura: A Religious Movement Among the Yoruba* (London: Oxford University Press, 1968), 26.

[32]Johnson, *The History of the Yorubas*, 113; Peel, *Religious Encounter*, 27, 26.

[33]Peel, *Religious Encounter*, 41.

[34]Johnson, *The History of the Yorubas*, 117-118.

was their primary responsibility, trading made it a lot easier for them to fulfill these functions.[35] Other forms of industries where women exercised monopoly included pottery, cloth dying, palm and nut oil processing, soap-making, and cloth spinning.[36]

The character of individuals and their behavior manifested in their interactions with others are believed to be reflective of the home or family the persons came from; this was often regarded as the benchmark of the child-rearing skills of the mother.[37] The bond between mother and child was often the closest in Yoruba society because it was the mother who gave birth, nurtured, and taught the child social virtues and behavior.[38] In celebration of womanhood the Yoruba had the *Gelede* spectacle, a ceremony that honored the power of women, and was intended to both placate and win the good will of those living and dead for purposes of fertility and to prevent harm.[39]

Marriage in the Yoruba community is a major event that brings together the lives

---

[35]Elizabeth Ojo, "Women and the Family," in *Understanding Yoruba Life and Culture*, ed. Nike S. Lawal, Matthew N. O. Sadiku, and P. Ade Dopamu (Trenton, NJ: Africa World Press, 2004), 243.

[36]LaRay Denzer, "Yoruba Women: A Historiographical Study," *International Journal of African Historical Studies* 27, no. 1 (1994): 6.

[37]Ojo, "Women and the Family," 239.

[38]Majorie Keniston McIntosh, *Yoruba Women, Work, and Social Change* (Bloomington, IN: Indiana University Press, 2009), 92.

[39]See Henry John Drewal and Margaret Thompson Drewal, *Gelede: Art and Female Power among the Yoruba* (Bloomington, IN: Indiana University Press, 1990); McIntosh, *Yoruba Women, Work, and Social Change*, 203.

of two individuals and their extended families.[40] In ancient times marriage typically had three stages: an early intimation, a formal betrothal which could last for a period of time, and the marriage proper.[41] Marriage customs varied according to region, period, and circumstances of the individuals; however, love was never a basis for marriage, since the choice of a partner was made by the family rather than by the individual.[42] A dowry was usually paid by the suitor, depending on the demands of the parents of the bride.[43]

Respect for the husband was a key element in marital relationships, and wives demonstrated this by kneeling or curtsying when greeting their husbands, who they never addressed by their given names.[44] Divorce was not commonly sanctioned among the Yoruba; all grounds for reconciliation had to be exhausted before this could be condoned. Chief among the reasons for granting a divorce were insanity, infertility of the wife, laziness of the husband, chronic illness, indebtedness, and extreme cruelty.[45]

Like many other societies in Africa, colonization, civilization, and urbanization have brought significant changes to traditional Yoruba communities. Some of the

---

[40]Emmanuel Babatunde, "Traditional Marriage and Family," in *Understanding Yoruba Life and Culture*, ed. Nike S. Lawal, Matthew N. O. Sadiku, and P. Ade Dopamu (Trenton, NJ: Africa World Press, 2004), 222.

[41]Johnson, *The History of the Yorubas*, 113.

[42]McIntosh, *Yoruba Women, Work, and Social Change*, 86.

[43]Geoffrey Parrinder, *Religion in an African City* (Westport, CT: Negro Universities Press, 1972), 73; Johnson, *The History of the Yorubas*, 114.

[44]McIntosh, *Yoruba Women, Work, and Social Change*, 86.

[45]Denzer, "Yoruba Women: A Historiographical Study," 4.

methods employed by the people to maintain their identities and patterns of living as they were displaced or parted from kin included: *oriki orile*, having "familiar names" defined by their community of origin; *ila*, facial tribal marks; *ewo*, food taboos associated with lineage or cult membership; and, *ori*, the sense of a protective personal destiny.[46]

Cultural Context

In studying Yoruba culture it needs to be understood that the contemporary culture is a dynamic affair consisting of several overlapping and partly conflicting systems of ideas with traditional practices.[47] That is to say, although the Yoruba are great respecters of tradition, nevertheless they pride themselves in being a people who desire to be seen as modern.[48] The following section will survey three dimensions of culture — affective, cognitive, and evaluative—of the Yoruba people. The affective dimension covers the ceremonies and festivals; the cognitive is concerned with the wisdom and knowledge systems of the people; and the evaluative dimension pertains to the moral values and judgments of the people.

Affective Facets of Yoruba Culture

It is almost impossible to separate elements of the cultural, social, or religious lives of the Yoruba people from one another. This is because, as Bolaji Idowu, a Yoruba religious scholar astutely observed, "the keynote of the life of the Yoruba is neither in

---

[46]Peel, *Religious Encounters*, 50.

[47]Benjamin C. Ray, "Aladura Christianity: A Yoruba Religion," *Journal of Religion in Africa* 23, no. 3 (August 1993): 267.

[48]Peel, *Religious Encounter*, 310.

their noble ancestry nor in their past heroes. The keynote of their life is their religion."[49] Thus, feasts and celebrations were not merely cultural issues but had religious and social functions, and were celebrated with great gusto that involved the entire community.[50] This is even more the case in contemporary times. Among the occasions that people gathered to celebrate were childbirth, naming ceremonies, birthdays, engagements, marriage or weddings, purchase of a car, building a house, funeral, and anniversaries. Since the religion of the people was inseparable from their culture[51] or daily living, each of these occasions in some way or the other involved prayer and worship.[52] N. A. Fadipe, a Yoruba sociologist, described the people as "gregarious and sociable."[53] During the rites of passages such as birth, marriage, and death, celebrations were conducted involving the entire community.

Music constituted a very important part of Yoruba life, and there is hardly any aspect of their existence that does not have special music designed for it.[54] Music was

---

[49]Bolaji Idowu, *Olodumare: God in Yoruba Belief* (London: Longmans, 1962), 5.

[50]McIntosh, *Yoruba Women, Work, and Social Change*, 39.

[51]Idowu, *Olodumare*, 5.

[52]P. Ade Dopamu, "System of Discipline," in *Understanding Yoruba Life and Culture*, ed. Nike S. Lawal et al. (Trenton, NJ: Africa World Press, 2006), 175.

[53]N. A. Fadipe, *Sociology of the Yoruba* (Ibadan, Nigeria: Ibadan University Press, 1970), 301.

[54]Lere Adeyemi, "Traditional Music," in *Understanding Yoruba Life and Culture*, ed. Nike S. Lawal, Matthew N. O. Sadiku, and P. Ade Dopamu (Trenton, NJ: Africa World Press, 2004), 589.

often accompanied by drumming and dancing.[55] Although music played a part in just about every facet of life from politics, to religion, the economy, and social life, it also served several other purposes.[56] One of the popular music forms was the *oriki*, or praise songs. Derived from *ori* (head or origin) and *ki* (to cite, or greet), it could be taken to mean "to cite one's origin."[57] Chiefs and prominent personalities all had their *orikis* describing their achievements, exploits, and character chanted as they approached the people; the singing was usually done by women and punctuated by the beating of the talking drums.[58] *Oriki*, however, also had a religious dimension that served as praise chants describing the characteristics of the divinities or *orisa*.[59] Although the *oriki* also provided the historian a source of oral history, it needed to be used with caution, since such music usually presented only the favorable and glorious aspects of an individual's life, with the primary objective being to exalt or glorify a person.[60]

Although drums in Yoruba societies served primarily musical purposes, like some

---

[55] McIntosh, *Yoruba Women, Work, and Social Change*, 202.

[56] Adeyemi, "Traditional Music," 590.

[57] J. A. Ayorinde, "Oriki," in *Sources of Yoruba History*, ed. Saburu O. Biobaku (Oxford: Clarendon Press, 1973), 63.

[58] See Ulli Beier's, *The Return of the Gods: The Scared Art of Susanne Wenger* (Cambridge: Cambridge University Press, 1975), 105-110; Ayorinde, "Oriki," 63.

[59] McIntosh, *Yoruba Women, Work, and Social Change*, 200.

[60] Ayorinde, "Oriki," 64.

other African drums, they also had rhythmic and communicative functions.[61] Drumming was used to lead people in dancing, working, or fighting; they also had therapeutic purposes, and could help sustain courage or warn of danger.[62] The *ilu* or drum, for instance, was worshiped as an *orisa* by a drummer who offered sacrifices to it.[63] During annual festivals and special ceremonies, drums were used to evoke the presence of the deities.[64]

Diverse types of drums were employed with varying rhythms; however, the *dundun* or talking drum filled a unique niche in the cultural ethos of the people. The special art of communication with the talking drum was a family profession that was passed down from father to son and required years of careful training and apprenticeship.[65] In Yoruba traditional religion the drum served two purposes: (1) to bridge the gap between the visible and invisible worlds, and (2) to foster a corporate spirit, in part by the construction of the drum, and in the making of its music.[66]

Among the tribes in Nigeria the Yoruba people stand out as having some of the

---

[61]Bade Ajayi, "The Talking Drum," in *Understanding Yoruba Life and Culture*, ed. Nike S. Lawal, Matthew N. O. Sadiku, and P. Ade Dopamu (Trenton, NJ: Africa World Press, 2004), 577. The drum messages have been described as "ancient text messages" in Amanda Villepastour, *Ancient Text Messges of the Yoruba Bata Drum: Cracking the Code* (Surrey, UK: Ashgate Publishing, 2010), 13.

[62]Ajayi, "The Talking Drum," 577.

[63]McKenzie, *Hail Orisha*, 78.

[64]Ademola Adegbite, "The Drum and Its Role in Yoruba Religion," *Journal of Religion in Africa* 18, no. 1 (February 1988): 22.

[65]Ajayi, "The Talking Drum," 583-584.

[66]Adegbite, "The Drum and Its Role," 24-25.

most elaborate and lively celebrations. Renowned for their colorful and matching clothing during occasions of festivities, the dressing of their women is particularly arresting, especially the impressive headgear known as the *gele*. During some occasions the members of an association or social grouping, *egbe*, dress in uniform fashion, usually referred to as *aso ebi* (literally meaning twin clothing) symbolizing their togetherness.[67]

Cognitive Facets of Yoruba Culture

A crucial element of the Yoruba worldview is belief in the existence of the enemy. The concept of *ota* (Yoruba word for enemy, enmity, or hostility) is prominent in Yoruba secular and religious beliefs.[68] In Yoruba communities, people at every level feared what their rivals (*ota*) might do to them through the agencies of witchcraft, evil-charms, or poison.[69] It was therefore important for the Yoruba to be able to identify their enemies so that they could beg, appease, or avoid them.[70] They believed that God alone could reveal who this enemy was, with the assistance of the *babalawo* (*Ifa* priest).[71] The

---

[67]Olugbemi Moloye, "Traditional High Fashion in Transition," in *Understanding Yoruba Life and Culture*, ed. Nike S. Lawal, Matthew N. O. Sadiku, and P. Ade Dopamu (Trenton, NJ: Africa World Press, 2004), 386.

[68]B. Akintunde Oyetade, "The Enemy in the Belief System," in *Understanding Yoruba Life and Culture*, ed. Nike S. Lawal et al. (Trenton, NJ: Africa World Press, 2006), 81.

[69]Peel, *Religious Encounter*, 80.

[70]Oyetade, "The Enemy in the Belief System," 84; Wande Abimbola, who has conducted specialized studies on the *Ifa*, describes the Yoruba universe as one in which constant conflict was the order of the day. Wande Abimbola, "Ifa: A West African Cosmological System," in *Religion in Africa*, ed. Thomas D. Blakely, Walter E. A. van Beek, and Dennis L. Thomson (London: James Currey, 1994), 115.

[71]Oyetade, "The Enemy in the Belief System," 84.

babalawo (diviner) using a complex system of divination would seek the best method to respond to the need of the inquirer.[72] In order to resolve the problem of the enemy, several courses could be followed. The *babalawo* may give medicine to be ingested, charms to wear around the body, and if the enemy was powerful, the services of *esu* (the divine trickster) could be appealed to.[73]

Another noteworthy aspect of Yoruba culture is its massive oral tradition expressed in myth, song, poetry, riddles, and proverbs.[74] Hardly a major decision is taken without recourse to a proverb—usually preceded by the preamble, "Our fathers/elders/ancestors say . . ." Although some of these oral traditions in earlier times were very important, over the years many have lost their value and significance. Riddles, for instance, had recreational and educational purposes, especially in the formation of children.[75] The traditional folktales also served their own purposes, and could be classified as: moral, tortoise, and why stories. The moral stories showcased moral lessons, the tortoise stories demonstrated the cleverness and cunning of this creature in Yoruba tales, while the why stories sought to explain some natural phenomena and the

---

[72] Peel, *Aladura*, 32-33.

[73] Oyetade, "The Enemy in the Belief System," 87-88.

[74] See, Ulli Beier, *Yoruba Myths* (Cambridge: Cambridge University Press, 1980). Beier, a German citizen, published several works on Yoruba culture and poetry.

[75] B. Ajayi, "Riddles and the Child," in *Understanding Yoruba Life and Culture*, ed. Nike S. Lawal et al. (Trenton, NJ: Africa World Press, 2006), 501.

continuance or discontinuance of certain customs.[76] For the purpose of contextualizing the gospel, knowledge of the local language and the body of proverbs, riddles, and folk tales will be of great value in developing an oral theology that will enhance gospel propagation and discipleship.[77]

A current missiological challenge posed by a number of Independent Churches in the Yoruba context is the manner in which oral poetry is incorporated in sermons and songs. For instance, certain songs formerly used in contexts reminiscent of the worship of Yoruba deities have been incorporated into choruses sung in Pentecostal congregations; they are also popular among many mission churches.[78] One pastor employed incantations and prayers usually employed in oracular verse by the *babalawo* in his sermons and child-naming ritual.[79]

---

[76] Ayo Bamgbose, "Traditional Folk Tales," in *Understanding Yoruba Life and Culture*, ed. Nike S. Lawal et al. (Trenton, NJ: Africa World Press, 2006), 555-557; Oyekan Owomoyela, *Yoruba Trickster Tales* (Lincoln, NE: University of Nebraska Press, 1997). A greater part of Owomoyela's tales focus on wiles and adventures of Ajapa, the tortoise.

[77] See W. Jay Moon, *African Proverbs Reveal Christianity in Culture: A Narrative Portrayal of Builsa Proverbs; Contextualizing Christianity in Ghana* (Eugene, OR: Pickwick Publications, 2009), 194-196; Prior Randall, "Orality: The Not-So-Silent Issue in Mission Theology," *International Bulletin of Missionary Research* 35, no. 3 (2011): 145.

[78] Rotimi Taiwo, "Discursive Practices in Nigerian Pentecostal Christian Songs," *California Linguistic Notes* 33, no. 2 (2008), http://hss.fullerton.edu/liguistics/cln/Sp%2008%20pdf/Taiwo-CDA.pdf (accessed November 2, 2008).

[79] Abdul Rasheed Na'Allah, "Influence of Traditional Oral Poetry on World Religions," in *Understanding Yoruba Life and Culture*, ed. Nike S. Lawal et al. (Trenton, NJ: Africa World Press, 2004), 569-570.

Evaluative Facets of Yoruba Culture

As in most parts of Africa, the Yoruba worldview is communal. Morality was therefore regulated by societal norms.[80] One's well-being was found in the maintenance of a harmonious relationship between self, God, nature,[81] and the community. Communal morals were believed to have their origin with God.[82] Therefore, there existed an intimate relationship between the religion of the people and their morality.[83] Yoruba people believe that the actions or conduct of a person within a community can affect other members for good or for evil.[84] As a result, Yoruba society is replete with moral and social sanctions for those who choose to disregard its ethics and norms.[85] While some offenses required public ridicule (such as sexual affairs and stealing), other abominable transgressions needed to be atoned for, such as when adultery was committed

---

[80]Geoffrey Parrinder, *Africa's Three Religions* (London: Sheldon Press, 1969), 89.

[81]Leonard Barrett, "African Religions in the Americas: The 'Islands in Between,'" in *African Religions: A Symposium,* ed. Newell S. Booth (New York: NOK Publishers, 1977), 185.

[82]Mbiti, *Introduction to African Traditional Religion,* 174.

[83]Samuel Waje Kunhiyop, *African Christian Ethics* (Grand Rapids, MI: Zondervan, 2008), 25.

[84]P. A. Dopamu and E. O. Alana, "Ethical Systems," in *Understanding Yoruba Life and Culture*, ed. Nike S. Lawal et al. (Trenton, NJ: Africa World Press, 2006), 156.

[85]Unfortunately, the advent of Christianity is considered to have resulted in the slackening of morals, because it did not "rely upon custom or sanction to bring about the moral life, but rather upon a change of heart." J. K. Parratt, "Religious Change in Yoruba Society: A Test Case," *Journal of Religion in Africa* 2, no. 1 (1969): 118; Dopamu and Alana, "Ethical Systems," 169.

with the spouse of a relative.[86] Other faults which caused social disorder and were considered dangerous were: jealousy, envy, theft, anger, injury, murder, armed robbery, rape, adultery, incest, meanness, disobedience, disloyalty, dishonesty, slander, lack of deference to seniors, and wickedness.[87] Secret offenses were punished by the ancestors who were the sentinels of family morality. The ancestors shared in this task of communal rectitude with the divinities, which were also there to punish those who attempted to wreak havoc on the community under the cloak of secrecy.[88]

Shame and honor were pivotal concepts for controlling and regulating social behavior. In communal contexts such as Yoruba societies, death was in certain cases better than shame or dishonor, as the Yoruba proverb stated, *"iku y'a j'esin"* (death is preferable to shame, dishonor, and indignity).[89] Because compounds were responsible for the behavior and conduct of their members they therefore policed themselves internally to avoid shame and hazard, usually under the threat of fearsome consequences for any lapses.[90]

---

[86] Dopamu and Alana, "Ethical Systems," 169.

[87] P. Ade Dopamu, "System of Discipline," 179.

[88] E. M. Uka, ed., "Ethics of African Traditional Religion," in *Readings in African Traditional Religion: Structure, Meaning, Relevance and Future* (Bern, Germany: Peter Lang, 1991), 191; Dopamu, "System of Discipline," 170.

[89] Lanre Abass and Bolatito Asiata, "Suicide and Human Dignity: An African Perspective," *Humanity and the Social Science Journal* 5, no. 1 (2010): 58.

[90] Peel, *Religious Encounter*, 59.

Religious Context

Religion is the integrating factor of Yoruba life and thought. Indeed it has been said of them that "they live religiously, eat religiously, and die religiously."[91] To the Yoruba, "the full responsibility of all the affairs of life belongs to the Deity; their own part in the matter is to do as they are ordered through the priests and diviners whom they believe to be the interpreters of the will of the Deity."[92] Yoruba traditional religion, like most of the traditional religions of Africa, has no codified set of doctrines; rather, its central teachings are discernable in its rich oral traditions. These oral traditions comprise (1) myths—stories, explanations regarding human origins and existence; (2) *odu* corpus—a body of recitals associated with an intricate system of divination that was connected with the cult of Orunmila; (3) liturgies—means of communication of the people with their gods, consisting of personal names of the Deity and divinities regarding their origins, attributes, capabilities, circumstances, and hopes reposed in them; (4) songs—which tell stories of the past, circumstances of the present, and the hopes and fears of the future; (5) proverbs, adages, and epigrams—which convey deep theological and metaphysical meaning.[93] Presently, the Yoruba traditional religion has attained an extended following from Nigeria to the Republic of Benin, in Brazil, Cuba, the West

---

[91]J. Olumide Lucas, *The Religion of the Yorubas* (Lagos, Nigeria: C. M. S. Bookshop, 1948), 33.

[92]Idowu, *Olodumare*, 5

[93]Ibid., 7-10.

Indies, and even some parts of North America, and among African diaspora in Europe.[94]

Fundamental features of Yoruba religion are worship, prayer, sacrifice, dance, and divination. The primary objective of Yoruba worship was to obtain the favor of the gods and ensure the physical, mental, and spiritual well-being of the worshiper.[95] For this reason Yoruba religious worship has been described as "a kind of commerce between men and gods."[96] Influenced by their cosmology, worship "begins, controls, and ends all the affairs of life."[97] Great importance was attached to the proper performance of the acts of worship by the people[98] and to a religion that was fundamentally ritualistic and liturgical.[99] Emotions also played a significant role in Yoruba religious worship experience and this ranged from admiration, awe, and reverence, to fear.[100]

Petitionary prayer lay at the heart and center of Yoruba religion.[101] The people believe in the efficacy of prayer—that prayer offered by a qualified person in a consecrated place or wherever demanded is bound to be answered.[102] The emergence,

---

[94]Peter McKenzie, *Hail Orisha!: A Phenomenology of a West African Religion in the Mid-Nineteenth Century* (Leiden, Netherlands: Brill, 1997), vi.

[95]Lucas, *The Religion of the Yorubas*, 177.

[96]Ibid.

[97]Idowu, *Olodumare*, 107-108.

[98]Lucas, *The Religion of the Yorubas*, 179.

[99]Idowu, *Olodumare*, 108.

[100]Lucas, *The Religion of the Yorubas*, 178.

[101]Idowu, *Olodumare*, 116.

[102]Lucas, *The Religion of the Yorubas*, 185.

growth, and spread of the Aladura Churches, an indigenous church movement that extended all across West Africa and Europe, is premised upon the conviction that their prayers are always efficacious.[103] J. D. Y. Peel, an authority on Christianity in Yorubaland, shares a typical prayer that is translated in his book, *Religious Encounter and the Making of the Yoruba*:

> May I avoid any dispute with the *Ase* [powers]. Whoever it may be who wishes against me, may I come out on top. The enemy who hurts me, may be a dead man. With my foot may I knock against things, not with my mouth. May I avoid any dispute with my neighbor. May I avoid troublemakers. May all my journeys be in peace. May I avoid sickness, sickness is an enemy. May I enjoy health. May I avoid loss. May everything I do turn out well. So shall it be.[104]

Commenting on this prayer Peel states, "The prayer is eloquent of the insecure and competitive life-world of nineteenth century Yoruba."[105] Surprisingly, contemporary prayers from many Yoruba Christians across Pentecostal, evangelical, and mainline faiths bear close parallels.

The corollary to answered prayer was a sacrifice of thanksgiving.[106] This sacrifice could comprise money, a creature, or property; a sacrifice could also be for the purpose of preventing any evil befalling the giver.[107] Sacrifices could also take the form of offering all kinds of foods and drinks; however, the offerings varied from one divinity to

---

[103]Ray, *Aladura Christianity*, 269.

[104]Peel, *Religious Encounter*, 90.

[105]Ibid., 91.

[106]Lucas, *The Religion of the Yorubas*, 209.

[107]Peel, *Religious Encounter*, 117.

another, since the taste of each divinity differed from one to the other.[108] For instance, *Orisa nla* delights in snails cooked in shea butter, *Orunmila* prefers rats and fish, *Ogun* specializes in dogs, roasted yams, and snails; *Esu*, the cock, and *Sango*, a ram. Almost all the divinities could be offered kolanuts, notwithstanding, there are certain foods and drinks that are considered taboo. *Sango* prefers bitter cola (*orogbo*) to the kola nut; *Orisha nla* does not drink palm wine (its worshipers also do not touch it); and *Esu* detests palm-kernel oil.[109]

According to traditional belief, "sacrifice was at the heart of devotional relationship in Yoruba religion: to 'worship' a deity was to sacrifice (*bo*) to it."[110] The purpose of the sacrifice determined the mode in which the sacrifice was offered. If the sacrifice was to redeem or to serve in exchange for the life of another, it could be offered in the following modes: (1) usually the sacrifice of a chicken or any animal could be taken to a street, crossroad, or highway and left there, (2) a sacrifice could be burned and the ashes thrown outside, (3) in the case of the *ebo irapada* (redemption or exchange sacrifice) the offerer touched the forehead of the animal with his own forehead and rubbed the entire body of the animal with his hands, after which the animal was carried

---

[108] Idowu, *Olodumare*, 118. In the country of Benin where Ogun is worshiped the sacrifices are similar. Robert G. Armstrong, "The Etymology of the Word 'Ogun,'" in *Africa's Ogun: Old World and New*, ed. Sandra T. Barnes (Bloomington, IN: Indiana University Press, 1989), 30.

[109] Idowu, *Olodumare*, 118.

[110] Peel, *Religious Encounter*, 99.

into a distant bush and allowed to escape. In such cases it was understood that the fate of the offerer had been transferred to the animal victim.[111]

In the case of the transference of guilt, the modes of sacrifice took the following forms: (1) the animal victim was taken across a river and led into the bush, (2) the animal victim could be thrown into a river or buried alive with or without chains around the neck, (3) a victim may be taken to the edge of a river and fastened in such a way to ensure death by hunger or drowning, and (4) the victim could be paraded through the streets allowing people to come out to lay their hands upon it, thereby transferring their guilt to it.[112]

Human sacrifice, in Yoruba religion, as with most other animistic societies was regarded as the supreme form of sacrifice. Usually, a warning would be made that within the next few days someone would be missing in that community. Following this announcement, during certain hours of the night those appointed would go in search of a hapless victim, usually a stranger.[113] Human sacrifices could be made annually or during times of great crises or stress. In certain cases infants could be sacrificed.[114] Among the Yoruba it is strongly believed that the most powerful *oogun* ("medicines, charms") are those containing human body parts, because human beings were the most powerful kind

---

[111]Lucas, *The Religion of the Yorubas*, 210-211.

[112]Ibid., 211-212.

[113]Idowu, *Olodumare*, 120.

[114]Lucas, *The Religion of the Yorubas*, 217.

of sacrificial offering that could be offered to the *orisa*.[115]

Some practices in Yoruba traditional religion have been observed to bear close parallels to Hebrew sacrifices such as the "Sin Offering on the Day of Atonement, the Scapegoat, the Passover, the Heave Offering and the consecration of [the] Priest and of [the] cleansed leper."[116] Idowu lists the major categories of Yoruba sacrifices as (1) meal and drink offerings, (2) gift of thanks offering, (3) votive offering, (4) propitiation, (5) substitutionary, (6) preventive, and (7) foundation—a combination of propitiation and preventive sacrifices offered at the foundation of a house, village, or town to appease the spirit of the earth and prevent evil from entering a place (in ancient times the victims were humans buried alive and armed as sentries).[117]

Dance was also another important feature in Yoruba religion. It expressed the people's joy in the presence of the deity demonstrated by joyous dancing through the streets or at a selected spot.[118] Sometimes spirit possession followed ecstatic dance rituals.[119] Ritual dances were another category that were symbolic re-enactments of the sacred or historic events and demanded a carefully observed pattern which if not followed could render inefficacious the ritual performed.[120] Although most religious

---

[115]Peel, *Religious Encounter*, 83.

[116]Lucas, *The Religion of the Yorubas*, 213.

[117]Idowu, *Olodumare*, 121-125.

[118]Lucas, *The Religion of the Yorubas*, 206.

[119]Geoffrey Parrinder, *West African Religion* (London: Epworth Press, 1949), 93.

[120]Lucas, *The Religion of the Yorubas*, 206.

festivals were followed by dancing, the solemn rituals at the shrines did not evoke such emotions.[121]

The Yoruba possess a complex and renowned system of divination known as the *Ifa*,[122] whose priest is the *babalawo* (father of mysteries).[123] There are, however, many other forms of divination besides the *Ifa*. Bade Ajayi, a Yoruba scholar, cites several forms of divination practiced by the Yoruba in his article, "*Ifa* Divination: Its Structure and Application."

> These include: *Erindinlogun*, which involves the casting of sixteen cowries, *Abigba*, which employs a set of separate strings with four markers each, and *Iyanrin tite* (sand printing). Others are: *obi dida* (kola casting), *omi wiwo* (water gazing), *atipa* or *abokuusoro wiwo oju* (eye gazing), and *digi wiwo* (mirror gazing).[124]

Of all these, *Ifa* is the most widespread, the most prestigious,[125] and also considered to be the most important and reliable.[126] It is believed that *Ifa* originated in Ile-Ife, the center of the Yoruba civilization, but it has spread throughout the Yoruba

---

[121] Idowu, *Olodumare*, 115.

[122] E. Thomas Lawson, *Religions of Africa: Traditions in Transformation* (San Francisco: Harper and Row Publishers, 1984), 55

[123] Newell S. Booth Jr., ed., "God and the Gods in West Africa," in *African Religions: A Symposium* (New York: NOK Publishers, 1977), 168; John Mbiti, *Introduction to African Religion*, 2nd ed. (Oxford: Heinemann Educational Books, 1991), 157.

[124] Bade Ajayi, "Ifa Divination: Its Structure and Application," in *Understanding Yoruba Life and Culture*, ed. Nike S. Lawal, Matthew N. O. Sadiku, and P. Ade Dopamu (Trenton, NJ: Africa World Press, 2004), 113.

[125] Abimbola, "Ifa: A West African Cosmological System," 101; Peel, *Religious Encounter*, 114.

[126] Ajayi, "Ifa Divination," 113.

world even beyond its borders to countries like Brazil, Cuba, and America.[127] *Ifa* divination is based upon sixteen basic and 256 derivative figures, known as *odus* (signs).[128] The basic purpose of *Ifa* is to determine the correct sacrifice necessary to secure a favorable resolution of whatever problem may confront the client.[129] In a divination ritual there are three important elements: the diviner (*babalawo*), the ritual apparatus, and the person consulting the diviner.[130]

Babalawo were considered the intellectuals of the Yoruba traditional society.[131] They were "adept at the analysis of novel situations in terms of precedents and prone to the rationalization of the cultural materials—myths, proverbs, *oriki*, maxims, fables, historical fragments—which were built into the *ese Ifa*."[132] Another function of the

---

[127]Cuban immigrants have also brought the Yoruba religion to cities in America such as New York. Mary Cuthrell Curry, "The Yoruba Religion in New York," in *New York Glory: Religions in the City*, ed. Tony Carnes and Anna Karpathakis (New York: New York University Press, 2001), 74; Thorpe, *African Traditional Religions*, 97.

[128]One of the earliest and most comprehensive studies on Ifa is William Bascom's, *Ifa Divination: Communication between God's and Men in West Africa* (Bloomington, IN: Indiana University Press, 1969); Thorpe, *African Traditional Religions*, 98.

[129]Booth, *African Religions: A Symposium*, 168.

[130]Lawson, *Religions of Africa*, 67.

[131]Peel, *Religious Encounter*, 114. One of the attractions of the *Ifa* priesthood was its lucrativeness. This idea is depicted in the proverb, *ebi ko le pa babalawo* (an *Ifa* priest can never starve). Lucas, *The Religion of the Yorubas*, 72.

[132]Peel, *Religious Encounter*.

babalawo was to interpret the dreams of the people[133] that were believed to be portentous and pregnant with meaning. J. D. Y. Peel, a scholar of Yoruba Christianity, adds insightfully concerning the *babalawo* and his *Ifa* divinatory system that

> if there was a keynote to the *Ifa* cult, it was control: control of circumstances through knowledge of the relevant precedents for action, a control which itself depended on the *babalawo's* own self-control. Unlike the other major *orisa*, *Ifa* or *Orunmila* did not possess his priests, and, again unlike the other cults, they were nearly always male.[134]

The ritual apparatus, as mentioned earlier, is a complex system founded on a mystical base of fours, which were used to interpret and determine responses to problems presented. While it is beyond the scope of this paper to delve into the details of this intricate and mysterious process, a brief survey will be provided of the functions of *babalawo*, and the *Ifa* divination.[135]

One of the functions of the *babalawo* begins at the birth of a child. The *Ifa* oracle was also consulted to ascertain what foods the mother-to-be is to eat and what sacrifice would be made to ensure a safe delivery of the child.[136] Furthermore, because of the strong Yoruba belief in destiny, the services of the diviner were sought to discover and

---

[133]Geoffrey Parrinder, *West African Psychology* (New York: AMS Press, 1976), 190.

[134]Peel, *Religious Encounter*, 114.

[135]Great sources on the *Ifa* system of divination are: Bascom's, *Ifa Divination: Communication between Gods and Men in West Africa*, and Wande Abimbola's, *Ifa Divination Poetry* (New York: NOK Publishers, 1977).

[136]S. A. Thorpe, *African Traditional Religions* (Pretoria, South Africa: University of South Africa, 1991), 101.

ensure the fulfillment of this destiny.[137] Also, because it was believed that each child had its own distinctive *orisa*, it was the duty of the *babalawo* through divination to direct each individual to discover his or her appropriate *orisa*.[138] Ingrained in the Yoruba worldview is the conviction that life without the *Ifa* would be worse, for "*Ifa* provides confidence and certainty in a world of anxiety," thereby performing a crucial stabilizing function.[139] It is for this reason that the *babalawo's* role is indispensable in the Yoruba society.

A better understanding of the impact and influence of divination and sorcery among the Yoruba can only be derived from a closer examination of what Lawson describes as the two levels of power foci in the belief system of the people. The first level is *Orun* (heaven) and the second *Aye* or *Aiye* (earth).[140] An examination of these concepts will shed light on Yoruba cosmology discussed in the following section.

Yoruba Cosmology

Although considered complex, Yoruba cosmology can be divided into two parts, *Orun* (skies or heaven) where the gods and divinities live, and *aiye* (world) where the humans and animals dwell. Three main elements at three different levels provide

---

[137]Lawson, *Religions of Africa*, 69.

[138]Steven S. Farrow, *Faith, Fancies and Fetich* (London: Society for Promoting Christian Knowledge, 1924), 92, 95; Peel, *Religious Encounter*, 115.

[139]Benjamin C. Ray, *African Religions: Symbol, Ritual, and Community* (Englewood Cliffs, NJ: Prentice-Hall, 1976), 110.

[140]Lawson, *Religions in Africa*, 66.

understanding for this complex world. These are: *Olorun*, the chief source of power, who is unapproachable directly; *orisa*, a level of power approachable through ritual action; and the ancestors, who in family worship play important roles.[141]

Olorun

Basically, Yoruba traditional religion, like its counterparts in the West African sub-region, consists of belief in the following entities: God (*Olorun* or *Olodumare*; owner of the heavens), the divinities, ancestors, spirits, the practice of magic (the metaphysical), and medicine (*oogun*).[142] Each of these beliefs in some way is interrelated with the practices of divination and sorcery.

Olorun (owner of the skies) is the originating power of the cosmos to whom all other forms of life and being such as the *orisa* (divinities), ancestors, and humans owe their existence.[143] *Olodumare* is another name for this Yoruba supreme deity. This name connotes the idea of One with whom man may enter into covenant and communion in any place and time, who is superlatively great, incomparable, unsurpassable, excellent in attributes, stable, unchanging, constant, and reliable.[144] Also known as *Edumare*, he is

---

[141]*Olorun* meant "Owner or Lord of Heaven," and was the most commonly used name for the Supreme Sovereign Ruler. Idowu, *Olodumare*, 37; Lawson, *Religions of Africa*, 57.

[142]Bolaji E. Idowu, *African Traditional Religion* (London: SCM Press, 1973), 139; Olu E. Alana, "Traditional Religion," in *Understanding Yoruba Life and Culture*, ed. Nike Lawal et al. (Trenton, NJ: Africa World Press, 2004), 69.

[143]Lawson, *Religions of Africa*, 58.

[144]Bolaji E. Idowu, *Olodumare, God in Yoruba Belief* (London: Longmans, 1962), 36.

"the king or chief who holds the scepter, wields authority and has quality which is superlative in worth, and he is at the same time permanent, unchangeable and reliable."[145] *Olodumare*, the Author of the essence of man and Determiner of human destiny is the One from whom the essence of human life (*ori*, literal translation, head) is derived.[146] The head in the Yoruba worldview is very complex, and is believed to possess both physical and metaphysical attributes, which have much to do in determining human destiny.[147] Olu Alana, a Yoruba scholar, states that a person's destiny, which is conferred at birth and sealed by God, is normally unalterable. However, it may be altered under certain circumstances—a good destiny could be preserved through good conduct, while an unpleasant destiny could be made promising through some good conduct.[148] This is where divination is beneficial. Success, prosperity, fortune, longevity, misfortune, illness, pain, and, untimely, death are all believed to proceed from a person's destiny. Consequently, the services of the diviner are needed to determine and deliver one from an unsavory existence.

---

[145]J. O. Awolalu and P. A. Dopamu, *West African Traditional Religion* (Ibadan, Nigeria: Onibonoje Press, 1979), 38-39.

[146]Alana, "Traditional Religion," 68.

[147]Michael O. Afolayan, "Defining and Conceptualizing Knowledge Among the Yoruba," in *Understanding Yoruba Life and Culture*, ed. Nike S. Lawal et al. (Trenton, NJ: Africa World Press, 2004), 190; Harry Sawyerr, *God: Ancestor or Creator?—Aspects of Traditional Belief in Ghana, Nigeria and Sierra Leone* (London: Longman, 1970), 41-42.

[148]Alana, "Traditional Religion," 68. Curiously the Yoruba worldview affirmed the dualistic concepts of fatalism and freedom in human existence. Ray, *African Religions*, 139.

Orisa

Orisa is the Yoruba word used to represent deity, divinity, god or goddess.[149] Their precise number varies from one scholar to another. Estimates for the number of divinities ranges between 201 and 700.[150] Although also placed at 401,[151] it is believed that this merely expresses a number that cannot be counted exactly, much like the English expression "a thousand and one."[152] The divinities can be divided into three categories: the primordial divinities, who existed from the beginning with the supreme deity; the deified ancestors, who were human beings that lived extraordinary lives and thus became deified as ancestors; and divinities that are merely personification of natural forces and phenomena.[153] Examples of the primordial divinities are: *Orisa nla* (*Obatala*), *Orunmila* (*Ifa*), *Ogun*, and *Esu*; of these *Orisa nla* (the archdivinity) is the head of the pantheon.[154]

Each Yoruba town had its own deities that played more prominent roles than

---

[149]Thorpe, *African Traditional Religions*, 90.

[150]Alana, "Traditional Religion," 69.

[151]Lawson, *Religions of Africa*, 59. Farrow believes that the actual number of orisas were at least 600. Farrow, *Faith, Fancies and Fetich*, 34.

[152]Thorpe, *African Traditional Religions*, 91.

[153]Alana, "Traditional Religion," 69.

[154]Parrinder lists the four most powerful gods in the Yoruba pantheon as Ifa, Ogu[n], Jakuta (Shango) and Obatala. *West African Religion*, 27; Alana, "Traditional Religion," 69.

others,[155] and each divinity had its own worshippers.[156] There were, however, *orisa* that were worshipped all over Yorubaland.[157] A recent study has shown that geographical and ecological factors may have significance in determining which divinity is worshipped from one locality to another.[158] Kalu also mentions two categories of pantheons which according to *Ifa* texts compete for universal domination. Of this number, 400 are the good gods, while the hostile ones are 200. Moreover, between them and the Supreme Being is the capricious trickster god, *Eshu*, who can aid or harm, depending on the sacrifice given.[159] The good gods want to bless, while the evil ones want to thwart personal and societal goals.[160] Such a scenario etched deep in the worldview of the people leads to a constant state of insecurity and anxiety that requires the services of diviners who act as mediators in order to avert adversity and evil. Curiously, although fear was characteristic in Yoruba religious worship, it was never directed towards *Olorun* (Supreme Deity); rather it was the *orishas*, especially *eshu,* that were dreaded.[161]

---

[155]Thorpe, *African Traditional Religions*, 91.

[156]Booth, "God and Gods in West Africa," 167.

[157]Lawson, *Religions of Africa*, 59.

[158]Ogbu U. Kalu, *Power, Poverty and Prayer: The Challenges of Poverty and Pluralism in African Christianity, 1960-1996* (Trenton, NJ: Africa World Press, 2006), 91.

[159]Blood sacrifices were first offered to *eshu* so that he may not prevent the orisa from granting the request of the supplicant. R. E. Dennett, *Nigerian Studies or the Religious and Political System of the Yoruba* (London: Frank Cass and Company, 1968), 94.

[160]Kalu, *Power, Poverty and Prayer*, 91-92.

[161]Farrow, *Faith, Fancies and Fetich*, 29.

Alana provides understanding of the various Yoruba divinities and their functions, which demonstrates the pivotal roles sorcery and divination play in the life and thought of the people:[162]

Obatala (Orisa nla)—deputy of *Olodumare* and agent of creation; his role, position and authority are derived from and delegated by *Olodumare*. He is the arch-divinity and head of the pantheon.

Orunmila or *Ifa*—oracle divinity among the Yoruba; deputy of *Olodumare* in matters of wisdom and foreknowledge. Traditionally *Ifa* is consulted by the Yoruba in every rite of passage.

Ogun—god of iron and war; he is the patron god of hunters and warriors.[163] Covenants and oaths made before him must be respected lest the blood of the violator of the oath is shed. Known to be ferocious, *Ogun* is believed to be the instrument of divine wrath and judgment.

Esu—deputy of *Olodumare* in matters of ritual and human conduct; he also looks into the conduct of divinities and men and brings back a report to *Olodumare*. *Esu* is ubiquitous, difficult to predict, mischievous, and is the intermediary officer between the heavens and the earth, accusing and defending divinities and men before God. Known to be sometimes benevolent, prayers and sacrifices are offered to him to secure his favor

---

[162]The following section is drawn from Alana's article, "Traditional Religion," 69-72.

[163]Sandra T. Barnes, "The Many Faces of Ogun," in *Africa's Ogun: Old World and New* (Bloomington, IN: Indiana University Press, 1989), 2.

and protection from evil. Esu determines the fate of humans, altering prosperously or adversely depending on the sacrifice offered to it.[164]

Sango—divinity of thunder and lightning. He is an example of a deified ancestor. Historically believed to be the fourth king of the Oyo Empire, after his death he took on the attributes of *Jakuta*, the earlier thunder divinity. A much-dreaded divinity representing divine wrath, *Sango* punishes lying, cheating, and stealing. Devotees petition him for peace, prosperity, longevity, and protection against misfortunes.

Osun—the goddess of the river Osun which flows through Osogbo, a town in Osun State, Nigeria. She is believed to be one of the wives of *Sango*. The custodian of fertility for both men and women, *Osun* is known for her benevolence and beneficence. She is worshiped by those seeking children, and water taken from her shrine is believed to enable women to become pregnant and have children. She blesses people materially and is known to prevent misfortune. *Osun* is also worshipped in the annual Odunde festival beside the Schulkyl river in Pasadena, Philadelphia.[165]

Evidently in the life and experience of the Yoruba, the divinities whose functions were considered more visible, played more prominent roles than the Supreme Deity, to whom prayers were made and through whom sacrifices were offered. Because the

---

[164]Femi Euba, *Archetypes, Imprecators, and Victims of Fate: Origins and Developments of Satire in Black Drama* (New York: Greenwood Press, 1989), 30.

[165]Begun in 1975 by Lois Fernandez, the *Odunde* festival is celebrated annually in the month of June in commemoration of the Yoruba New Year, with fruit and flowers offered to the river goddess Osun. Mark J. Stern, Susan C. Seifert, and Domenic Vitiello, "Migrants, Community, and Culture," *Creativity and Change* (January 2008): 9. http://www.plancincinnati.org/documents/working_groups/Arts_Culture/plans/SIAP%20-%20Migrants.pdf (accessed November 25, 2013).

divinities were needed to survive and thrive in a world filled with capricious deities, constantly changing circumstances, and communal demands, the aid of diviners and sorcerers was often sought.

Ancestors

In the West African belief system, ancestors are regarded as some of the most powerful spiritual forces.[166] To the Yoruba, at death a person enters into the realm of the living-dead, or ancestors.[167] These ancestors referred to as *Baba-nla* (great fathers),[168] even before their death, as elders, were credited with power beyond the average because by their words they were able to produce effects by curse or blessing.[169] Consequently, after their death they are believed to assume superhuman powers, a simple extension of

---

[166] Geoffrey Parrinder, *Africa's Three Religions* (London: Sheldon Press, 1969), 69.

[167] Thorpe, *African Traditional Religions*, 95. There were two classes of ancestors: family ancestors—pertaining to a local family; and deified ancestors—not tied to particular families, but were persons who once lived, but at death attained considerable spiritual power, and are worshiped. Caleb Oluremi Oladipo, *The Development of the Doctrine of the Holy Spirit in the Yoruba (African) Indigenous Christian Movement* (New York: Peter Lang Publishing, 1996), 75-76.

[168] Simeon Abiodun Ige, "The Cult of Ancestors in African Traditional Religion," *An Encyclopedia of the Arts* 10, no. 1 (2006): 26, http://assets00.grou.ps/0F2E3C/wysiwyg_files/FilesModule/mtofolives/ 20100927151021-mitrtueogmxwpafbx/Ancestors_and_ African_Religions.pdf (accessed November 25, 2011).

[169] The deceased are never considered to be in the graves, but they continue their roles as the parents they were before death in a more powerful manner. Idowu, *Olodumare*, 192; Peel, *Religious Encounter*, 94.

the place and functions they had while alive.[170] One function the ancestors performed in heaven was to determine people's destinies, or fate (*ori*), even before they were born.[171]

Yoruba society, like most African communities, was considered as comprising the living and the ancestors. These ancestors are thought to have power to hurt or help their living kin, depending on the recognition and respect shown to them by the living.[172] Traditionally it is believed that the ancestors can influence life for good, they can bring rainfall or good harvest, promote prosperity, or give protection and general well-being to living family members.[173] Among the Yoruba, ancestors have shrines where sacrifices and prayers are offered to them, known as *Igbo Igbale*.[174] The priests and priestesses were the eldest members of the family. However, the priestess could not be a woman married into the family.[175]

Annually two festivals are celebrated in honor of the ancestors in Yorubaland: the *Egungun* and *Oro*.[176] The *Egungun* is the cult of the dead ancestors who are believed to

---

[170] Peel, *Religious Encounter*, 94-95.

[171] Ray, *African Religions*, 136.

[172] Thorpe, *African Traditional Religions*, 95.

[173] Alana, "Traditional Religion," 74.

[174] Ige, "The Cult of Ancestors in ATR," 28; other *orisa* which represent the spirits of the ancestors are, Iro, Oro, Egun, or Egungun, and Eleko. Dennett, *Nigerian Studies*, 28.

[175] Alana, "Traditional Religion," 74.

[176] A basic difference between the *Oro* and *Egungun* was that while the devotees of the former could never be seen appearing in public at daytime, the latter paraded during the day robed from head to toe in colorful cloth. Parrinder, *West African Religion*, 143; Alana, "Traditional Religion," 74.

have descended to the world of the living in order to celebrate with their descendants.[177] This ancient cultic festival was celebrated to welcome the ancestors, who had returned to right the wrongs in the community and to bless with human, and crop fertility.[178] During these festivals, the masquerades entertain with dance and witty philosophical sayings; they chased young men and women around with whips, which they freely used.[179] Barren women were known to seek help and blessings from some of the powerful *Egungun* during their public displays.[180] Because of the belief that ancestors serve as intermediaries between humans and the divinities, food and animal offerings are made to them accompanied by prayers.[181] The new yam festival, usually in early June, was never celebrated until the *Egungun* festival had been done. It was only after its weeklong festivities were concluded that the harvesting of yams was permitted.[182]

---

[177]Jacob K. Olupona, "The Study of Yoruba Religious Tradition in Historical Perspective," *Numen* 40, no. 3 (1993): 248, http://www.jstor.org/stable/3270151 (accessed November 25, 2011). The word *Egungun* means "bone" or "skeleton"; its devotees impersonated the dead. Parrinder, *West African Religion*, 143.

[178]P. S. O. Aremu, "Between Myth and Reality: Yoruba Egungun Costumes as Commemorative Clothes," *Journal of Black Studies* 22, no. 6 (1991): 6, http://jbs.sagepub.com/content/22/1/6.full.pdf (accessed November 25, 2011).

[179]Isola Olomola, "Contradictions in Yoruba Folk Beliefs Concerning Post-life Existence: Ado Example," *Journal des Africanistes* 58, no. 1 (1988): 113, http://www.persee.fr/web/revues/home/prescript/ article/ jafr_0399-0346_1988_num_58_1_2255 (accessed November 25, 2011).

[180]Olomola, "Contradictions in Yoruba Folk Beliefs," 113.

[181]Alana, "Traditional Religion," 74.

[182]Thorpe, *African Traditional Religions*, 96.

The *Oro* cult was a secret society that represented the spirits of the departed, and aroused great fear among the Yoruba.[183] Peel submits that both the *Oro* and *Egungun* cults served similar ideological roles: "To expose the living to the power of the dead and so to underwrite society."[184] Festival celebrations could last for one day, or go on for three to seven days.[185] During the celebrations sacrifices are offered by the worshippers to ward off epidemics, evil, and misfortune.[186]

The *Oro* cult is a male secret society whose celebration is mainly nocturnal, in the bush, and required that women stayed indoors all through the celebrations.[187] It is believed that if a woman saw the *Oro* she would be carried away in the night.[188] The *Oro* instrument is the bull-roarer, which produced a high shrill sound, or a deep guttural note—depending on its size—which was weird and awe-inspiring.[189] The cult also had a

---

[183] Parrinder, *West African Religion*, 141; Thorpe, *African Traditional Religions*, 97.

[184] Peel, *Religious Encounter*, 58.

[185] P. A. Dopamu, "Traditional Festivals," in *Understanding Yoruba Life and Culture*, ed. Nike S. Lawal et al. (Trenton, NJ: Africa World Press, 2006), 658.

[186] Oro was regarded as a giver of children, but was also responsible for arresting disease and sickness. Dennett, *Nigerian Studies*, 38; Dopamu, "Traditional Festivals," 659.

[187] Thorpe, *African Traditional Religions*, 97.

[188] Dopamu, "Traditional Festivals," 659.

[189] Made from the whirling of a flat stick, the noise began as a low moan, then rose to a scream; it was a capital crime to imitate such a sound. Dennett, *Nigerian Studies*, 46. Farrow, *Faith, Fancies and Fetich*, 69-71, provides a fuller description of the *oro* stick; see also Dopamu, "Traditional Festivals," 659.

normative function, which included in ancient times the execution of thieves and witches,[190] or their expulsion from the town.[191]

Celebration of the *Egungun* and *Oro* festivals constantly reinforced in the subconscious of the Yoruba the powerful role that the ancestors played to their well-being and existence. Because these ancestors wield power over their prosperity and longevity, it was in their own interests to seek the intervention of the diviners and sorcerers to either secure their benediction or nullify a malediction.

Apart from the traditional religion of the Yoruba people, two other religions that have influenced and made significant impact on the history and existence of this people group are Islam and Christianity. The effect of Islam is evident in the many loan words from that religion that have entered and been assimilated into the Yoruba vocabulary. Christianity became the adopted religion of several Yoruba tribes to the extent that a new form of indigenous Christianity was birthed, known as the Aladura. The rise and spread of the religion of Islam and the major features of Aladura Christianity will be the subjects of the following sections. This brief overview is to simply highlight how the Yoruba people have accommodated and transformed these foreign religions and indigenized them.

Islam in Yorubaland

As early as the eleventh and twelfth centuries Muslims could be found in Bornu

---

[190]Peel, *Religious Encounter*, 57.

[191]Dopamu, "Traditional Festivals," 659.

and Hausaland.¹⁹² It was not until the 1900s, however, that Islam finally penetrated and became institutionalized in Northern Nigeria and parts of Yorubaland.¹⁹³ Usman Dan Fodio through a jihad established a theocratic Muslim empire that ruled in the Hausa states of Northern Nigeria, but it was itinerant Hausa traders who brought the religion to Yorubaland in the mid-eighteenth century.¹⁹⁴ Muslim traders and missionaries from Mali promulgated the new religion to the Yorubas, which is why Islam is known as Imale (that is, the religion of the people of Mali).¹⁹⁵ A local poem aptly portrays the relationship between Yoruba traditional religion, Islam, and Christianity:

> We met *Ifa* in the world
> We met Islam in the world
> But Christianity arrived right
> in the "afternoon"
> We shall perform our traditional rites
> We shall perform our traditional rites
> Christianity does not prevent us
> From performing our traditional rites
> We shall perform our traditional rites.¹⁹⁶

Another convincing argument of Islam as a precursor is evident from the number of Songhai, or Arabic loan words, that can be found in Yoruba today. Ironically, some of these words were also adopted by Christianity. Examples of these are: *alufa* or *alfa*

---

¹⁹²Peel, *Aladura*, 45.

¹⁹³Gabriel Maduka Okafor, *Development of Christianity and Islam in Modern Nigeria* (Wurzburg, Germany: Echter Verlag, 1992), 57.

¹⁹⁴Peel, *Aladura*, 46.

¹⁹⁵Yushua Sodiq, "The Practice of Islam," in *Understanding Yoruba Life and Culture,* ed. Nike S. Lawal, Matthew N. O. Sadiku, and P. Ade Dopamu (Trenton, NJ: Africa World Press, 2004), 137-138.

¹⁹⁶Okafor, *Development of Christianity and Islam in Modern Nigeria*, 55-56.

(Muslim cleric, now used for Christian pastors); *iwasu* (preaching or sermon).[197] This occurrence is traceable to Samuel Ajai Crowther, the indigenous bishop in Yorubaland, and writer of one of the earliest works in the Yoruba language; some of the borrowed words are: *alufa* for priest, *woli* (Muslim word for saint that represented a prophet), and *adura* (prayer). Other loan words included the names for God like *Ubangiji* (Lord) and *Alanu* (merciful).[198] Such integration and assimilation resulted in Islam attaining a position that was second only to the traditional religion.[199]

A notable feature of Islam in Yorubaland is that it was a rather tolerant and mild breed that did not push its converts too hard.[200] In contrast to the traditional rulers of Northern Nigeria, when the Yoruba chiefs accepted Islam they never abandoned their traditional cults, or the rituals of their ancestors.[201] Indeed, scholars have noted that with Yoruba Muslims, they were first Yoruba before they were Muslims[202] (or even Christians).[203]

Two major reasons have been advanced to account for Islam's relative success in

---

[197]Peel, *Religious Encounter*, 190.

[198]Ibid., 196.

[199]Okafor, *Development of Christianity and Islam in Modern Nigeria*, 56.

[200]Peel, *Aladura*, 47. Many Yoruba Muslims did not see anything wrong in practicing various forms of divination. Patrick S. Ryan, *Imale: Yoruba Participation in the Muslim Tradition* (Missoula, MT: Scholars Press, 1978), 155.

[201]Okafor, *Development of Christianity and Islam in Modern Nigeria*, 56.

[202]Peel, *Aladura*, 47.

[203]Sodiq, "The Practice of Islam," 148.

Yorubaland; its magico-spiritual techniques—where the *alufa* (also spelled *alfa*—Muslim cleric) were engaged like the *babalawo*, and exercised spiritual power through prayer, charms, and offering;[204] and its social affability—they employed practical offers to attract converts and made few demands of cultural renunciation on them.[205] Regarding religious conversion among the Yoruba, it has been astutely observed that the superiority of any religion was not as important as the usefulness of the belief; in other words the people were utilitarian in their beliefs.[206] Patrick Ryan, who wrote his dissertation on the accommodation of Islam into Yorubaland, observed that, "a purist version of Islam, demanding complete renunciation of the cultural attitudes of the Yoruba, might not have succeeded in striking roots in Yorubaland."[207]

Yoruba Christianity

Several attempts had been made by various Catholic orders to establish Christianity in the Benin kingdom during the fifteenth and sixteenth centuries, but they failed to establish any lasting presence in the country of Nigeria. It was not until the

---

[204]Warriors especially came to the *alufas* to obtain charms for protection in battle. Ryan, *Imale*, 126-127; Peel, *Religious Encounter*, 214, 198.

[205]Peel, *Religious Encounter*, 205. Other practices that the Muslim *alfas* incorporated into their version of Islam to make it relevant to the Yoruba context included divination and the interpretation of dreams. Ryan, *Imale*, 155, 174.

[206]Sodiq, "The Practice of Islam," 148-149.

[207]Ryan, *Imale*, 165.

1840s that mission in earnest began in Yorubaland.[208] The progress of missionary efforts among the Yoruba was slow for the first half century, due to a number of cultural and missiological factors. Among these were the charges that Christians were cowards and womanly because of their refusal to fight during a period of continual battles among the tribes.[209] Because engagement in war indicated a sense of honor, Christianity was despised by young Yoruba men. Another factor was the significance burial customs had in the society. Christian converts were taunted that when they died they would be buried in the bush, a dreadful prospect for people who valued the role of ancestors in the community.[210] Curiously it was partly through the agency of returned slaves that Christianity was finally able to spread in Abeokuta and Ibadan, two prominent cities of the Yoruba.[211] The other factors that facilitated the spread of Christian missions from the 1890s was the annexation of Yorubaland by the British, which resulted in Christian missions now being regarded with new status and appreciated for their educational and other benefits.[212] The Ijebus, for instance, massively adopted Christianity, the religion of

---

[208]Okafor, *Development of Christianity and Islam in Modern Nigeria*, gives 1842 as the date when the Church Missionary Society (C. M. S.) commenced missions among the Yoruba; Peel in *Aladura* mentions 1842 as the date of the arrival of T. B. Freeman of the Methodist mission to Abeokuta; Law concurs that Christian missionaries did not penetrate the interior of Yorubaland before the 1840s.

[209]Peel, *Religious Encounter*, 138.

[210]Farrow, *Faith, Fancies and Fetich*, 113.

[211]Peel, *Religious Encounter*, 240.

[212]Peel, *Aladura*, 50.

their conquerors, because their defeat discredited the gods, who failed to protect them.[213] During this same period, however, a series of secessions by the African Church movement led to the eventual emergence of African Indigenous (Independent) Churches.[214] A significant characteristic of the Yoruba, demonstrated in their assimilation of Islam and their engagement with Christianity, is their exceptional ability to adopt and adapt a religion and make it their own.[215] Corroboration for this is evidenced in the growth and spread of the Aladura churches.

Aladura

Benjamin Ray, an expert in sub-Saharan African religions, defined Aladura Christianity as "a distinctive form of Christianity that bears the full imprint of Yoruba traditional religion."[216] The emergence of such African churches was attributable to the commitment of the Yorubas to Christianity, and to the refusal of missionary societies to give Africans more than token representation at the administrative level.[217]

In recent times four identifiable strands of Aladura churches have emerged, all founded by Yoruba men. These are the Apostolic Churches, the Cherubim and Seraphim

---

[213] Peel, *Religious Encounter*, 149.

[214] It was the hesitation to hand over the highest position of the church to Africans by the missionary societies that in major part led to the emergence of the African churches. James Bertin Webster, *The African Churches Among the Yoruba: 1888-1922* (Oxford: Oxford University Press, 1964), 41; Peel, *Religious Encounter*, 149.

[215] Peel, *Aladura*, 54.

[216] Ray, "Aladura Christianity," 266.

[217] Peel, *Aladura*, 55.

Church, The Church of the Lord, and the Celestial Church of Christ.[218] Beliefs that they hold in common are "the efficacy of prayer (*adura*), the reality of the spirit world, the power of God's kingdom on earth, the ritual of holy water, the power of biblical words, the extraordinary popularity of the psalms, and the power to heal."[219]

Divination through the assistance of the *babalawo* helps the traditional Yoruba worshiper in explaining and predicting events, while sacrifice serves the purpose of appeasing spiritual beings, averting of danger, and controlling evil powers. Aladura in response to those cosmological fears and needs of the people employs prayer (*adura*), prophecy, visions, and dreams in place of these.[220]

There are several syncretistic practices prevalent in Aladura churches such as wrapping and sewing up portions of Ps 108 in black leather with a cube of camphor, and writing Ps 126 on paper around a piece of camphor and hanging it around the neck for healing and protective purposes.

---

[218]Matthew N. O. Sadiku, "The Practice of Christianity," in *Understanding Yoruba Life and Culture,* ed. Nike S. Lawal, Matthew N. O. Sadiku, and P. Ade Dopamu (Trenton, NJ: Africa World Press, 2004), 128.

[219]Other beliefs and practices include an imminent and evocable divinity, witchcraft explanations to account for suffering, and religious dance. Deidre Helen Crumbley, *Spirit, Structure, and Flesh: Gendered Experiences in African Instituted Churches Among the Yoruba of Nigeria* (Madison, WI: The University of Wisconsin Press, 2008), 19; Sadiku, "The Practice of Christianity," 128.

[220]Afe Adogame, "Building Bridges and Barricades," *Marburg Journal of Religion* 3, no. 1 (March 1998): 5, http://archiv.ub.uni-marburg.de/mjr/pdf/1998/adogame1998.pdf (accessed November 5, 2013).

There are other recipes for sickness, protection against witches and evil spirits, which use a variety of traditional means. It is easy to see why Yoruba Christians in the adaptive climate of their culture, sought to appropriate the power of Christianity, while retaining as much of the power of traditional medicine as well. Thus to seek the best of both worlds seems both sensible and reasonable to the average Yoruba Christian.[221]

Aladura Christianity is regarded as a precursor for the charismatic or Pentecostal movement that swept through Nigeria, making its first appearance about 1930-1931.[222] Although derisively called "white garment churches," the Aladura churches share basically similar worldviews with the Nigerian Pentecostal churches, such as belief in the power of prayers to guarantee healing, prosperity, guidance and success, in addition to belief in the prevalence of evil forces—demons, and ancestral spirits for which protection is needed, and deliverance should be sought.[223]

Aladura churches were representative of the indigenous spiritual awakening that swept through Africa in the 1920s, with "a precarious worldview [that] was suffused with a keen awareness of the presence of evil and who saw life as the tapping of the resources of good gods against the machinations of evil ones."[224] As the Nigerian missiologist

---

[221]Peel, *Aladura*, 118.

[222]Peel, *Religious Encounter*, 314. Kalu argues that the Aladura and AICs may be considered as the first phase of African Pentecostalism. *Power, Poverty and Prayer*, 135-136.

[223]Peel, *Religious Encounter*, 315.

[224]Kalu, *Power, Poverty and Prayer*, 35. Aladura Churches reflected cosmological continuities between the traditional religion and Christianity. Walls, *The Cross-Cultural Process*, 126.

Ogbu Kalu perceptively observed, power and spirituality lay at the center of these indigenous church movements.[225]

---

[225]Ibid., 35.

CHAPTER III

CONVERSION AND WORLDVIEW TRANSFORMATION

Introduction

Conversion is synonymous with change or transformation, and Christianity is a religion premised on this experience.[1] A sign that initial change has occurred is the commitment of a believer's life to the lordship of Christ through baptism. Although the history of Christianity bears ample record to the radical transformation that faith in Christ has brought to individuals, communities, and to nations, regrettably, that has not always been the case in every instance. Evidence of this can be found in a survey of Christianity in Yorubaland.

An irksome and pervasive missiological issue is the reality of Christians who claim to be converted never come to reflect transformation at the worldview level. Far too often orthodoxy has been stressed as evidence of conversion even when the underlying assumptions of belief and reality remain unaffected.[2] Affirmation of this predicament can be found in reports of dual allegiance, immorality, and various forms of discrimination in present-day church life. Extremely bothersome is the fact that some

---

[1]Andrew F. Walls, *The Cross-Cultural Process in Christian History* (Maryknoll, NY: Orbis Books, 2002), 67.

[2]Paul Hiebert, "Conversion and Worldview Transformation," *International Journal for Frontier Missions* 14, no. 2 (April-June 1997): 83-84.

who claim to be Christians are primarily creatures of their culture and only secondarily Christians—such as is the case sometimes with Yoruba Christianity. This is the underlying cause behind genocide, ethnocentrism,[3] racism, discrimination, and the practices of divination and sorcery among some Yoruba Christians. Evidently, Christianity needs to go beyond seeking external conformity to norms and codes, to internal transformation of worldviews, which govern behavior and attitudes, especially in times of crises.

This chapter will examine conversion and worldview transformation. Various models will be considered with the aim of employing a multidisciplinary approach towards a holistic model that will lead to discipleship and worldview transformation.

Conversion

Conversion is a concept that is primarily found in the religions whose origins trace their roots to the Middle East—Judaism, Christianity and Islam.[4] Alfred Nock in his seminal work on this subject states that in the rival religions contemporaneous with Judaism and Christianity "there was no possibility of anything that can be called

---

[3] Antoine Rutayisire, "The Rwandan Martyrs of Ethnic Ideology," in *Sorrow and Blood: Christian Missions in Contexts of Suffering, Persecution and Martyrdom*, ed. William David Taylor, Antonia Van der Meer, and Reg Reimar (Pasadena, CA: William Carey Library, 2012), 249. The Rwandan occurrence is here regarded as a "failure in mission."

[4] Paul G. Hiebert, "Conversion in Hinduism and Buddhism," in *Handbook of Religious Conversion*, ed. H. Newton Malony and Samuel Southard (Birmingham, AL: Religious Education Press, 1992), 9.

conversion."[5] This is because Greco-Roman religions of ancient times did not insist on a decisive break with the past,[6] and the religions of the East were accommodating by nature. It is significant to observe that among the primal traditions, or non-universal religions, conversion was virtually unknown.[7] Hence, conversion was peculiar only to those three monotheistic, missionary religions that emerged from the Middle East.

Definition

The term conversion means different things in different disciplines, as Bailey Gillespie points out. To the scientist it refers to the change from one state to another; to the financier it means the change of a security, currency, or coinage to another type; in law it refers to the unlawful appropriation and use of another's belongings; in logic it is the producing of a new proposition by transposing the subject and predicate of the original proposition; in mathematics it involves the change in form of a quantity or an expression without a change in value—the basic connotation, as Gillespie notes, that what runs through the gamut of meanings in all these disciplines is "change," "transformation," and "transposition."[8]

---

[5]A. D. Nock, *Conversion: The Old and the New in Religion from Alexander the Great to Augustine of Hippo* (London: Oxford University Press, 1933), 14.

[6]Stephen J. Chester, *Conversion at Corinth: Perspectives on Conversion in Paul's Theology and the Corinthian Church* (London, T & T Clark, 2003), 5.

[7]M. Darrol Bryant and Christopher Lamb, eds., "Conversion, Contours of Controversy and Commitment in a Plural World," in *Religious Conversion: Contemporary Practices and Controversies* (London: Cassell, 1999), 3.

[8]V. Bailey Gillespie, *Religious Conversion and Personal Identity* (Birmingham, AL: Religious Education Press, 1979), 9.

The definitions for the word conversion are as diverse as the authors themselves. Derived from the Latin word *convertere*, conversion means "to revolve, turn around or head in a different direction."[9] It is also "defined as a perceptible change in one's religious identity, a conscious self-transformation, which is often discussed and proclaimed for all to see."[10] Conversions are considered processes involving a series of events, often complex, happening over a period of time, even lasting for several years.[11] Lewis Rambo is another scholar whose work on the subject of conversion is often cited, and who has sought to provide a holistic model of this process. Rambo also avers that conversion is a process rather than a specific, one-time event. He posits that the word *converting* better captures the phenomenology of the process of conversion.[12]

Although in recent times this concept can be found outside Christian circles, it started out as a theological notion, necessary for entry into a community of the faithful. In the New Testament the word translated as conversion is *epistrophe*. Three other related word groups also translated as conversion are: *epistrepho, metanoeo, and*

---

[9]Frank K. Flinn, "Conversion: Up from Evangelicalism or the Pentecostal and Charismatic Experience," in *Religious Conversion: Contemporary Practices and Controversies*, ed. Christopher Lamb and M. Darrol Bryant (London: Cassell, 1999), 51.

[10]Benjamin Beit-Hallahmi and Michael Argyle, *The Psychology of Religious Behaviour, Belief and Experience* (London: Routledge, 1997), 114.

[11]Gordon T. Smith, *Transforming Conversion: Rethinking the Language and Contours of Christian Initiation* (Grand Rapids, MI: Baker Academic, 2010), 6

[12]Lewis R. Rambo, *Understanding Religious Conversion* (London: Yale University Press, 1993), 7.

metamelomai.[13] In Hebrew society the concept of "turning," or "returning" (*shuv*), was usually a group experience and entailed a return to God and His covenants.[14] It needs to be understood that "God's transformation of all things—the heavens and the earth, humans and all creatures—is at the heart of biblical theology."[15] Unfortunately, however, as Gordon Smith observes, conversion is often confused with salvation.[16] As a result some persons trace their "conversion" to a date and time when they gave their lives to Christ. Nonetheless, a person may profess to be Christian without necessarily demonstrating evidence of life-transformation. Evidence of this can be found all through Christian history, especially during the Crusades, when the vilest crimes were done in God's name.

While it has been demonstrated that conversion to a religion may produce a more virtuous pattern of behavior, it is controverted whether true transformation is attained.[17] It is for this reason that missiologists prefer to employ the expression "worldview

---

[13]Richard V. Peace, *Conversion in the New Testament: Paul and the Twelve* (Grand Rapids, MI: William B. Eerdmans, 1999), 346.

[14]Charles H. Kraft, "Conversion in Group Settings," in *Handbook of Religious Conversion*, ed. H. Newton Malony and Samuel Southard (Birmingham, AL: Religious Education Press, 1992), 263.

[15]Frederick J. Gaiser, "A Biblical Theology of Conversion," in *Handbook of Religious Conversion*, ed. H. Newton Malony and Samuel Southard (Birmingham, AL: Religious Education Press, 1992), 94.

[16]Gordon T. Smith, *Transforming Conversion: Rethinking the Language and Contours of Christian Initiation* (Grand Rapids, MI: Baker Academic, 2010), 3.

[17]William Sims Bainbridge, "The Sociology of Conversion," in *Handbook of Religious Conversion*, ed. H. Newton Malony and Samuel Southard (Birmingham, AL: Religious Education Press, 1992), 188-189.

transformation," referring to a deeper level of change in the life of a believer than the less precise "conversion." Although the two words may appear synonymous, this study is focused on the level of conversion that results in worldview transformation. Kraft, however, provides a caveat that is important as studies on worldview change are engaged upon. He states,

> Another thing to note is that when we speak of the conversion of a worldview, we are not talking of a complete conversion. A complete exchange of one worldview for another is as far as we know totally impossible. We are, rather, looking at partial conversion in terms of the number of assumptions (subparadigms, paradigms, subthemes, etc.) that are changed, though speaking of significant conversions in terms of the importance of the changes and the significance of the people's new commitment.[18]

The following section will discuss the nature of conversion, the stages involved, and the various views of the subject in areas of studies such as psychology, sociology, religious education, and theology. It shall be followed by a survey on worldviews and how worldviews can be transformed.

Nature of Conversion

Conversion from the biblical standpoint emphasizes change in these important areas of life: belief, emotion, and behavior (Rom 10:9; 2 Cor 5:17; Rom 6:22; 8:2-4; 9:25; Gal 5:22-23).[19] Warren Brown and Carla Caetano explain these changes that take place at conversion. Conversion, they state, has a propositional aspect, which however

---

[18]Charles H. Kraft, *Worldview for Christian Witness* (Pasadena, CA: William Carey Library, 2008), 448.

[19]Warren S. Brown and Carla Caetano, "Conversion, Cognition, and Neuropsychology," in *Handbook of Religious Conversion*, ed. H. Newton Malony and Samuel Southard (Birmingham, AL: Religious Education Press, 1992), 148-149.

goes beyond mere statements. It is also accompanied by the emotion of joy and ecstasy, and is evidenced by a change in behavior.[20]

Smith makes three observations about conversions based on what he considers to be the theological vision of Ephesians: (1) Conversion is a human response to divine intervention, (2) Conversion is an act of faith; a self-abandonment to the will of God, and (3) Conversion needs to be both radical and comprehensive; radical because sin is pervasive, comprehensive because the problem of sin is complex.[21]

Outlining the history of conversion through the ages, Gooren describes a time when conversion was about repentance and rebirth. Following the conversion of Constantine and the rise in power of the church, conversion became synonymous with living a devout, religious, and monastic life.[22] During the Reformation, Luther's approach was considered to place more emphasis on individual conversion experiences, while the Calvinistic ideal was more sudden and individual. By the seventeenth and eighteenth centuries, as Gooren observes, personal conversion and heartfelt religion was the thrust of Puritan, Pietist, and Methodist movements. Furthermore, he states, while the Great American Awakening of 1730-1750 was more or less a family phenomenon, the modern individual concept of salvation, which has become a benchmark of Western evangelistic campaigns, can be traced to the Second Awakening of this period.[23]

---

[20]Ibid.

[21]Gordon T. Smith, *Transforming Conversion: Rethinking the Language and Contours of Christian Initiation* (Grand Rapids, MI: Baker Academic, 2010), 26.

[22]Gooren, *Religious Conversion and Disaffiliation*, 12.

[23]Ibid., 12-13.

Factors Affecting Conversion

Several factors are responsible for the conversion of any individual or group. Rambo asserts that four important components in varying degrees affect the conversion experience of people.[24] These components are cultural, social, personal, and religious. Each of these matrices, depending on the history, context, needs, and circumstances of persons/individuals, in unique ways contributes to the process of conversion. Such an occurrence could be instantaneous (as with the conversion of Paul) or gradual and protracted (which is often the case with a majority of converts). In the past, various disciplines sought to discover the single factor they felt was responsible for conversion,[25] but this attitude has since changed as more recent studies indicate, which see the great benefit in a multi-disciplinary approach.

Reviewing conversion experiences in early church history, Alan Kreider observed that in an age when conversion to Christianity was a life-threatening experience, "attractiveness was the key to the churches' growth."[26] Kreider stated that Christians were people "in touch with the miraculous," and that conversion evidently changed the convert "into a better person."[27]

---

[24]Rambo, *Understanding Religious Conversion*, 7-11.

[25]M. Scott Fletcher, "On Conversion," in *Psychological Insight into the Bible: Texts and Readings*, ed. Wayne G. Rollins and D. Andrew Kille (Grand Rapids, MI: William B. Eerdmans, 2007), 228.

[26]Alan Kreider, *The Change of Conversion and the Origin of Christendom* (Harrisburg, PA: Trinity Press International, 1999), 13.

[27]Ibid., 13, 16-20.

Stages of Conversion

Rambo in his book *Understanding Religious Conversion* outlines seven stages converts have undergone in their journey towards conversion. In a later published article with Charles Farhadian they explained that conversion "is a process of religious change that takes place in a dynamic force field of people, events, ideologies, institutions, expectations and experiences."[28] Rambo's stages of conversion are context, crisis, quest, encounter, interaction, commitment, and consequences. The context is subdivided into macro and micro contexts. The macro context includes those factors such as "political systems, religious organizations, relevant ecological considerations, transnational corporations, and economic systems." The micro context refers to "the more immediate world of a person's family, friends, ethnic group, religious community and neighborhood."[29] In a later article Rambo and Farhadian added a meso context, which constituted the dimension between the macro and micro aspects, such as local government, regional politics, and economics.[30]

Internal and external forces trigger crises that lead people in a quest for meaning, purpose of life, and salvation. Encounter is the stage that describes the contact between the potential convert and the advocate/proselytizer, and involves learning the benefits of one's decision. In the interaction stage, prospective converts learn more about the

---

[28]Lewis R. Rambo and Charles E. Farhadian, "Converting: Stages of Religious Change," in *Religious Conversion: Contemporary Practices and Controversies*, ed. Christopher Lamb and M. Darrol Bryant (London: Cassell, 1999), 24.

[29]Rambo, *Understanding Conversion*, 21-22.

[30]Rambo and Farhadian, "Converting: Stages of Religious Change," 25.

teachings, lifestyle, and expectations of the group to be joined. At the commitment stage, prospective converts are confronted with a choice between life and death, forcing the individual to make a decision. The final stage, consequences, involves assessment of the cumulative effect of various experiences, effects, and beliefs that may hinder or facilitate conversion.[31]

In a similar vein Gooren outlines fives stages converts pass through in their journey towards conversion. The stages he describes are pre-affiliation, affiliation, conversion, confession, and disaffiliation. Pre-affiliation is used to describe the worldview and social context of potential members. Affiliation refers to the one who has attained formal membership, although group identity may not form a central aspect of the person's life or identity. Conversion is the stage where radical personal change of a person's worldview and identity has occurred. Confession is the theological expression used to describe a high level of participation in the new group joined, and a strong "missionary attitude" towards non-members—employing testimonies of their personal conversion experience to evangelize. The last stage Gooren describes is disaffiliation, which is depicted by rejection of former membership or inactive membership.[32]

Having examined the definition, nature, factors, and stages of conversion, the next section will examine various paradigms of conversion. Conversion will be examined through the lenses of various disciplines in order to develop a model incorporating relevant insights.

---

[31]Ibid., 23-33.

[32]Gooren, *Religious Conversion and Disaffiliation*, 48-49.

Psychological Paradigm

Psychologists have always attached great importance to the study of conversion since the inception of this discipline in the late nineteenth century.[33] Generally, they tend to view religious phenomena from a purely scientific and empirical perspective. Solely psychological factors are often attributed to conversion to the extent that God is entirely left out of the picture. Employing the metaphor of a computer solving a mathematical equation, Warren Brown and Carla Caetano explain that neuropsychological views of conversion have inherent limitations because they ignore meaning and reality which faith affirms in the conversion experience.[34] Two different neurocognitive models of conversion are known. The first views conversion as the result of abnormal experiences which originate from the malfunctioning of the brain, while the other regards conversion as an extension of normal mental activity in content and perceived significance.[35] Explaining these concepts, Brown and Caetano reject the idea that conversions are associated with abnormal brain activities such as seizures. Rather, they view Christian conversion as "involving the adoption of a better-fit life-schema, with all the accompanying sense of satisfaction, release from anxiety, and joy."[36]

Commenting on Paul's conversion, for instance, Scott Fletcher states that the

---

[33]Lewis R. Rambo, "The Psychology of Conversion," in *Handbook of Religious Conversion*, ed. H. Newton Malony and Samuel Southard (Birmingham, AL: Religious Education Press, 1992), 159.

[34]Brown and Caetano, "Conversion, Cognition, and Neuropsychology," 148.

[35]Ibid., 149.

[36]Ibid., 150, 157.

defect of some psychologists is that "they wish to find one element only that will account antecedently for the sudden change."[37] Rambo observes that early psychological studies focused primarily on conversion as a dramatic, radical change involving adolescents and young adults.[38] Presently, three types of conversion are recognized by psychologists: sudden, gradual, and unconscious. Sudden conversion may take place within hours, while gradual conversion takes a longer period and involves a cognitive and rational process. Unconscious conversion—where the individual cannot remember ever not believing the faith—is considered the result of social learning.[39]

Studies carried out on the issue of conversion from a psychological viewpoint indicate that dramatic religious conversions are most likely to occur among people with a history of poor parental relationships.[40] Other research reports suggest that dramatic religious conversions are most likely to occur during periods of severe distress, depression, and high stress.[41] The preponderance of studies carried out by psychologists on conversion reveals that childhood and adolescence was the period when the majority

---

[37]Fletcher, "On Conversion," 228.

[38]Rambo, "The Psychology of Conversion," 159.

[39]Raymond F. Paloutzian, Steven L. Jackson, and James E. Crandall, "Conversion Experience, and Belief System, and Personal and Ethical Attitudes," in *Psychology and Christianity: Integrative Readings*, ed. J. Raymond Fleck and John D. Carter (Nashville, TN: Abingdon, 1981), 217.

[40]Lee A. Kirkpatrick, "Attachment Theory and Religious Experience," in *Handbook of Religious Experience*, ed. Ralph W. Hood Jr. (Birmingham, AL: Religious Education Press, 1995), 458.

[41]Ibid.

of the religious phenomena occurred.[42] Some of the postulated reasons find links for this in puberty, sexual instincts, need for meaning, seeking purpose, and a sense of identity.[43]

Another concept that psychology has demonstrated that influences conversion is the social influence theory. This theory holds that three concepts exert influence on an individual's religious stance: the social roles a person is called on to play; social norms which provide prescriptions; and reference groups, which are the particular audience the person values and to whom they turn to for direction and approval.[44] It is also well known that the presence of continued group support is critical in stabilizing and cementing commitments and creating solidarity for new believers.[45] Psychological research has also shown the significance of the emotional state in conversion experiences which reveal that the experience of being loved and the hope of future emotional care is an attractive factor to converts.[46]

Sociological Paradigm of Conversion

Sociology, like psychology, experiences difficulty in researching issues that have to do with the supernatural, with the result that the divine aspect is left out of the

---

[42] Kalevi Tamminen and Kari E. Nurmi, "Developmental Theories and Religious Experience," in *Handbook of Religious Experience*, ed. Ralph W. Hood Jr. (Birmingham, AL: Religious Education Press, 1995), 296; Kirkpatrick, "Attachment Theory," 459.

[43] Kirkpatrick, "Attachment Theory," 459.

[44] Chana Ullman, *The Transformed Self: The Psychology of Religious Conversion* (New York: Plenum Press, 1989), 78-79.

[45] Ibid., 85.

[46] Ibid., 98.

equation.[47] It is nevertheless helpful to look at the factors sociologists identify as influencing conversion, besides divine intervention. Two popular sociological theories are the social influence theory and the strain theory. The former posits that people join a religion because of social attachments they have formed with the members of a group and because their ties to other nonmembers are weak. The strain theory explains that people join a religion "to satisfy conventional desires that unusual personal or collective deprivations have frustrated.[48] A contrary view to these two theories is the personality traits theory that deems conversion as dependent upon the predisposing effects of various personality traits. This view perceives the causes of conversion as residing within the psyche of the individual, rather than arising from the influence of situational and societal factors outside the person.[49]

Another explanation for conversion is the "seekership" theory, which states that those who are predisposed to conversion undergo transformation because "they are in active pursuit of just such a self-transformation."[50] In other words, conversion takes place in such individuals because they willingly and voluntarily have made this their goal.

An additional sociological theory suggests that the social attributes and structural availability of converts predispose them to conversion. Snow and Machalek explain that

---

[47]Bainbridge, "The Sociology of Conversion," 178.

[48]Ibid., 178-179.

[49]Snow and Machalek, "The Sociology of Conversion," 180.

[50]Ibid.

recent studies have identified specific social attributes and specified categories of people amenable to conversion. They state that most research describes these converts to new religious movements as in their twenties, from the middle class, with more education than previously acknowledged, and from stable family environments.[51] What is of special note in this case is that this theory conflicts with the widely accepted strain theory, which suggests that people turn to religion because of their relative deprivation.[52] Accordingly, instead of the marginalized, materially indisposed, and the alienated seeking refuge in the cults, this study shows that the young, free, and single are structurally available and turning to religion.[53]

Educational Paradigm of Conversion

One of the foremost religious educators in contemporary times who has conducted research into how faith is developed is James Fowler. Fowler conducted studies with the assistance of his graduate students on 359 persons ranging in ages from four to eighty. Following his research Fowler developed a six-step model of how faith grows in the lives of individuals of various age brackets. These steps were:

1. Intuitive-Projective—This is the stage of pre-school children whose fantasy and reality get mixed up. What is known about God is obtained from parents and/or society. It is the basic level of faith-formation.

---

[51] Ibid., 181-182.

[52] Bainbridge, "The Sociology of Conversion," 179.

[53] Snow and Machalek, "The Sociology of Conversion," 182.

2. Mythic-Literal—As children grow up they understand their faith in a literal manner as told them by their faith community. Some adults get stuck in this stage, though, and may never advance beyond this level.

3. Synthetic-Conventional—This stage is where teenagers usually get stuck; they find it difficult to see outside the box of the belief system which they have put together. Their authority resides in an authority figure (person or institution) and they get upset if anyone challenges their accepted beliefs.

4. Individuative-Reflective—During this stage of young adulthood, people begin to look outside their boxes. This is a very tough stage for some, and it sometimes results in disillusionment and the abandonment of faith. It is a usually a time for questioning and doubt for those stuck in this stage.

5. Conjunctive Faith—Persons at this stage discover the paradoxes in life and later settle down to accepting the mystery of life, often returning to the stories learned in earlier years. It is rare for persons to get to this stage before mid-life.

6. Universalizing Faith—Few persons arrive at this stage in life. When they do, they devote their lives in service to others. Other concerns matter more than self-interest at this last stage.[54]

Fowler derived his model by leaning heavily on the research contributions of psychologists such as Jean Piaget and his former colleague at Emory, Lawrence

---

[54]James W. Fowler, *Stages of Faith: The Psychology of Human Development and the Quest for Meaning* (New York: HarperCollins, 1981).

Kohlberg.[55] His model, however, provides more insight on the stages of faith development than it does on the conversion process.

In recent years advances in brain science have stirred a wave of excitement in educational circles. Within the last decade alone knowledge in the field of neuroscience has been growing at a breathtaking and dizzying pace and has had an impact on the studies of evangelism, discipleship, and missions. Educationist William Yount, explaining the import of this development, states, "The brain wires itself according to the choices we make, [and] the lives we lead." What Yount finds exciting about neuroplasticity—that is, changes in neural pathways due to changes in behavior—is the fact that what people focus upon today can open new neurological doors to a new way of thinking.[56] This uncanny ability of the brain to remap itself has serious implications for missiologists, for it implies that by assisting converts to refocus their minds on new images, methods, and ideas, changes can be initiated that can result in transformation. Bible studies, ministry opportunities, worship services, fellowships, witnessing, and visiting the sick produce many kinds of stimuli in converts which serve as reinforcement for the new ideas, attitudes, and actions they are taught, thereby creating new pathways leading to transformation.[57]

Anthropological Paradigms of Conversion

One of the earliest and most respected pioneers in the field of Christian

---

[55] James W. Fowler, "Faith Development at 30: Naming the Challenges of Faith in a New Millennium," *Religious Education* 99, no. 4 (Fall 2004): 409-410.

[56] William R. Yount, *Created to Learn* (Nashville, TN: B & H Publishing Group, 2010), 550.

[57] Ibid., 552.

anthropology was Alan Tippett. Tippett conceptualized the conversion process in three clear-cut units of time—period of awareness, period of decision, and period of incorporation—interjected by two critical points, point of realization and point of encounter.[58]

Awareness results from a number of factors: natural causes, imposed pressures, or directed programs—in other words, factors could be natural, circumstantial, stimulated, or due to a complex combination of these factors.[59] No conversion or paradigm shift may occur without the intervention of one of these factors.

For any individual or group, the period of decision may be spread over a number of years and could result in four different possibilities. The first reaction could be rejection, such as is found in resistant areas like the regions of some of the major world religions—Hinduism, Islam, and Buddhism. The second possible reaction is total acceptance. Acceptance with modification is the third, and could in turn produce two well-known patterns: syncretism—as is found in regions where folk versions of the world religions are found—and a situation where adjustment to the advocated belief is made by the acceptors into their cultural structures. An example of this is the indigenous churches such as the Aladura. Noteworthy in this scenario is the fact that it is the acceptors, not the advocates, who determine the adjustments.

The fourth possible reaction in the point of decision is fission, where some

---

[58] Alan R. Tippett, "The Cultural Anthropology of Conversion," in *Handbook of Religious Conversion*, ed. H. Newton Malony and Samuel Southard (Birmingham, AL: Religious Education Press, 1992), 195.

[59] Ibid., 196-197. The following section explaining these concepts is derived from the referred article.

segments of the group may accept, and others reject the religion. This usually occurs in large communities where competitive values exist, and frequently happens on the basis of social structure.

During the period of incorporation the group members (or individuals) have separated themselves from the old context and are vulnerable until they can quickly achieve a new contextual entity. After instruction and training, the process is finally completed by means of an act of incorporation, such as baptism. Tippett shares deep insight when he states that it is only those religious rites and forms which fit into the frame of reference of the locals that stand the chance of finding permanent acceptance, rather than those perceived to have foreign character. He adds that "for any religious conversion to be permanent its new structure should both meet the needs of the converts and operate in meaningful forms."[60]

Furthermore, Tippett observes, if the new religion is to be adopted, it must meet the specific needs the people have, and demonstrate that it can satisfy those needs better than the old religion. Ultimately, Tippett advocates "two conversions" for people from non-Christian backgrounds; the first faith experience of a power encounter should be from heathenism to Christianity. The second faith experience, coming a little later, should lead to a positive assurance of new birth, and should further result in the experience of sanctification. The total conversion process should entail rapid, quantitative discipling, but not without its essential qualitative concomitant dimension.[61]

---

[60]Ibid., 197.

[61]Ibid., 195-205.

Another prominent personality in Christian anthropology who has contributed immensely to the discourse on conversion/worldview transformation is Paul Hiebert states that "conversion to Christ must encompass all the three levels of culture: behavior and rituals, beliefs, and worldview."[62] The transformation of the worldview, he states, "is not simply a mental assent to a set of metaphysical beliefs, nor is it solely a positive feeling toward God. Rather it involves entering a life of discipleship and obedience in every area of our being and throughout the whole story of our lives."[63] Charles Kraft, another Christian anthropologist, is a leading figure in contemporary missiology who also believes that the impulse for worldview change always has its origin in external or outside sources.[64] Although he admits in his book, *Worldview for Christian Witness*, that his primary context was not Christian conversion, Kraft maintains that the primary focus in worldview change is the conversion of allegiances.[65]

Like other anthropologists such as Anthony Wallace, Kraft subscribes to a three-stage process of worldview change. The first stage is the equilibrium, or steady state stage, which represents a community before change occurs. The second stage is epitomized by the entry of a crisis situation. This could take the form of war, or natural calamity, which calls to question familiar valuations, allegiances, guidelines, and rules.

---

[62] Paul Hiebert, *Transforming Worldviews: An Anthropological Understanding of How People Change* (Grand Rapids, MI: Baker Academic, 2008), 315.

[63] Ibid., 310.

[64] Charles Kraft, *Worldview for Christian Witness* (Pasadena, CA: William Carey Library, 2008), 448.

[65] Ibid., 449.

This leads to dissonance, imbalance, and disequilibrium. The third stage is the new steady state, which is the result of the resolution of the crisis and the survival of the society.[66]

Again, following the pattern of Tippett, Kraft prescribes four fundamental responses to worldview change.[67] The first response is demoralization, where the worldview of the people is so damaged that it cannot be rescued, causing the entire society to break down. In this scenario, neither traditional nor novel adaptations effectively answer the problems and challenges brought about by external pressure on a worldview; the result is the absence of a will to live. The second radical response to worldview change is submersion, due to external pressures. In this case, new perceptions and thinking patterns are promoted, but the only way the traditional worldview can survive is to be submerged under the veneer of the new. Such is usually the case in the face of military oppression or invasion. Kraft describes the first response to severe external pressure, defeatist; the second, survivalist; and the third response, conversion. In the conversion situation, traditional perceptions are challenged and, ultimately, new perceptual paradigms and fundamental presuppositions, valuations, and allegiances emerge. Kraft concedes that it is practically impossible to achieve a complete exchange of one worldview for another, instead, what may occur would be partial conversions in terms of a number of assumptions.

The fourth response is revitalization. In this case, change is brought about not

---

[66]Kraft, *Worldview for Christian Witness*, 429.

[67]Ibid., 434-461.

because of a response from external pressure but due to the attitude of the people. It differs from the first three responses in that while the others are initial responses, revitalization is a secondary response. In other words, change arises from pressures within to revive and revitalize a society that has lost or nearly lost its "accustomed equilibrium or cohesion."

Commenting on the change that comes through revitalization, Hans Kasdorf summarizes by explaining, "Revitalization describes the conversion process as a religious change of an ethnological system from its pagan context to the Christian way of life." He further states that "the concept of renewal has been applied to describe the spiritual restoration of reverted and paganized Christians or post-Christian neo-pagans; it refers to the transformation of such nominal Christians both within the camp of second-, third-, fourth-, or tenth-generation Christianity."[68] Evidently in Western Christian contexts renewal is constantly needed.

Conversion and worldview transformation are processes that are in need of continual re-evaluation.[69] As Hiebert explains, "Cultures are constantly changing, and these changes often lead to changes in worldviews, which tend to change more slowly because they are at the subconscious level."[70] This is especially true in the African traditional religious context. Perceptively Hiebert states,

---

[68]Hans Kasdorf, *Christian Conversion in Context* (Scottdale, PA: Herald Press, 1980), 141.

[69]Charles Kraft, ed., "Contextualization and Time: Generational Appropriateness," in *Appropriate Christianity* (Pasadena, CA: William Carey Library, 2005), 261.

[70]Hiebert, *Transformational Worldviews*, 316.

> Recent studies reveal that initial conversion is generally followed by a period of evaluation during which the new life is critically reexamined. If the new is no better than the old, or the cost of adopting it is too high, the person or group turns back to traditional ways. But those who choose a new way and reevaluate it are open to knowing and experiencing it more fully. Enduring transformations are the result of many decisions to adopt and develop a new worldview.

It is for this reason that the process of discipleship is of crucial importance for the retention of converts after their initial commitment or conversion. In the following section, principles derived from various disciplines that have previously been considered will be discussed.

The Biblical Paradigm: Conversion in Acts

The greatest historical records of the early Christian church are found in the book Acts of the Apostles. It details the birth, spread, and supernatural growth of this movement that eventually reached every corner of the earth. Although known as Acts of the Apostles, some prefer to refer to it as the Acts of the Holy Spirit, because all through the book the Spirit is seen directing, empowering, and establishing believers and the nascent church.

While a number of conversion narratives are scattered throughout the early chapters of the book, strangely enough there exists a dearth of literature devoted to this important study. This section will examine a number of the personal conversion narratives found in the book, with the view to drawing contemporary missiological lessons from them. It will seek responses to the questions: How did conversion take place in the Apostolic times? And, What lessons can be drawn from these accounts in order to effect true discipleship in our age?

Conversion narratives which this study shall pay particular focus to are: (1) Simon Magus (Acts 8:9-24), (2) The Ethiopian Eunuch (Acts 8:26-39), (3) Paul (Acts 9:1-19),

(4) Peter/Cornelius (Acts 10), (5) Bar-Jesus (Acts 13:4-12), (6) Lydia (Acts 16:11-15), and (7) Slave diviner (Acts 16:16-24). Four important components play crucial roles in individual or group conversions, according to Lewis Rambo. These are the cultural, social, personal, and the religious components of the convert's life.[71] Other studies affirm that conversion is "a process of religious change that takes place in a dynamic force field of people, events, ideologies, institutions, expectations and experiences."[72] In this study, particular attention will be paid to the following elements as much as they relate to the pericope in question: Context, Convert, Community, Crisis, Change, and Consequence.

Simon Magus

Context: Persecution of the believers in Jerusalem drove many out the city. It was this event that led Philip, one of the recently ordained deacons, to go to Samaria where he began preaching the gospel. Prior to Philip's arrival, a magician, Simon, had held the Samaritans in awe of his power, resulting in him being regarded as the Great Power, "a designation that seems close to the inscriptional evidence about a god who is less than the supreme god but nonetheless very powerful."[73] It is notable that the setting of this encounter is a city in the province of Samaria (no particular town is mentioned), for there

---

[71]Rambo, *Understanding Religious Conversion*, 7-11.

[72]Rambo and Farhadian, "Converting: Stages of Religious Change," 24.

[73]Ben Witherington III, *The Acts of the Apostles: A Socio-Rhetorical Commentary* (Grand Rapids, MI: William B. Eerdmans, 1998), 254.

had been a 1,000-year dispute between the Jews and the Samaritans by this time.[74] Simon, who had previously amazed the whole town, eventually became himself amazed by the works of Philip, and ended up following him around.[75]

Convert: Simon was a magician by profession and one who seemed to be very good at his art—the reason the people had so much faith in him, which is why prior to Philip's arrival many people believed in him.

Community: The people in the community were those who had praised and hailed the power of the magician. Simon must have realized the superiority of Philip's power and sought to discover the secret of this power. His ulterior motive was eventually revealed when he requested Peter to sell him that power. He probably sought to regain his influence and status in that Samaritan community.

Crisis: As Rambo has indicated, crisis in the life of a person usually had a function in their conversion. For Simon, it must have been the loss of status in the eyes of the people. He must have wondered how he could regain his position of honor among the people. In this case, a power encounter (the loss of eyesight) demonstrated the superiority of Philip's message and of His God.[76]

Change: Although Simon was baptized, it would appear that in his heart nothing

---

[74]John R. W. Stott, *The Message of Acts: The Spirit the Church and the World* (Leicester, UK: InterVarsity Press, 1990), 146-147.

[75]F. Scott Spencer, *Acts* (Sheffield, UK: Sheffield Academy Press, 1997), 86.

[76]Paul Hertig, "The Magical Mystery Tour: Philip Encounters Magic and Materialism in Samaria: Acts 8:4-25," in *Mission in Acts: Ancient Narratives in Contemporary Context*, ed. Robert L. Gallagher and Paul Hertig (Maryknoll, NY: Orbis Books, 2004), 105.

much had changed. In his attempt to purchase the Holy Spirit from Peter, Simon revealed that his intent was to profit from the ability to purvey the Spirit for a price, profit financially from this, and regain his standing as a "the Power of God," called the Great Power.[77] Another issue that comes to the fore in this account is Simon's magical worldview, which led him to view "the Spirit as a commodity that can be bought and sold," and to consider Peter's call for repentance as "a curse from a more powerful magician against another."[78] Talbert concludes by stating that Simon the magician is baptized but not changed.[79]

Consequence: Simon's conversion, which is shallow, selfish, and calculating, comes with a terrible consequence—a stern rebuke from Peter, even a curse—"To hell with you and your money (8:20)."[80] It is from this narrative and attitude that the medieval term "simony"—the buying and selling of church offices—was derived.[81]

This account has several implications for conversion in the church today. As Paul Hertig observes, baptism is not a safeguard against evil motives; baptized believers need to guard their hearts from influences that can quench the work of the Holy Spirit in

---

[77]Paul W. Walaskay, *Acts* (Louisville, KY: Westminster John Knox Press, 1998), 83.

[78]Charles Talbert, *Reading Acts: A Literary and Theological Commentary on the Acts of the Apostles* (New York: Crossroad Publishing Company, 1997), 87.

[79]Ibid.

[80]Hertig, "The Magical Mystery Tour,"106.

[81]Walaskay, *Acts*, 83.

them.[82] This also has relevance for Yoruba converts from folk religious backgrounds.

Another remarkable feature of this conversion account, the first personal conversion account of a Gentile in the Apostolic Church, is that it was mediated by a power encounter. Charles Talbert observes that "in a power-oriented society, as Samaria is portrayed in this story, a demonstration of power serves as a catalyst for people's becoming open to the gospel."[83] He adds that "the thrust of scene one is the superiority of Jesus' name to magic."[84] While this mooted point may be passed over by some in Western contexts where magic is regarded as mere superstition, to persons from non-Western contexts, like the Yoruba, this is extremely significant.

Another noteworthy feature of this power encounter is the contrast between Simon the magician and Philip the evangelist. Philip obviously has divine power that is blatantly superior, yet is presented as humbly performing his duty, while Simon the pretender, who reveled in the acclaim of being someone great, is eventually humbled in the face of superior power. As in other power encounters in Scripture, God makes clear to all that He is the Supreme Ruler, the King of kings and Lord of lords.

It has been observed that the two conversion accounts located in this chapter seemed to portray baptisms following spontaneous responses. Unfortunately, however, repentance did not precede Simon's baptism.[85] Another point that must not be overlooked

---

[82]Hertig, "The Magical Mystery Tour," 107.

[83]Talbert, *Reading Acts*, 85.

[84]Ibid., 86.

[85]Hertig, "The Magical Mystery Tour," 106.

is that the power encounter of Philip in this passage was followed by a truth encounter (8:12), which led to mass baptisms among the Samaritans.[86]

Another feature worthy of mention is the sending of Peter and John. Their coming was primarily to inspect what was taking place,[87] but they also established the faith of the converts, since power encounters are insufficient to make converts into disciples.

A second objective for the appearance of the apostles was to introduce the powerful agency of the Holy Spirit. It is this power alone that can transform people from animistic contexts into true disciples of Christ. The Holy Spirit came down in Pentecost-like manner, sometimes referred to as the "Samaritan Pentecost" upon the Samaritans, demonstrating that even Gentiles have a place in the plan of God.

Ethiopian Eunuch

Context: During a return trip home from a religious pilgrimage from Ethiopia to Jerusalem, Philip encountered a foreigner reading from the book of prophet Isaiah.[88] Philip's obedience to the voice of the Holy Spirit led him in an opposite direction from what he would have preferred, going instead towards the desert to meet with a high official from the Ethiopian court. While running beside the chariot he heard the traveller reading uncomprehendingly from Isa 53 concerning the suffering Messiah. Upon his invitation Philip mounted the chariot and began to explain the passage to him.

---

[86]Talbert, *Reading Acts*, 85-86.

[87]F. F. Bruce, *The Acts of the Apostles*, rev. ed. (Grand Rapids, MI: Eerdmans, 1988), 168

[88]R. Kent Hughes, *Acts: The Church Afire* (Wheaton, IL: Crossway Books, 1996), 120.

Convert: This is the second personal conversion story in Acts and it also involves a foreigner, thus highlighting the fact that in fulfillment of the Lord's promise and command, the gospel was indeed going to all the world—from Jerusalem, to Judea, Samaria, and the uttermost ends of the earth (Acts 1:8; Matt 28:18-20).

The convert was an Ethiopian national, a black man, as was evident from his countenance, and a man of authority and power.[89] Introduced not only as a high official, this pilgrim was a eunuch, a castrated male whose condition restricted him from entry into the Jewish temple, due to his impairment.[90] Outstanding in this Ethiopian's religion is a faith so strong and a commitment so pure that he undertook a journey so distant that some estimates believe it would have taken him not less that five months of travel each way, not to mention the hazards encountered along the way.[91] One more issue that should not be ignored is that this man was literate, an educated person who could read, though without understanding the deep meaning of the passage.

Community: While there may not have been an immediate community around the Ethiopian official that played a crucial role in his conversion, nevertheless there are some observable points. As a eunuch he must have felt rejected or despised, like the Messiah he was reading about. While he was reading the scriptural passage, which

---

[89]R. C. H. Lenski, *The Interpretation of the Acts of the Apostles* (Minneapolis, MN: Augsburg Publishing House, 1964), 337.

[90]Keith H. Reeves, "The Ethiopian Eunuch: A Key Transition from Hellenist to Gentile Mission—Acts 8:26-40," in *Mission in Acts: Ancient Narratives in Contemporary Context*, ed. Robert L. Gallagher and Paul Hertig (Maryknoll, NY: Orbis Books, 2004), 117.

[91]Bruce Milne, *Acts: Witnesses to Him* (Ross-shire, UK: Christian Focus Publications, 2010), 198.

discussed the humiliation and suffering of Christ, he was brought into contact with Philip by the Holy Spirit—this may have suggested to the pilgrim divine acceptance into the community of God's people.

Crisis: Did any crisis contribute to the Ethiopian eunuch's quest for conversion? The main crisis mentioned in the passage was that of incomprehension. The pilgrim had made a long hazardous journey as an expression of his devotion, and he had also gone to great lengths to acquire a scroll of the Scriptures, which were not easily obtainable. While reading his prized possession yet without understanding anything, Philip appeared. His crisis resolved, understanding obtained, he found occasion to demonstrate his joy in the Lord by requesting and obtaining baptism.

Change: The events that led to the baptism of the Ethiopian eunuch were carefully orchestrated by God.[92] This is evident from the sending of Philip to the desert road, to the providential availability of water out in the desert for his baptism to be performed. A transformation had indeed occurred—from perplexity and alienation, to joy and communion with the people of God.

Consequence: As in the previous conversion account, this story again demonstrates the fulfillment of the command and promise that the gospel shall be taken to the ends of the earth—in those days Ethiopia, the region of the black race, was regarded as the ends of the earth.[93]

Although his pilgrimage had been made because of the importance of Jerusalem

---

[92] Witherington III, *The Acts of the Apostles*, 293-294.

[93] Spencer, *Acts*, 91.

as the city of God, the eunuch was brought to realize that it was not where he worshiped, but who he worshiped that mattered.[94] The eunuch, who had once been relegated to the fringes of the faith, now enjoyed full fellowship through baptism. Here is another vital lesson: God has room for all in His kingdom and wishes to bring down walls that separate race, ethnicity, sexuality, and caste/status in order to save people. His followers, therefore, should be like Him. The baptism of the Ethiopian eunuch was symbolic of the entrance of the gospel "to an entire nation or a whole continent," as well as declaring that "the last days are here, whereby a foreigner also has a place in the house of the Lord."[95]

This conversion narrative also turns the spotlight on the importance of a spiritual guide, mentor, or teacher in the conversion process. The rhetorical question, asked by the eunuch, "How could I understand unless guided by someone?" (Acts 8: 31) reveals the important role of a teacher or guide to help connect the personal story of a prospect and integrate it into the broader metanarrative of salvation history.

Another question posed by the eunuch also has significance. He demanded, "What can hinder me from being baptized?" (Acts 8:36). There must have been something in Philip's explanation of Scripture that caused the eunuch to perceive that God's kingdom was an inclusive community of believers. As F. Scott Spencer asserts, "In the inclusive messianic community founded by the suffering Jesus, the eunuch finds the

---

[94]Howard Brant, *Acts: Courageous Witness in a Hostile World: A Guide for Gospel Foot Soldiers* (Eugene, OR: Wipf and Stock, 2013), 84.

[95]Justo L. Gonzalez, *Acts: The Gospel of the Spirit* (Maryknoll, NY: Orbis Books, 2001), 117.

understanding and acceptance he has been seeking."[96] These accounts in Acts 8 powerfully demonstrate that "all sorts of people are included in the messianic community: Ethiopians, Samaritans, eunuchs, women as well as men, magicians as well as those impressed by magic."[97]

Paul of Tarsus

Context: Empowered by the stoning of Stephen, Saul of Tarsus obtained permission from the Jews to round up, persecute, eliminate, and exterminate the Christian sect (Acts 22:4-5). In perhaps one of the most dramatic conversion narratives in all of Scripture, Saul of Tarsus while on his way to Damascus gets converted, blinded by a strange light from heaven, after a very short conversation with Jesus. He became helpless, powerless, and blind, until a few days later Ananias was sent by the Lord to the house where Paul was staying to baptize him. Saul's conversion was too sudden for many to trust its genuineness. Many today question whether Paul's experience can be employed as a benchmark for conversion experiences.

Convert: Prior to his conversion Saul was a person whose "heart was filled with hatred and his mind was poisoned by prejudice."[98] His commission to conduct the business of persecuting the Christians was from the Sanhedrin, and for this purpose he was given a group of Levite police who were to assist him in hauling the people he

---

[96] Spencer, *Acts*, 94.

[97] Talbert, *Reading Acts*, 93.

[98] Stott, *The Message of Acts*, 169

arrested to prison.[99] However, when Saul received the vision of Christ, those who were with him only heard a sound but saw nothing.

Community: Saul's conversion experience was not complete until he received the visit and ministration of Ananias. Keenly aware of the persecutor's reputation, Ananias was not overexcited about his assignment; however, when he arrived at the home he had been directed to go to, he laid his hands over the blind persecutor, called him Brother Saul, told him God would restore his eyesight, and eventually baptized him. By calling Saul "brother," Ananias demonstrated not only closeness, but also acceptance into the family of Christ.[100] Lenski in affirmation states, "That word admitted him into the communion of 'saints' (v. 13), all his past guilt was erased."[101] Later in this chapter Barnabas's pivotal role in mentoring Paul and introducing him into the community of faith in Antioch where he later began his ministry is indicated.

Crisis: The vision of blinding light from heaven resulted in Saul losing his eyesight. The conversation with the Lord further caused the persecutor intense crisis, and he struggled to understand what direction all this was headed. A salient observation has been made that when Ananias was told in vision that Saul, chosen for a special mission, would be found praying, this was an indication of the deep distress Saul was in.[102] Ironically, the loss of his physical sight eventually led to the opening of Paul's spiritual

---

[99]Lenski, *The Interpretation of the Acts of Apostles*, 351.

[100]Brant, *Acts: Courageous Witness*, 88.

[101]Lenski, *The Interpretation of the Acts of Apostles*, 365.

[102]Ibid., 360.

eyes. Another evidence of the severe crisis Saul was passing through at that time was further revealed by the fact that he fasted until the visit of Ananias.

Change: Although Saul was initially distrusted due to the suddenness of his conversion, it became evident to all, especially the Apostles, that Saul indeed had been transformed. The hunter became the hunted, and the persecutor became the persecuted.[103] On the way to Damascus, Saul became transformed from adversary to advocate, but even more, he received a call from Christ to be His special witness.[104] Such was the transformation that the raging lion had turned into a bleating lamb.[105]

Consequence: Several profound lessons can be learned from the conversion of Saul. Among them is the importance of having more members like Ananias to introduce and welcome people into the Christian community after baptism, and to befriend them without scruples.[106] Heaven alone has the records of those who may have been turned away due to lack of acceptance by those in the community of faith.

Charles Talbert makes an intriguing observation that "in Mediterranean culture generally, religious vocation was often based on divine manifestation to the person." He continues, "In like manner, Acts says that when God gets ready to move out to the Gentiles, He chooses and commissions His servant through a Christophany."[107]

---

[103]Hughes, *Acts*, 126-127.

[104]Walaskay, *Acts*, 96-97.

[105]Lenski, *The Interpretation of the Acts of Apostles*, 360.

[106]Stott, *The Message of Acts*, 178.

[107]Talbert, *Reading Acts*, 95.

Saul's conversion is also a powerful reminder to all Christians that God can choose and use anyone for a special purpose of His designation. However, as Stott cautions, the church should never be satisfied with mere conversion but should continue to disciple until people are conformed into Christ's image.[108]

According to Talbert, the evidence from the conversion accounts reveals five stable components from ancient conversion stories: (1) the context; (2) the catalysts leading to conversion; (3) the counterforces that pose an obstacle or opposition; (4) the conversion itself; and (5) the confirmation of the genuineness of the conversion from post-conversion evidence.[109]

Peter and Cornelius

Context: The setting of this particular story is Caesarea, where a strong military regiment was headquartered. On this occasion one of the disciples of Jesus, Peter, was involved. As in previous accounts, a most unusual prospect for the kingdom of God is revealed. Although the principal character is Cornelius, a Roman centurion, there are others in this narrative who also undergo a conversion/worldview transformation. These included the Apostle Peter himself, his Jewish entourage, and the entire household of Cornelius. Also, as with the previous chapter, visions feature prominently in the experiences of the two protagonists, Cornelius and Peter.

Converts: Cornelius was the leader of a centurion band known as the Italian regiment. He was also a God-fearer, whose entire household had been converted to the

---

[108] Stott, *The Message of Acts*, 180.

[109] Talbert, *Reading Acts*, 97.

worship of Jehovah. He had given liberally to the needy and was regarded as a man of prayer. What is most amazing is that, "among the Roman soldiers who lived lives of cruelty, immorality, and ruthless power," a person such as Cornelius could be found.[110]

Peter, a former fisherman-turned-disciple, was a man with strong prejudices. His repeated reaction to the troubling visions he received prior to the arrival of the centurion's envoys had been met with the negative, "Not so, Lord!" (Acts 10:14). This was a strong indication of his unwillingness to ritually defile himself and was also reflective of his resolute aversion to change.

Community: Cornelius's religious experience was one that was shared with the members of his household. Not only were family members worshippers of the God of heaven, but, even his soldiers had become believers. Noteworthy in this chronicle is the realization that although Cornelius seemed to be doing all the right things as a believer—worship, prayer, and generosity—nevertheless he is told to send for Peter.

Peter, on the other hand, was already an Apostle of great standing, one of the inner circle who had walked with Jesus. Yet, he needed to make this visit to Cornelius in order for his knowledge and faith in God to grow.

Crisis: The text portrays events as going fine in the lives of Cornelius and Peter until they each received the set of visions that brought perplexity to their lives. Cornelius was told to send for Peter, while the Holy Spirit informed Peter not to be afraid to accompany the envoys from Caesarea. Cornelius was alarmed, like most other persons in Scripture who have had angelic visitations. Peter was "thoroughly perplexed," wondering

---

[110]Brant, *Acts*, 96.

about the meaning of the vision.[111] What would the Holy Spirit have to do with uncircumcised Gentiles, and why would He ask Peter to accompany them? These crises form the background for the conversion experiences that followed.

Change: Evidence of the profound transformation this experience brought to Cornelius was seen in his reaction to Peter's arrival at his home. Cornelius "'fell at his feet in reverence'; *'proskuneo'* literally means 'to kiss forward,' and is used for offering homage to deity and angels and sometimes men."[112] The main focus of the conversion experience, however, seemed to be Peter rather than Cornelius—it was he who experienced a radical transformation as opposed to the centurion.[113] It would seem that "Peter was a changed man with an enlarged heart."[114]

Consequence: Conversion has sometimes been considered to be a one-time event. However, as was demonstrated in the life of Peter, it is a process where there is opportunity for continuing transformation to occur. This was "at least the third in a series of conversions in the life of Peter."[115] Another pertinent feature of this account is the great desire and impatience of the Holy Spirit to come down upon the gathered Gentiles,

---

[111]Lenski, *The Interpretation of the Acts of Apostles*, 405.

[112]Hughes, *Acts*, 150.

[113]Charles E. Van Engen, "Peter's Conversion: A Culinary Disaster Launches the Gentile Mission—Acts 10:1-11:18," in *Mission in Acts: Ancient Narratives in Contemporary Context*, ed. Robert L. Gallagher and Paul Hertig (Maryknoll, NY: Orbis Books, 2004), 136.

[114]Hughes, *Acts*, 153.

[115]Van Engen, "Peter's Conversion,"135.

so much so that Peter's sermon is finally interrupted before his conclusion (Acts 10:44). This indicated that the initiative and prerogative were entirely from the Holy Spirit rather than from any human agency.

Mission scholar Charles Van Engen observes that this narrative has profound theological and missiological significance because it provided an explanation for the outpouring of the Holy Spirit, and for the church's impetus to accept its mission to the Gentiles.[116] Also, as Walaskay explains, God "changed the rules of the game."[117]

Bar-Jesus

Context: Barnabas and Saul had been ordained and sent out on what was their first missionary expedition. They were invited to the island of Paphos by the Roman proconsul, who was described as an intelligent man, so that he could hear the gospel. There they encountered a sorcerer who tried to oppose the ministry of the evangelists, and who sensed that his status and position would be diminished once the proconsul became a believer. Against this backdrop where a magical worldview was prevalent and where it was commonplace for leaders to have diviners and magicians as their counselors, a conversion occurs.

Convert: Sergius Paulus, the Roman proconsul, was a man of authority, who also sought to know more about the Christian way. Described as intelligent, he seemed to

---

[116]Ibid., 140-141.

[117]Walaskay, *Acts*, 108.

have harbored an intellectual and spiritual hunger that made him want to hear the word of God.[118]

Community: Present with Sergius Paulus was Elymas, regarded as a Jewish sorcerer and a consort to the king. The name Elymas had an Arabic origin and meant the "skillful one." He was also known as Bar-Jesus, and possessed touted magical powers.[119] Elymas however had no desire to lose his control and influence over the proconsul and so resisted the ministry of the evangelists.

Crisis: Paul, recognizing the opposition presented by the sorcerer, pronounced a curse on Elymas that resulted in his immediate loss of sight and the need to be led by the hand away from the gathering. This power encounter, which resulted in the blinding of the false prophet, was instrumental in leading the proconsul to faith. In other words, it was this demonstration of the supremacy of the might of God that led to faith.[120]

Change: No mention is made in Scripture that the punishment Elymas received eventually led to his conversion. However, for Sergius Paulus it was recorded that he believed, and archaeological inscriptions bearing his name have been found that give credence to the conviction that he and his entire family became Christians.[121]

Consequence: Paul's audacious confrontation of the magician may also be seen as a lesson in courage for Christian witnesses who sometimes appear weak and powerless

---

[118]Stott, *Acts*, 219.

[119]Hughes, *Acts*, 177.

[120]Talbert, *Reading Acts*, 128.

[121]Hughes, *Acts*, 179.

in settings where power quotients mean everything. Lenski observes that Elymas, the "Son of the Expert," is denounced as the son of the devil, and publicly humiliated by the genuine messenger of God.[122] Prominent among the missiological outcomes of this conversion narrative is that, "in a power-oriented society, change of faith has to be power-demonstrated."[123] This point is sometimes lost sight of when missionaries operate in cross-cultural contexts.

It is also significant that Luke, the author of Acts, brings to the attention of his readers how the gospel found its place in the courts of power and among the rich, thereby indicating that the message of Christ has the power to reach and save all.

Lydia

Context: Acts 16 is the setting of the last two conversion narratives to be considered. Philippi was a prominent Roman city that was famous for its school of medicine.[124] It is also believed by some to have been the home city of Dr. Luke, the author of Acts,[125] and it was a strategic gateway that connected the Middle East to Rome and the rest of Europe. It was therefore significant for the westward thrust of the gospel message.[126] This encounter took place on a Sabbath by the river, for it seems there were no Jewish men, or not enough men to form a synagogue.

---

[122]Lenski, *The Interpretation of the Acts*, 501.

[123]Talbert, *Reading Acts*, 128.

[124]Wittherington III, *The Acts of the Apostles*, 490.

[125]Stott, *The Reading of Acts*, 262.

[126]Brant, *Acts: Courageous Witness*, 163.

Convert: This narrative is the account of Europe's first convert, a woman of significant status and wealth, a dealer in purple cloth, the garment of royalty.[127] Lydia was a native of Thyatira, where it is believed she probably found her faith in God. She was a businesswoman, householder, and woman of great generosity, who appeared to be the leader of the group that met by the river for worship. After her conversion, her house became the place where the community of believers gathered to hear the word of God.[128]

Community: Lydia, in this account, is surrounded by people: her female counterparts, with whom she worshiped, and her household that later joined her in baptism. While these may not have played any crucial role in her conversion, her conviction is what resulted in the baptism of her entire household and her home provided an abode for further missionary activities in the region.[129] Lydia opens not only her heart to the Lord, but her home to the disciples.[130]

Crisis: In this story there does not appear to be any crisis that precipitates this conversion. Rather, as Luke notes, it is the Lord who opens Lydia's heart to receive the gospel. Lenski, however, provides a plausible explanation for the absence of men and for the all-female congregation as owing to the expulsion of the Jews from Rome by Claudius, which was an example followed by the city of Philippi.[131] Although she was a

---

[127] Lenski, *The Interpretation of the Acts*, 656-657.

[128] David L. Matson, *Household Conversion Narratives in Acts: Patterns and Interpretation* (Sheffield, UK: Sheffield Academic Press, 1996), 149.

[129] Lenski, *The Interpretation of the Acts*, 659.

[130] Smith, *Transforming Conversion*, 50.

[131] Lenski, *The Interpretation of the Acts*, 655.

wealthy householder, Lydia was most likely a widow,[132] which explains why the evangelists accepted the offer to reside in her house.

Change: The primary evidence of Lydia's conversion is seen in her plea for the disciples to lodge at her abode: "if you have judged me to be faithful to the Lord," a statement observed to be a "powerful rhetorical approach."[133]

Consequence: Easily ignored in this story is the unusual act of Paul the former Pharisee sitting down to study with a group of women, an inconceivable thing for one of his training.[134] Of significance also from this account is the "standard apostolic practice" of household conversions.[135] This is also evident in Peter's baptism of the household of Cornelius. In group-oriented communities, due to their communal nature this is still a model worthy of imitation.

Also, the significance of a woman as the first European convert is not lost on many scholars, as already indicated. Once again, the author of Acts seeks to demonstrate that the gospel, in transcending cultural frontiers, was also doing the same in many other dimensions.

Slave Diviner

Context: On another Sabbath as the disciples went out for prayer they encountered a slave girl who had the gift of divination with which she made profit for her

---

[132] Wittherington III, *The Acts of Apostles*, 493.

[133] Ibid.

[134] Walaskay, *Acts*, 157.

[135] Lenski, *The Interpretation of the Acts*, 661.

owners. She followed the disciples around for several days, proclaiming that they were servants of the Most High God. This soon offended Paul, who commanded the spirit to leave her. Immediately, she lost her power of divination. This event occurred in the same town of Philippi where Lydia had been converted.

Convert: Not too much is known about the person in question, save that she was a slave, had several owners, signifying her worth and the success of her profession. The fact that she was a slave is indicative of not being a Roman citizen, but a foreigner. The slave girl was described as possessed by the spirit of Python. Local myths had it that "Python was a snake that guarded the Temple of Apollo, and was eventually killed by Apollo. Later the word Python came to mean a demon-possessed person through whom Python spoke."[136]

Community: Apparently, the former diviner's clientele and her patrons were displeased with her conversion, for the disciples were imprisoned. This was evidently a community that was resistant to change and opposed to foreign influences, a fact exploited by the aggrieved patrons of the slave girl. Although it has been commonly believed that Paul's exorcism was predicated upon irritation or annoyance, Stott avers that it may rather have been out of dismay for her condition of exploitation.[137]

Crisis: The immediate consequence of the exorcism was accusation, flogging, and eventual imprisonment for the disciples. It is noteworthy that the confession of the possessed slave girl bears close resemblance to the demons who confessed their

---

[136]Hughes, *Acts*, 214.

[137]Stott, *The Message of Acts* 265.

knowledge of Jesus' identity as the Son of God (Luke 4:33-35; 8:28-35). Ben Witherington is of the opinion that it was a crisis of confusion that prompted Paul to act, lest there be a wrongful association between the spirit in the girl and that of their God.[138] Affirming this view David Peterson states, "Paul's concern was that she was saying these things under the influence of an evil spirit. . . . Bystanders could have imagined that Paul and Silas were possessed by similar spirits from the underworld."[139]

Change: The immediate change in the former diviner resulted in the financial loss of her owners. Her change led to false charges against the disciples.

Consequence: Providentially the imprisonment of the disciples on vengeful charges ended up in the baptism of the entire household of the jailor. As Walaskay affirms, "The heart of this story is about the salvation of the jailer and his household."[140] It is possible that with more than one owner, and a gift that earned them a steady income, there was possibly no way that the slave girl could have ever obtained her personal freedom. The only way that could have happened was if she lost her "gift." Her gift had become her bond. Ironically, the loss of her divining abilities made her worthless in the sight of her former owners, but useful to the church of God.

A clear distinction between divination, magic, or sorcery and miracles is that while the former usually come with a big price tag, the latter comes at the instance of

---

[138]Witherington III, *The Acts of Apostles*, 495.

[139]David G. Peterson, *Acts of the Apostles* (Grand Rapids, MI: William B. Eerdmans, 2009), 464.

[140]Walaskay, *Acts*, 159.

God and is free. Also, while the focus of the former is on self, in the latter case the glory goes to God.

Another salient issue observed from this conversion narrative was that it involved divination, which is a very thorny issue confronting persons from animistic backgrounds. Lenski observes that while most of the practice of divination is by charlatans, in this particular case it involved demonic influences. However, it is ironic that the divining spirit could not see that its eviction was imminent.

The survey of conversion from the paradigm of the social sciences provides valuable insights into the factors and processes involved in conversion. However, these influences and processes without the supernatural intervention of the Holy Scriptures and the Holy Spirit will neither be lasting nor authentic, for conversion itself is a spiritual and supernatural event. The social sciences can be regarded as serving diagnostic purposes—bringing to focus the extent and nature of the problem, while the Scriptures serve prescriptive and curative functions—responding in life-transforming manner to the specific issues unveiled by the diagnosis.

From the book of Acts the importance of elements such as the context, crisis, and community to produce change in the lives of converts can be learned. In the following section the account of conversion in the Yoruba context will be presented. It will reveal the successes and the failings of the missionary evangelistic enterprise in the pre-colonial church in Yorubaland.

Conversion in the Yoruba Context

Conversion to Christianity in Africa has often been equated with the religious change that took place during the Roman Empire. Never since then has a continent adopted Christianity, a new religion, as it has happened in Africa. Although syncretism may appear to be the norm, as the converts mix pre-Christian practices they are familiar with in their worship of God,[141] it is a well-known fact that "conversion involves a mingling of a traditional religion with biblical religion, since nobody comes into the Christian faith with a religious vacuum and nobody can sweep out every trace of [the] former religious background."[142]

Clearly the most significant study and analysis of religious conversion in Yorubaland is John Peel's *Religious Encounter and the Making of the Yoruba*.[143] In the chapter he entitled, "Leaf Becomes Soap," Peel employs a known Yoruba proverb, *Bi ewe ba pe yio di ose* ("leaves when they have been long in soap become soap") to discuss the process of Christianization in the Yoruba context.[144] Kalu explains that unlike the experience in Igboland (Eastern Nigeria) where there was wholesale adoption of Christianity in a rapid manner, with the Yoruba, who received Christianity earlier, the process took much longer.[145]

Peel notes that for the early Yoruba converts it was a struggle against their

---

[141]Peel, *Religious Encounter*, 277.

[142]John S. Mbiti, *Bible and Theology in African Christianity* (Nairobi, Kenya: Oxford University Press, 1986), 128.

[143]Kalu, "Osondu: Patterns of Igbo Quest for Jesus Power," in *The Collected Essays of Ogbu Uke Kalu,* Volume 2*, Christian Missions in Africa: Success, Forment and Trauma*, ed. Wilhemina J. Kalu, Nimi Wariboko, and Toyin Falola (Trenton, NJ: Africa World Press, 2010), 99.

[144]Peel, *Religious Encounter*, 248-249.

[145]Kalu, *Collected Essays*, 98.

heathen environment to keep from what the missionaries considered as "backsliding." However, as the influence of Christianity permeated the community, the lifestyles the "backsliders" slid into became greatly affected by Christian influence so that they still could retain much of the Christian formation they had received.[146] This goes to illustrate the importance of the community in spiritual formation or discipleship.

Among the other factors that Peel demonstrates eventually led the Yoruba people to accept Christianity were the effectiveness of prayer, complemented by the power of a public testimony depicting God's working among the people. He illustrated this with the prayers of a converted *babalawo*, who enlisted the power of God to furnish the same protection and help that the *orisas* had provided to its devotees.[147]

The rapid spread of Christianity in Yorubaland is attributed to the work of indigenous ministers, who, understanding the worldview of the people, sought to apply local logical methods in their evangelization. In spite of their accomplishments, local evangelists also struggled with vestiges of the traditional worldview and did not disregard the power of the *orisa*, or the predictions of *Ifa*. Peel shares several accounts in his book to corroborate this assertion.[148] In the need to respond to the continuing belief in the existence of evil supernatural powers, the missionaries acquiesced to the Yoruba worldview of spiritual causation by demonizing the *orisa* and an increased consciousness

---

[146]Peel, *Religious Encounters*, 250.

[147]Ibid., 259.

[148]Ibid., 261.

about the personality of the Devil.[149]

The indigenous ministers were successful in evangelizing the people by using local logic patterns such as idioms and proverbs, and by highlighting continuities and discontinuities between the two religions. For instance, since *Orunmila* (another name for *Ifa*) meant "Heaven only knows the Mediator," they explained that this name demonstrated the need for Christ, our Mediator; moreover, they concluded, "Where the *Ifa* fails, there our Jesus begins."[150] Another crucial factor in the conversion process that played a pivotal role in the shaping of the Yoruba identity was the translation of the Bible into the Yoruba language.[151]

Alongside the search for power, which Peel describes as the "dominant orientation of the Yoruba toward all religions," were the superior answers given to the questions of meaning. Coming after the internecine ethnic wars, which Peel refers to as the Age of Confusion, these explanations contributed immensely to the rapid conversion among the Yoruba.[152]

Peel also mentions two important factors that Yorubas have contextualized in shaping and creating their unique brand of Christianity. Since conversion entailed a "trade-off between the attractions of Christianity and its costs," for the Yoruba it meant

---

[149]Ibid., 262-263.

[150]Ibid., 183.

[151]Kalu, *Collected Essays*, 102.

[152]Peel, *Religious Encounter*, 217, 230.

"the capacity to deliver pragmatic benefits such as healing."[153] This explains the prominent role healing plays in the Aladura Churches. The second factor was the emphasis on the spiritual issues.[154] An expression of this spiritual vitality is the heartfelt devotion to prayer that is evidenced in the Aladura Churches; for this reason they are popularly referred to as Spiritual Churches.[155]

Missiological Implications

From the foregoing conversion accounts, a few general features are discernable and applicable from the various contexts and are listed in no particular order of importance.

1. Conversion is largely the premise and prerogative of the Holy Spirit but also involves the human will. While human agencies are directed and employed, it is always the Holy Spirit who superintends the process.

2. Without discipleship, conversion can be short-lived. Careful instruction is needed to lead converts to spiritual maturity in order to prevent reversion to old ways and allegiances that could follow.

3. Spiritual mentors play pivotal roles in leading converts to become disciples. It is from these mentors, who serve as spiritual guides, that converts learn about the new faith and grow in an environment of nurture and care to themselves become disciplers.

---

[153]Ibid., 232-233.

[154]Ray, "Aladura Christianity," 268. Ray contends that one of the essential elements of Aladura Christianity was the belief in invisible spiritual forces, especially of malevolent spiritual powers (266-291).

[155]Peel, *Religious Encounter*, 264-265.

4. Conversion is possible without worldview transformation occurring. Cultural and environmental factors may hinder spiritual development in the life of a convert; it is through the working of the Holy Spirit and the application of Scripture to blind spots in a convert's life that elements of the worldview can be transformed.

5. Conversion and discipleship occur better in community. Communities provide an enabling, supportive structure for converts to thrive and flourish, even though each individual is called to make personal decisions regarding salvation.

6. Conversion may occur as an event or a process in the lives of individuals. The New Testament, especially the book of Acts, provides ample evidence that both cases are possible depending on the circumstance, person, or occasion.

7. The Holy Scriptures are a primary agency for making converts disciples and for their continuous spiritual growth and progress.

8. The church must be open to the direction of the inclusive leading of the Holy Spirit as He breaks down barriers and establishes new frontiers for the kingdom that may be contrary to the inclinations of even the church leadership. Each conversion context and community has unique case-sensitive and environmental features that need to be considered in the discipleship-making process.

As with the people in the book of Acts, even so are these principles applicable to the church in Yorubaland. Worldview transformation is imperative if true disciples are the goal and reversion to pre-Christian practices is to be avoided. Chapter 4 will examine the results of field research conducted among selected pastors, members, and diviners in a region of Yorubaland. It will present the data and conclusions from personal interviews and focus group discussions from the qualitative research on the significance of the continued practices of divination and sorcery among converts to the Adventist Church.

CHAPTER IV

FIELD ANALYSIS ON DIVINATION AND SORCERY

AMONG ADVENTISTS IN YORUBALAND

Introduction

At the heart of much missiological research is qualitative research,[1] because description, interpretation, and understanding lie as the basis of all qualitative research.[2] Characteristics of qualitative research enumerated by John Creswell include: (1) data collection in a natural setting, (2) the researchers themselves as key instruments in data collection, (3) multiple sources of data, (4) inductive and deductive data analysis, (5) a focus on participants' meanings rather than the researchers' meanings, (6) the production of an emergent design, (7) reflexive analysis, and (8) a goal of an holistic account.[3] Qualitative research methodology "involves the studied use and collection of a variety of empirical materials—case study, personal experience, introspective, life story, interview,

---

[1]Edgar J. Elliston, *Introduction to Missiological Research Design* (Pasadena, CA: William Carey Library, 2011), 74.

[2]John Swinton and Harriet Mowat, *Practical Theology and Qualitative Research* (London: SCM Press, 2006), 46.

[3]John W. Creswell, *Research Design: Qualitative, Quantitative, and Mixed Methods Approaches* (Thousand Oaks, CA: Sage, 2014), 185-186.

observational, historical, interactional, and visual texts—that describe routine and problematic moments and meanings in individual lives."[4]

This chapter presents the results of four weeks of field research conducted among a sub-section of the Adventist Church in Yorubaland. It begins with a description of the research context, proceeds to describe the research design that was deemed most appropriate for the study, and concludes with an analysis of the results of a grounded theory qualitative research project.

Description of the Research Context

The history of Christian missions to Yorubaland can been traced back to the 1840s. However, it was not until seventy years later that the first Adventist missionary arrived in the little village of Erunmu, in Western Nigeria.[5] This year, 2014, the Adventist Church is celebrating a century of missions in Yorubaland. Within this period it has been able to reach a number of milestones, including the founding of a hospital and school of nursing at Ile Ife, and the initiation of a publishing house, which was later moved to Ghana. Perhaps most notable was the establishment of the Adventist Seminary of West Africa in 1959 (which later evolved into Babcock University), and a teacher

---

[4]Norman K. Denzin and Yvonna S. Lincoln, "Entering the Field of Qualitative Research," in *Strategies of Qualitative Inquiry*, ed. Norman K. Denzin and Yvonna S. Lincoln (Thousand Oaks, CA: Sage, 1998), 3.

[5]David Agboola, *A History of Christianity in Nigeria: The Seventh-day Adventists in Yorubaland—1914-1964* (Ibadan, Nigeria: Daystar Press, 1987), 2.

training college at Ede.⁶ Last year the Adventist Church in Western Nigeria was organized into a union conference, having grown in membership and financial strength to support its operations and evangelistic missions in the region. Despite the significant accomplishments of the church in Yorubaland, recent research reveals a challenging proclivity for dependence on the services of diviners and sorcerers among the rank and file of its membership. Among Yoruba converts to Christianity, two practices associated with the traditional religion that in times of crises often result in lapses to pre-Christian conduct include divination and sorcery. Etched deep in the worldview of the people is the conviction that the *babalawo* (diviner) can discover the cause of life's problems and deliver the solution as well. Although in recent times some effort has been made to understand the factors that predispose members to the practice of dual allegiance⁷ and the phenomenon of spiritism,⁸ no comprehensive study has yet been undertaken regarding the significance of divination and sorcery in the worldview of this influential people group.

In order to understand the nature of this missiological challenge and to find

---

⁶Adekunle A. Alalade, *Limiting Factors to the Success of the Seventh-day Adventist Church in Africa: The Nigeria Case Study* (Ibadan, Nigeria: Agbo-Areo Publishers, 2008), 49-50.

⁷A good example of this is the dissertation by Paul Adekunle Dosunmu, "A Missiological Study of the Phenomenon of Dual Allegiance in the Seventh-day Adventist Church Among the Yoruba People of Nigeria" (PhD dissertation, Andrews University, 2011).

⁸Kwabena Donkor, ed., *The Church, Culture and Spirits: Adventism in Africa* (Silver Spring, MD: Biblical Research Institute, General Conference of Seventh-day Adventists, 2011), and the edited study by Philemon O. Amanze and Michael O. Akpa, *Seventh-day Adventist Response to Spiritism: The Nigerian Experience* (Ilishan Remo, Nigeria: Babcock University Press, 2011).

answers to the research questions of this project, a qualitative research design was adopted. The following section will describe the field research design and how it was employed.

Field Research Design

Central to the practices of divination and sorcery are worldview assumptions that undergird the predilection to resort to pre-Christian solutions to problems encountered. A grounded theory methodology was therefore adopted in order to unravel the predisposing factors that lead to the phenomenon of sorcery and divination. Grounded theory will facilitate the development of a model for worldview transformation that takes into account the fears and needs that induce dual allegiance.

Grounded Theory (GT)

Grounded theory is an inductive research approach that relies on observations to develop understandings, processes, laws, and protocols with the ultimate aim to construct substantive and formal theory.[9] It is a methodology grounded in systematic gathering and analysis of data from which theory emerges through the continuous interplay of analysis and data collection.[10] Grounded theory was developed in the mid-1960s by psychologist Barney Glaser and sociologist Anselm Strauss, with the aim of using observations from reality to construct meaning and theory—a departure from the previous method of theory

---

[9]Carol Grbich, *Qualitative Data Analysis: An Introduction* (Thousand Oaks, CA: Sage, 2013), 80.

[10]Anselm Strauss and Juliet Corbin, "Grounded Theory Methodology: An Overview," in *Strategies of Qualitative Inquiry*, ed. Norman K. Denzin and Yvonna S. Lincoln (Thousand Oaks, CA: Sage, 1998), 158.

that was directed to theory-generating research.[11] For Glaser and Strauss the discovery of theory from data provides opportunity for relevant predictions, explanations, interpretations, and applications through the process of comparative analysis.[12] It is for these reasons that grounded theory methodology is amenable for this research on worldview transformation.

In later years both Glaser and Strauss developed different emphases, leading to new approaches to this methodology. Glaser took a more hermeneutic approach that focused on theory verification, while Strauss adopted a stage-based coding that entailed open coding, axial coding, and selective coding to generate theory.[13]

Kathy Charmaz, representing a new school in the development of grounded theory, takes a different position from Glaser and Strauss. She believes that neither data nor theories are discovered, rather, researchers are a part of the world they study and the data they collect. As a result "any theoretical rendering offers an interpretive portrayal of the study's world, and not the exact picture of it."[14] Essentially, the features of grounded theory, no matter the approach, consist of the grounding of theory upon the interplay of data through data-theory analysis, constant comparisons, asking theoretically oriented

---

[11]Grbich, *Qualitative Data Analysis*, 80.

[12]Barney G. Glaser and Anselm L. Strauss, *The Discovery of Grounded Theory: Strategies for Qualitative Research* (Chicago, IL: Aldine, 1967), 1.

[13]Grbich, *Qualitative Data Analysis*, 80-81. A more detailed discussion on the history and development of this methodology can be found in Kathy Charmaz's, *Constructing Grounded Theory: A Practical Guide Through Qualitative Analysis* (Thousand Oaks, CA: Sage, 2006).

[14]Charmaz, *Constructing Grounded Theory*, 10.

questions, and theoretical coding, leading to the development of theory.[15] Grounded theory has been discovered to be effective in three particular circumstances: (1) when there is a paucity or little information on a subject, (2) when existing concepts or theories are inadequate, and (3) when the researcher wishes to explore alternative modes of conceptualization.[16]

Researcher's Background and Limitations

An unavoidable aspect of qualitative research is the role of the researcher, who functions as an instrument in the research paradigm.[17] A researcher's background, gender, culture, history, and socio-economic conditions impact upon the research findings and interpretation.[18] For this reason, this section will explore the factors that may influence the data collected and their interpretation. Of advantage to the research was my knowledge of Yoruba, having been born in Lagos. This was beneficial in my interaction with the diviners and some members who struggled with communication in English. Previous background knowledge of the Yoruba worldview from teaching classes in African Traditional Religion at Babcock University and from my doctoral research for a Doctor of Ministry degree also proved helpful.

---

[15] Strauss and Corbin, "Grounded Theory Methodology," 179.

[16] Steven Engler, "Grounded Theory," in *The Routledge Handbook of Research Methods in the Study of Religion*, ed. Michael Stausberg and Steven Engler (New York: Routledge, 2011), 256.

[17] Catherine Marshall and Gretchen B. Rossman, *Designing Qualitative Research*, 2nd ed. (Thousand Oaks, CA: Sage, 1995), 59.

[18] Creswell, *Research Design*, 202.

Because divination and sorcery are practices frowned upon by the church and may constitute grounds for apostasy, this factor had a significant impact on the paucity of subjects available for personal interviews. This was the case in spite of earlier studies that indicated the existence of such practices.[19] There was obvious reluctance to discuss this unflattering subject with me, as I am a pastor and a familiar person. A former colleague privately admitted to having wrestled with the temptation to seek the services of a diviner when he had felt unjustly treated by a senior colleague. Of the persons interviewed, none admitted to a visit to the diviner at any time as recent as a decade ago. Perhaps if I had been a complete stranger and not a minister whose respect they desired, admitting to this practice might have been easier. On the other hand, when interviewing the diviners I posed as a research student from nearby Babcock University, and said nothing about the objective of the research—to develop a transformative model that would curtail the visits of members to diviners.

A major limitation I experienced was the shortage of informants to be interviewed. I often wondered if I would not have had more subjects for interview if I had a longer period for data collection. It is also possible that my gender may have influenced the unavailability of female members for face-to-face interviews. Another limitation was distance. I sometimes was informed of certain individuals who had confessed to such practices but who were inaccessible for an interview due to great distances involved.

I sought to compensate for any inadequacy through varying the modes of data collection by conducting interviews with ministers and diviners. Also, recognizing the

---

[19]See Amanze and Akpa, *Seventh-day Adventist Response*, and Dosunmu's "A Missiological Study."

sensitivity of this topic, another mode for data collection employed was through the use of focus groups.

Purposive Sampling

Data for the research were collected through face-to-face interviews and focus group discussions using semi-structured interview questions. Informants interviewed were selected by the use of combination purposive sampling due to the nature of the phenomenon under study. This method employs a "combination of various types of purposive sampling to obtain a single sample." In the case of this research, it was a combination of homogeneous and snowballing sampling.[20]

Human Subject Protection

Research can be threatening to the subjects interviewed and to the researcher involved. This is more so the case with sensitive topics where the research is concerned with behavior that can have emotional, psychological, or spiritual repercussions on those involved.[21] Six foundational ethical concerns are considered invaluable in order to protect the participants in the research. These were (1) voluntary participation, (2) informed consent, (3) risk of harm, (4) confidentiality, (5) anonymity, and (6) right to service.[22]

---

[20]Lawrence T. Orcher, *Conducting Research: Social and Behavioral Science Methods* (Glendale, CA: Pyrczak Publishing, 2005), 104. Snowball sampling, also known as chain sampling or network sampling, depends upon a system of referral and is ideal for hard-to-find participants, while homogeneous sampling involves individuals who are similar in important ways (ibid., 102-103).

[21]For a fuller discussion on this subject see Claire M. Renzetti and Raymond M. Lee, *Researching Sensitive Topics* (Newbury Park, CA: Sage, 1993).

[22]Elliston, *Introduction to Missiological Research Design*, 104-105.

A foundational element in the ethical process of the research entailed an application to the Institutional Review Board (IRB) of Andrews University, and obtaining approval for the project.[23] Gatekeeping access to the research sites was obtained through duly signed official letters of consent from the pastors in charge of the districts where the focus groups were held, even before the research process commenced.[24]

Inclusion criteria for the research allowed participants who were members or ministers above twenty-one years of age, of sound mind, and who had served in the Adventist Church in Western Nigeria. It was required that no names of persons currently involved in divination or sorcery were to be mentioned during the course of the research.

Prior to commencing an interview or group discussion, informed consent forms were signed by participants to acknowledge their willingness to contribute voluntarily without coercion, for the benefit of the research. Subjects were informed of the nature, purpose, and objective of the research and accepted to have the sessions recorded through the use of a digital audio device, while handwritten field notes were also taken. Subjects were informed that they had the right to leave the interview or focus group at any time without apology or explanation. Participants were assured of confidentiality and anonymity in the reporting of the research findings.

Data Collection Procedures

The primary method of data collection entailed groups of face-to-face interviews

---

[23] Creswell, *Research Design*, 95.

[24] Anne Celnik, "Ethics in the Field," in *Research Training for Social Scientists*, ed. Dawn Burton (London: Sage, 2000), 100.

and focus group discussions employing a set of semi-structured open-ended questions. Among the groups interviewed were pastors who had experience with the topic, church members who had at some time in the past engaged the services of diviners but had quit the practice, and diviners from different locales in the research area.

Interviewing Process

A total of five pastors were interviewed during the course of the study. To allow for diversity and breadth of scope, two long-serving ministers were interviewed who had been administrators of the church in Western Nigeria. Two other pastors interviewed had conducted doctoral research on themes related to Yoruba religious beliefs and practices and taught courses on African Traditional Religion. The fifth minister had pastoral and medical experience in Yorubaland and hailed from a traditional religious background. Their ages ranged from late forties to late eighties. Their period of service in ministry ranged from twenty-three to almost sixty years. Typically the interviews lasted about an hour, although in one case it extended for over two hours.

Due to the sensitive nature of the research topic it was difficult to obtain subjects to interview from among church members who admitted having consulted diviners in the past. The focus groups and contacts obtained by networking were helpful in providing connections with such members. Eventually, four persons were interviewed in this category.

A research assistant was provided by one of the pastors interviewed, who served as a guide and interpreter, in one case, to the four diviners. Homogeneous sampling led to the four diviners interviewed, chosen randomly from four different towns in Remo Local Government Area, namely, Ilishan, Irolu, Iperu, and Ogere. In only a single case did a diviner choose to have the interview conducted in the local language, Yoruba, even though he clearly understood English.

Focus Groups

Focus group discussions were conducted among a cross section of informed members from two churches, Ilishan Number 1 Church and Orile Iganmu Church in Lagos. These churches were purposefully selected, the former representing a rural setting, and the latter an urban context. Among the reasons why focus group discussions were selected as a means for data collection was that they provided the researcher an occasion to corroborate viewpoints; observe debate, body language, and group interaction; and check differences of opinion.[25] Also, the fundamental strengths shared by focus groups and qualitative methods are (1) exploration and discovery of poorly understood people or subjects, (2) context and depth behind people's thoughts and experiences, (3) and interpretation, by providing understanding of why things are and how they became that way.[26] Above all, focus groups were employed because they are ideal for topics that are hard to talk about due to external circumstances, such as social stigma.[27]

In Ilishan, nine persons comprised the focus group, which had persons ranging from the mid-twenties to a retired minister in his seventies. Among the group were a

---

[25]Elliston, *Introduction to Missiological Research Design*, 146.

[26]David L. Morgan, *Focus Group Guidebook* (Thousand Oaks, CA: Sage, 1998), 12.

[27]Anna Davidson Bremborg, "Interviewing," in *The Routledge Handbook of Research Methods in the Study of Religion*, ed. Michael Stausberg and Steven Engler (New York: Routledge, 2011), 313.

woman, three elders, and the local pastor. The church hall was the venue for the focus group discussion which took place on a Sabbath evening. The meeting lasted almost two hours.

Orile Iganmu Church in Lagos was selected due to its uniqueness of being the church in Lagos with the largest body of homogeneous Yoruba membership. The focus group met after service on Sabbath because it would have been impossible to meet at any other time. In spite of several appeals to reduce the size of the group to fewer than ten, nineteen persons stayed behind and participated in the discussion. Among the group, which ranged from persons in their mid-twenties to the sixties, were five women, an equal number of youth over the age of twenty-one, and several church elders. Notwithstanding external distractions and control issues, the focus group discussions were extremely information rich. Interpretation was done for some older members present. The discussions lasted for over an hour.

The hub of the research was Babcock University, Ilishan Remo, because it provided a rich source of informants and access to the villages where the diviners were located. Also, due to travel, time, and financial constraints, it provided me with greater access to the resources and persons needed for the research purposes.

Data collection continued until saturation was attained. Saturation is the point where repetition of information was obtained confirming previously collected data.[28] Other goals soon began to appear as priority, indicating that the stage of withdrawal had

---

[28] Janice M. Morse, "Designing Funded Qualitative Research," in *Strategies of Qualitative Inquiry*, ed. Norman K. Denzin and Yvonna S. Lincoln (Thousand Oaks, CA: Sage, 1998), 76.

been reached.[29] It was time to move on to the next stage of the project.

Examples of Interview Questions

The interview protocol consisted of semi-structured open-ended questions which began with some initial questions to establish rapport, followed by a core set of questions for the research participants.[30] Other questions sought to probe for inner motivations and meanings for why the subjects acted or behaved in a certain manner.[31] Opportunity was also provided for concluding thoughts to wrap up the sessions.

Sample of Questions to Members

1. When were you baptized?
2. How did you come to know the Lord?
3. Have you ever served in any leadership position in the church?
4. Have you ever visited a diviner?
5. How long ago was this?
6. Where did this happen?
7. What factors led to this incidence?
8. Who exactly did you meet with?
9. Did any church member play any role in this episode?

---

[29]Ibid, 78.

[30]Orcher, *Conducting Research*, 131.

[31]Michael Sheppard, *Appraising and Using Social Research in the Human Services: An Introduction for Social Work and Health Professionals* (London: Jessica Kingsley Publishers, 2004), 140.

10. Did you feel any sense of guilt, and how did you resolve it?

11. Were you at this time in any leadership position in your church?

12. Were your parents Christians?

13. Did your parents or any other member of your family ever have the need to consult a diviner or sorcerer?

14. Do you have friends who consult diviners or traditional healers?

15. Did you believe that there were certain ailments that only diviners or traditional healers could solve?

16. Have you been attacked, harassed, or disturbed by evil spirits or powers?

17. What made you quit such practices?

18. Why is it not possible that some other day you may return to the practice of consulting diviners?

19. As a person who has once indulged in such practices what counsel would you give to one considering such a course?

20. In what way can you help the church respond to such issues?

21. Do you believe that there may be other church members involved in such practices?

22. What should the church do regarding this issue?

Sample of Questions to Pastors
1. How long have you been in ministry?
2. Where have you pastored?
3. Have you had experiences of members visiting diviners for help?
4. How did you get to know about their experiences?

5. Was this before or after they became Adventists?

6. Can you tell their primary motivation for such practices?

7. Did they hold positions of leadership in the church at that time?

8. How did they get to know about the diviner they consulted?

9. Did they have to deal with feelings of guilt or shame?

10. What led to their repentance from such practices?

11. How long had they been in the church before this incident?

12. In your experience would you say that this is a current issue among church members or is the practice dead?

13. As a pastor, how do you get to know if there are issues of dual allegiance among members of your church or district?

14. Have you ever conducted open discussions or Bible studies on such issues in your church?

15. How have you sought to respond to allegations of the practice of dual allegiance in your church or district?

16. Have you received training or instruction on how to handle issues of this nature in your church or district?

17. Typically, what sorts of needs or fears motivate members to seek the help of diviners?

18. Can you provide a profile of a typical member who gets involved in dual allegiance?

19. How can the church eliminate this practice among its members?

Sample of Questions to the Diviners

1. How did you become a traditional healer?
2. Where did you acquire your training?
3. What types of cases do you deal with?
4. Which of your services are in greater demand by your clients?
5. Could you describe what a typical client of yours looks like?
6. Do you also have Christians who visit you?
7. How do you know that they are Christian believers?
8. Why do they come to you?
9. Can you tell how they came to know about you?
10. What are some of the issues for which they seek your help?
11. Do your clients ask you for protection from spiritual powers?
12. Have your clients ever asked for your help to hurt some other person?
13. Even the Christians too?
14. On average how many clients do you have weekly?
15. Is there a period when your clientele increases?
16. During what seasons do you experience a decline in services?
17. Do you have prior interaction with your clients before they seek your services?
18. Have you any idea of the backgrounds of your clients?
19. Would you know why your Christian clients visit you rather than go to their pastors/priests?
20. What could run you out of business?
21. Do your patrons feel discomfort about being found seeking your services?
22. In what way has the growth of the churches in the area affected your services?

23. Describe for me, if you please, your typical Christian client?

Sample of Questions to Focus Groups

1. Is the issue of church members visiting diviners a problem in the church?

2. In your opinion what are the reasons why people seek the services of diviners?

3. To what extent are the practices of divination or sorcery a problem in the society?

4. Do such practices concern the church?

5. How should the church respond to these issues and relate to those alleged to be involved in such?

6. What can the church do to make our members immune to such temptations?

Research Analysis

Analysis of research data can generally take one of two forms, the classical research model or the emergent model.[32] The classical model is a linear staged process that begins with the definition of the research problem, and proceeds to data gathering, or findings, then to categorization and ordering, concluding with a neat structured presentation of recommendations and conclusions.

The emergent model on the other hand more closely resembles the reality of human life and the nature of qualitative research. Rather than the sequential stages moving in the neat ordered manner of classical research, in the emergent model all the various stages happen throughout the entire research process, and involve evaluating and

---

[32]Sheila Keegan, *Qualitative Research: Good Decision Making Through Understanding People, Cultures and Markets* (Philadelphia, PA: Kogan Page, 2009), 203-209. Keegan's description, which follows, applies to a marketing context; however, the simplified analysis fits this research goal.

backtracking at every stage. Ultimately, however, analysis is the interplay between the researcher and the data collected.[33] It is this constant interaction that results in the conclusions arrived at.

In recent years, computer software programs have gained recognition and acceptance as being reliable for analyzing and storing qualitative research data. This research could not have been completed in such a timely and cost-effective manner without such assistance.

Computer Software

The process of qualitative analysis requires four components: "the exploration, organization, interpretation, and integration of research materials."[34] Qualitative software programs have greatly aided researchers in organizing, sorting, and searching through data with greater speed and efficiency than if it had been done manually.[35] Other advantages include accuracy, safe storage, and multiple levels of analysis and presentation formats. Qualitative researchers employ the software to "retrieve, rethink, compare subsets, and identify patterns, and relationships" as data analysis is conducted.[36]

For this project the data analysis software program used was Dedoose, a relatively

---

[33] Strauss and Corbin, *Basics of Qualitative Research*, 13.

[34] Judith Davidson and Silvana Di Gregorio, "Qualitative Research and Technology: In the Midst of a Revolution," in *The Sage Handbook of Qualitative Research*, 4th ed., ed. Norman K. Denzin and Yvonna S. Lewin (Thousand Oaks, CA: Sage, 2011), 628.

[35] Creswell, *Research Design*, 195.

[36] Davidson and di Gregorio, "Qualitative Research and Technology," 628.

new program in research analysis compared with older programs such as NVivo and MAXqda. Dedoose was selected for this project primarily because of its cost advantage, user-friendliness, and attractive presentation formats.

To begin, data from the interviews were transcribed and uploaded into the Dedoose program. Identifiers were then assigned to each transcription before the next stage, coding, commenced. Tutorials and videos were helpful in facilitating this time-saving process.[37]

Constant Comparative Analysis

A characteristic feature of grounded theory research is the application of a constant comparative process in which data are collected for the development of theory.[38] This process allows for modifications and adjustments of the definitions of themes and categories as emerging information is provided by new cases.[39] In their seminal work, Glaser and Strauss describe this process as comprising four stages: (1) comparing incidents applicable to each category, (2) integrating categories and their properties, (3) delimiting the theory, and (4) writing the theory.[40] All through the process "the analysis focuses on similarities and differences in the data that might be accounted for by a core

---

[37] A list of academic publications that have employed the Dedoose research program can be found at http://www.dedoose.com/InTheField/Publications.

[38] Grbich, *Qualitative Data Analysis*, 295.

[39] Sheppard, *Appraising and Using Social Research*, 190.

[40] Glaser and Strauss, *The Discovery of Grounded Theory*, 105.

idea."[41] The researcher's background and experience were applied to frame questions and develop initial concepts. These were tested during data collection by observing emerging patterns and honing subsequent interviews. The process of coding continued to be adjusted and redefined as interview transcripts were pored over during the analysis stage.

Coding and Categorization

Although no precise formula exists for conducting grounded theory analysis, it is established upon concepts and categories derived from the data collected.[42] These categories and concepts originate from codes obtained from research transcripts. Coding has been defined as "naming segments of data with a label that simultaneously categorizes, summarizes, and accounts for each piece of data."[43] Coding is the next step in the analytical process after the researcher has read through the interviews, and is helpful for classification into meaningful units.[44] The grouping of codes into higher order categories while searching for patterns and relationships is known as categorizing.[45]

Principle grounded theory has three levels of coding: open coding, axial coding, and selective coding. Strauss and Corbin define open coding as "the analytic process through which concepts are identified and their properties and dimensions are discovered in data." Axial coding is "the process of relating categories to their subcategories, termed,

---

[41]Orcher, *Conducting Research*, 164.

[42]Engler, "Grounded Theory," 257.

[43]Charmaz, *Constructing Grounded Theory*, 43.

[44]Bremborg, "Interviewing," 317.

[45]Ibid., 317.

'axial' because coding occurs around the axis of a category, linking categories at the level of properties and dimensions." Selective coding is described as "the process of integrating and refining the theory."[46] In practice, not all the steps are imperative for the grounded theory methodology to be accepted as applicable to a research project. For this project, initial coding was followed by open coding, then selective coding. In other words, "other codes became subservient to the key code under focus"—what Dedoose refers to as the root code.[47]

The Dedoose software made the coding process extremely easy and adjustable. Codes could be edited and expanded to incorporate secondary codes under root, or primary codes. Another feature which was quite convenient was the file for "Great Quotes." This feature captured special quotes that could be stored and recalled for use in the course of the project writing. Dedoose codes were quite user-friendly and provided direct links with the excerpts that were highlighted.

Memoing

Another integral aspect of grounded theory is memoing. Strauss and Corbin simply define memos in qualitative research as "written records of analysis that vary in type and form."[48] Memos are a way of recording the insights, concepts, and the properties and dimensions associated with the concepts that arise from the researchers' interaction with data collected; without this process essential aspects of the developing story could

---

[46]Strauss and Corbin, *Basics of Qualitative Research*, 101, 123, 143.

[47]Engler, "Grounded Theory," 259.

[48] Strauss and Corbin, *Basics of Qualitative Research*, 217.

be lost.[49] Memoing is recognized as a crucial aspect of grounded theory which occurs through all the phases of the research process and includes notes, diagrams, charts, or lists.[50] New ideas and insights can be gained through this process of self-conversation which seeks to capture thoughts, comparisons, and connections in concrete ways on paper.[51] Carol Grbich lists the purpose of memoing as (1) to follow the pathway from indicator to concept, (2) to develop the properties for each category, (3) to identify hypotheses relating to categories, and (4) to link categories and generate theory.[52]

Although memoing scarcely occurred in the earlier phase of this project, memos did contribute greatly to the later stage of theory formulation. The Dedoose software provided the platform for memo writing and for attaching these to individual transcripts of data collected.

Rigor of the Qualitative Process

Issues of reliability and validity lie at the heart of every research project. This is even more so in the case with qualitative research projects, which do not set out to test theories or hypotheses, but to develop theory, such as can be obtained with grounded theory. The rigor involved in qualitative research must be applied throughout the entire project. John Creswell explains that for qualitative research, reliability and validity have

---

[49] Juliet Corbin, "Strauss' Grounded Theory," in *Routledge International Handbook of Qualitative Nursing Research*, ed. Cheryl Tatano Beck (New York: Routledge, 2013), 176.

[50] Engler, "Grounded Theory," 259-260.

[51] Charmaz, *Constructing Grounded Theory*, 72.

[52] Grbich, *Qualitative Data Analysis*, 85.

different meanings from that of quantitative research. He describes qualitative validity as meaning that the researcher has checked for the accuracy of the findings by employing certain procedures, while qualitative reliability signifies an approach that is consistent among different researchers and in different projects.[53] A number of methods for ensuring qualitative rigor are known, most of which are associated with reliability and validity checks, Janice Morse supplies a listing of these:[54] (1) criteria of adequacy and appropriateness of data, (2) the audit trail, (3) verification of the study with secondary informants, and (4) multiple raters.

Triangulation is another method recommended to give the data "more rigor, breadth and complexity."[55] Briefly explained, triangulation is a social science method that seeks to take information from two or more vantage points; it implies that the use of diverse methodologies will validate one's findings.[56] This use of various approaches with variations in practice and applicability is an important principle in religious research.[57]

Besides triangulation, Creswell cites seven other "validity strategies" for verifying the trustworthiness, authenticity, and credibility of a research project. Listing them from

---

[53]Creswell, *Research Design*, 201.

[54]Morse, "Designing Funded Qualitative Research," 76.

[55]John Swinton and Harriet Mowat, *Practical Theology and Qualitative Research* (London: SCM Press, 2006), 215.

[56]Sheppard, *Appraising and Using Social Research*, 234; David Silverman, *Interpreting Qualitative Data: Methods for Analysing Talk, Text and Interaction* (Thousand Oaks, CA: Sage, 1993), 156-157.

[57]Wade Clark Roof, "Research Design," in *The Routledge Handbook of Research Methods in the Study of Religion*, ed. Michael Stausberg and Steven Engler (London: Routledge, 2011), 74.

most frequently used to least used, they are (1) member checking, (2) the use of rich thick description, (3) clarification of researcher bias, (4) the presentation of negative or discrepant information, (5) spending prolonged time in the field, (6) the use of peer debriefing, and (7) the use of an external auditor.[58]

To ensure reliability of this research project, data were collected from a number of different sources. These were through interviews of a diverse range of individuals from different spheres of life: pastors, members, and diviners. Furthermore, where pastors were interviewed, effort was made to check that there was diversity in background, experience, and orientation. Although this effort at maintaining diversity was not possible with the members interviewed due to the small number that were found and the sensitive nature of the topic, with the diviners, the four interviewed were selected from different contexts, had diverse backgrounds, and represented different age brackets.

Another way that triangulation was incorporated into the research design was by having focus group discussions. Focus groups have been observed to be "particularly valuable for verifying the quality or reliability of data based on observations or interviews."[59]

In the following section the research findings will be discussed by presenting in detail the concepts that emerged from the data, which explain the basis for the phenomenon of divination and sorcery in Yorubaland and the agencies whereby the

---

[58]Creswell, *Research Design*, 201-203.

[59]R. Daniel Shaw, "Qualitative Social Science Methods in Research Design," in *Introduction to Missiological Research*, ed. Edgar J. Elliston (Pasadena, CA: William Carey Library, 2011), 146.

worldview orientation can be transformed. The categories that emerged from the data were employed to develop a theory for worldview transformation to move Yoruba Adventists from the practice of divination and sorcery to biblically appropriate responses.

Findings

Data collected from the research confirmed that the primary cause for the practices of divination and sorcery by Christian converts in Yorubaland was due to established worldview foundations that had not been transformed upon conversion. Other equally important influences that induced Christians to visit diviners were the quest for supernatural power to control their world, and protection from perceived evil. Also, the appeal for the services of the diviners derived from the pressure for solutions to existential needs and fears which spawned shame, sorrow, or pain.

The study also revealed the need for leaders and members of the church to have a deeper relationship with Christ that would be reflected in their words and deeds. In order to achieve this end, members and pastors concurred that education and training would be required in the church for all levels of the body of believers for transformation to occur.

As a result of these findings, a theoretical model was developed, which takes into account the authority of Scripture combined with insights from the social sciences in order to foster worldview transformation among the Yoruba people. The theoretical paradigm derived from the research findings is that worldviews can be transformed by offering better biblical explanations to the causes and remedies of evil and afflictions, through an encounter with the power of the gospel, and through an experiential relationship with Christ. In the following sections these concepts shall be discussed, presenting excerpts from the research, which shall be employed to validate this theory and to form the bedrock for a missiological model for transformation.

Worldview Transformation by Explanation, Encounter, and Experience

Explanation

A predominant reason that disposes Christians in Yorubaland to visit a diviner is the influence of their worldview. Data obtained from all the personal interviews and the focus groups indicate the overwhelming influence of the Yoruba worldview stemming from parental and external sources. Belief in mystical causation and the perennial specter of evil pushes people to seek safety and protection. The studies demonstrate that despite their positions, years in the church, education, international exposure, and the spread of Christianity in the region, the practices of divination and sorcery are current and frequent. The appeal of this phenomenon is largely transmitted by means of the oral lore that has kept the traditional religion alive. It is evident that far from declining, there is a resurgence in Yoruba traditional religion and reinforcement of its worldview constructs. Excerpts from the interviews and focus groups will serve to underscore the significance of the worldview issue and the need for new biblical explanations that will respond to this missiological challenge.[60] Corroborating the view regarding the significance of the worldview to the people, one of the informants, pastor Papa, explained it in this way:

> It has been discovered that Africans of all status and all levels tend to come back home when they meet dead ends in every front of life. They tend to see the African religion as a panacea, so to say, for any challenge they cannot surmount. . . . They come back home, they have that understanding.

---

[60]The names of the subjects have been coded in this manner: pastors begin with "P," members with "M," and diviners with "D."

Causation

Causation is the belief that every event or occurrence has a supernatural origin and this view is prevalent among Yoruba and many African people. This sentiment was aptly depicted in the interview with one of the pastors, Pasho, who described it this way:

> Except for those who are ingrained in the truth, for us in Africa anything that happens to you is caused by a demon. A road accident is [caused by] a demon, the car refuses to start, even when it has given sufficient warning [signs] it's a demon. When the power goes out and the food goes bad, it's a demon. So everybody is chased by demons, except for those who have come to rest in the Lord.

A similar idea was reflected right at the beginning of the focus group in Ilishan, when one of the elders candidly stated, "There's an African adage that no African dies a natural death—there's always a supernatural cause. We believe there is evil in the society and the devil comes in different ways to attack people with different problems."

In the other focus group at Orile Iganmu, it was also emphatically proclaimed, "There are problems and there are powers in Africa that make people to be frustrated, oppressed, and suppressed." It was further added that the "majority of the problems that we have, trace their origins [to] our villages, or homes of origin; they may not have come from the individual." This is illustrative of the belief in the influence of generational curses and cultic covenants made by a person's forebears which could cause shame, sorrow, and misery all through one's existence unless something is done to correct this.

Parental and Societal Influence

In every instance where a Christian visited a diviner the reason could be traced in part to the influence of parents who had no inhibitions about such practices because of their backgrounds. Suggestions or pressure from friends and other members in the community were also mentioned.

Pastor Poja explained the source of these beliefs, stating, "You know we don't have a written tradition, it was passed from parents to children and so on, and that is how it has been."

The role of the diviner is to find out the cause of misfortunes or mishaps in the lives of people in the community. The diviner, or *babalawo*, does this by consulting the Ifa oracle to determine the cause and cure of the problem. One of the pastors who had waited for several years before the birth of their first child shared how his in-laws increased pressure on them saying, "'Go and find out, do some investigation.' What did that mean? [It meant] 'go to the diviner and find out what is the cause of this childlessness.'"

Childlessness is one of the major contributory factors that leads women to the diviners. A woman from the Ilishan focus group explained,

> I didn't know anything about dual allegiance until the time I sought a child. You know that your relations will not allow you to wait. If your faith is not strong, people will come to you and ask you to go see the diviner, and if you refuse to go they will say that it may be that you are the cause of your problem.

Sometimes, however, the pressure does not come from without, rather it is a factor programmed into the very DNA of the culture. This insight can be inferred from the interview with the Ilishan diviner who factually asserted, "Yoruba people believe that they originated from Ile Ife. Our people believe in tradition, and it will never go back from us. Whether Christian or Muslim, you must participate in it." A Yoruba proverb in consonance with this view states, "Religion does not mean you cannot help yourself." This was affirmed by Pasho who quoted the same proverb as saying, "Christianity does not forbid us from keeping our traditions."

Pastor Poja grew up under strong traditional influences and explained it this way:

There is affinity between you and your parents or grandparents, it takes something strong to break what they have taught you. I was brought up in heathenism by grandparents. Every morning they had to consult the *babalawo* before the king would go out. Because the problems of today are different from those of yesterday, the *babalawo* must be consulted every day.

Currency and Frequency

The aim of two of the questions directed at the pastors was to discover if the practice of consulting a diviner was current, and to know the extent of the problem. In response, all the pastors interviewed admitted unequivocally that the practice was ongoing and was pernicious. Pastor Poja, one of the senior pastors who had served as an administrator, unabashedly confessed the following:

> It is a serious problem which the leaders of the church do not have an answer to. They assume that some may be doing it. It is generally assumed that only a few are going. A pastor may assume that in his congregation of about 300 only about 5 may be going, but it may be more than 5, because we don't have the statistics to measure, but many may be going because there is nobody in Africa who does not have problems.

When asked how he had responded to the allegations of such practices among his members, he admitted with chagrin, "I won't lie to you, I deny the allegations because I don't want a stain on the name of the church, I leave such to individuals."

Pastor Pad posited that traditional religion and the practice of consulting a diviner are experiencing a resurgence:

> A revival is going on and it is becoming more refined. In Lagos they have what is like a seminary and they are now advertising on TV or radio, "Come and learn how to be a diviner." There is an open program on LTV [Lagos State Television], which holds twice or thrice every year where they promote their goods and sell their wares openly. People register, and on TV and radio, people share their specializations, they tell their booth numbers, phone numbers, etc. They claim to be traditional healers but they may use incantations and divinations; you can't tell the difference any longer. And the government is really promoting these practices in the name of herbal medicine.
>
> For instance during an IT commissioning program, several religious leaders were invited to pray. They included an Islamic leader, a pastor and a traditional religionist.

> . . . You wouldn't believe that such a person [the governor] would associate himself with such. [But] it is becoming fashionable to recognize and visit traditional religionists these days. People are not ashamed because they feel these people give them what they want so why should they be ashamed. This revival in traditional religion is posing a challenge to us as ministers.

Pastor Papa, an authority who has written on this subject, when asked how serious the problem was, responded, "It is a serious problem but I don't think that the church is doing enough to address the problem."

While it was impossible to obtain any statistical data in the course of this qualitative research to convey the frequency of this practice, the perception from those interviewed suggested a widespread prevalence of such practices. In addition, one of the participants has co-authored a book on this topic that documents the fact that Christians are visiting diviners.[61]

Insignificant Influences

The study demonstrated that certain influences and characteristics did not appear to preclude persons in these contexts from practicing divination or sorcery. Those influences that had little significance on the proclivity to such practices were education, years in the church, position, and the influence of Christianity. Pasho, who had served in Ijebuland, the region where this study took place, averred that although the Ijebus were among the earliest to accept the missionaries and to be educated, "education has not changed anything."

---

[61] Amanze and Akpa, *Seventh-day Adventist Response to Spiritism*.

Pastor Pajja, who initially maintained that this practice was mainly among the uneducated, when pressed on this point admitted that "we also have professors, lawyers and others who, in spite of education, visit the diviners."

Asked concerning the profile of the typical client of a diviner, Pastor Pad responded, "I will say it cannot be limited to any particular cadre whether educated, or uneducated, [it could be] a professor who wants to hold his chair for a long time, the farmer who wants [a] good harvest, so it is not limited to a particular level or status."

Pastor Papa shared his personal experience when his father fell strangely ill and was taken to the Ogun State Teaching Hospital. With humor in his voice he recalled the following:

> At the end of the day, the consultant physician, a professor of geriatrics asked some questions, "Where did this man come from?" "Has he any children?" "Who is the wife, is she the current wife, the wife of his youth?" "Is he enjoying the wife?" "Are they living peacefully?" The man [doctor] explained that they had done all the tests, sputum, blood, urine, feces, ECG, after everything the man [his father] was not found to be sick based upon medical investigation. Yet the man [his father] was going down to the grave. He said, "Take him back to the village."

Being an expert on traditional religion he understood the professor of medicine as saying, "Take him to the diviner, there's absolutely nothing medically wrong with your father."

It was also fascinating to observe that among the diviners interviewed one had an education in insurance from a polytechnic institution, while another had left an accounting profession to take over from his dead father. A third diviner informed the researcher that although his children are presently going to school to get an education, they were also being groomed to succeed him upon his death.

Age or years of church membership and even positions in the church did not seem to be of any real significance in this study. Pastor Pasho, who had listened to confessions from a few of his members with such experiences, calmly mentioned the following:

> I won't really say that [age in the church] matters. For instance, the elder I told you about had been in the church for over 40 years. The second case, the lady, had been in the church for over 25 years. The third person had been in the church for over 40 years too. It is not a matter of how long you had been in the church because the rich also cry.

Another pastor, Poja, shared this story:

> I know a friend of mine whose wife divorced him because she said he had a habit of visiting diviners. She said to me, "The friend you know is not the person he really is." And what made this so sad was the fact that he was an elder, a second generation Adventist, since 1959.

Mami is a third-generation Adventist himself, yet it was his grandmother, a traditional healer, who gave him directions, and insisted that he visit a diviner, when she discovered his son was born with a neonatal condition; she also paid the diviner's fee and gave a token by which the diviner would recognize who had referred him there.

Pastor Papa remembered a couple he had to counsel regarding a visit the wife had made to a diviner. Although they had been members for over fifteen years, her barrenness left her insecure concerning her husband's affection.

> I met a sister who went to a diviner to give her some objects, love objects, so that the husband may love her more. See, she had no child, and was of the opinion that her husband was on the move to go and get another lady, so she was trying to woo the man back to herself, and the thing leaked out . . . and I got to know about them.

Just about every subject interviewed and participants in both focus groups admitted that even pastors were not immune to the temptation to visit diviners. While some may rationalize about this, others are shameless about it, as though the end justified the means.

Diro, a diviner, cited an example of the kind of cases for which his services were required by clergy. "For instance reverends who are not supposed to marry may have had an indiscretion and they don't want it reported, so they would want the pregnancy covered up, because if it is known he would be disgraced."

Poja related his own personal experience with a pastor colleague when after four years had gone by and he and his wife were still childless. Here was his account:

> We had been married for 4 years without children. He [the district pastor] said one day, "There is a goddess in Okitipupa, from where I was transferred it is called Ayelala, still there till today," he said, "I have sent many there and they get their children. Poja why are you doing this to yourself, we get children from the devil's way and we train them in the way of the Lord!" The following year we had our first child without going to Ayelala. He [the district pastor] was there at the naming ceremony and shared this incident openly there, with his own lips.

One of the former administrators interviewed, when asked if those who visited the diviner held leadership positions in the church, replied, "Some. Some were elders, deacons, holding lofty positions, some names if I mentioned them would shock you. But they go there in the night so they would not be seen."

The fact that people from this culture had gained exposure through travel abroad and living in countries like Europe and America did not seem to make a difference in their worldview orientation. Almost all the diviners indicated that some of their clientele even called them from abroad and cell-phone business was conducted with them.

Diro, the Irolu diviner, claimed to have the ability to control the outcome of a court case in America in favor of his client. "Sometimes we use incantations, and other times we use a padlock to do it. We have a particular leaf that we use, if the case is in America, on the day that the case goes to court we will hold the leaf up in the air and the judgment shall go in favor of the client."

When asked if he ever received requests from clients abroad to help solve personal issues, Dili replied, "A lot! Both from home and abroad."

Although Christianity arrived in the western region of Nigeria in the 1840s and the country has become an influential center for the growth of Pentecostalism on the continent, the growth of churches does not seem to have hindered the business of diviners in any notable manner. One question put forward to each diviner sought to know if the spread of churches to virtually every street corner had in any way hampered business for them.

Diro responded that nothing could shut up his business, "Except my death." Doge dismissively stated regarding the churches, "They are of no concern." Dipo confidently explained, "That is not likely to happen. We also have a fellowship that is international that meets every Sunday, Ojulawo Orunmila, that attracts Christians and Muslims from all over, and the crowd is very large during our services from 10 a.m. to noon."

Dili's rejoinder was by far the most disturbing, "It hasn't affected anything, it has boosted it."

Diro further declared,

> Formerly people believed that they could find healing in the churches but now they have seen the light. In the churches they pray for prosperity not healing. They claim they perform miracles in these churches. . . . So people are seeing the light and they know that not everything needs a miracle, but with leaves and medicine healing can be obtained.

Orality

African Traditional Religions in general have thrived for millennia without written creeds or codes because they have relied on oral traditions. Other than the recent attempts discovered during the course of the study by modern diviners to begin documenting what they refer to as "accounts," the Yoruba religious worldview that has shaped and reinforced the beliefs of the people has largely been transmitted orally.

When asked about the stories that shape the worldview of the people, the Ilishan focus group responded, "It is also interesting to know that most of these practices are being recorded now as accounts. Accounts, as they call them, are the records of *juju* solutions to problems we face today."

When I probed a little further they explained: "The accounts are like a book. They are instructions such as: pluck this leaf, bind them together—they tell you what to do, if you want to kill a person, or treat a problem; it is found in families, and is inherited."

As a result of the manner in which the tradition is transmitted, the group attested that "what I have come to realize is that, like I said, we live with this problem, and hardly will you ever see any child that is born that has no knowledge of *juju*, in our society."

Poja confirmed the origin of the oral tradition that shaped the societal worldview, explaining, "You know we don't have a written tradition, it was passed from parents to children and so on, and that is how it has been. There were no hospitals, so whatever medicine they [the diviners] gave like herbs, were what we took and were healed."

He mentioned a recent societal phenomenon that has further strengthened the traditional worldview. "Another contributory factor is home videos, which have helped many to consider *baba* as the solution to their problems."

Hence the appreciation that "*Baba* is the answer," and that the "last bus stop" for every possible malaise is the diviner, views that are largely attributable to the issue of orality.

The foregoing findings are eloquent calls for the need for new worldview explanations to replace the deeply entrenched worldview constructs that precipitate visits to the diviners and healers. Such an explanation must by nature be more tenacious than the myths and oral traditions that have endured for centuries. It should offer more coherent responses concerning the origin and existence of evil and suffering and demonstrate the love, power, and justice of God. This is precisely the role that the Scriptures can play in the transformation of the worldview of the Yoruba people.

Encounter

Yorubaland, like much of Africa, can be classified as a power-oriented society. Aside from the hierarchical nature of the culture in which control is exerted from those at the top over persons below, the issue of supernatural control and power was discovered by the study to be a significant factor as to why people seek the services of a diviner.

Quest for Power

Diviners are generally acclaimed to be persons of power who have supernatural resources to solve virtually every type of problem. In contrast to the typical Christian faith declaration, "Jesus is the answer," common to Christian communities, in the Yoruba context what seems more commonplace is, "*Baba* is the answer!" (*Baba* is the shortened form of the local word for "diviner.") As Pastor Poja explained, "There is a general belief that the *babalawo* has the solutions to all the problems."

Supernatural power is sought primarily because life's challenges are believed to have supernatural origins. The diviners are consulted because they are the mediators between the divinities/deities and the people. Among the major reasons why the diviners play such a crucial role in the society is because they meet needs and allay the fears of their clients. They also are the agencies whereby the shame and pleas of the people can find redress. Diviners also seem to serve as a ballast, maintaining balance in the societal order and arbitrating power equations in the community.

Rapid Response

The most impressive attraction for the services of diviners among those of the church was their celerity. This factor was expressed at the Orile focus group when one of the group stated, "Yorubas have a proverb that states, 'I call on God and He doesn't come in twenty years.' But when they turn to the diviners they have instant help."

Pastor Papa in his research uncovered a humorous but perturbing dimension to the perceived speed of the diviner,

> Some responses are that the diviners' solutions tend to be faster, and quicker. They call them, "Panasharp!" [an allusion to a pain killer, Panadol, believed to be the most effective remedy for pain relief; also, sharp connotes speed]. The other one is "Panadull" so they say, "Pastor, *baba's* own is Panasharp. Prayer is Panadull." It's interesting! So the diviners tend to give rapid response, kind of, to those sorts of problems. They respond quickly, you see the results almost immediately. But prayer works to those who believe, they will work only for those. The thing is that prayer is a little too slow for their liking.

Apart from the diviners, every subject interviewed, along with both focus groups, agreed that a primary motivation for seeking the diviner was the rapid response sought for problems.

Needs and Fears

Generally, it was people's needs and fears that led them to seek help from diviners. These existential needs ranged from childlessness, healing, prosperity, job promotion, marital bliss, success, and issues that would bring respect, or honor, or at the same time remove perceived shame. The fears included death, witchcraft, evil, and spiritual attacks. An excerpt from the Ilishan focus group is illustrative of the common responses from the research:

"Childlessness is one of the reasons. Another is promotion. Some people might have embezzled money in the office, so they will go to the diviner so that he can do something to cover them, so that accusing fingers will not be pointed at them." Other responses included, "Lingering illness," "spiritual attack," "protection." When I asked why they needed protection, they replied, "from accidents, from witches and wizards," "untimely death" "because of money; that is prosperity" "marriage; if parents are longing that their children should have a good family in the future. They want to go and see (divine), to know if this person is the right one." Others said, "We do it to know the future also." Another person suggested, "It is also in our tradition that when a child is born, on a particular day we bring the child before the gods to inquire regarding the child's destiny." One respondent reported that "some people, when they want to travel abroad, go to the herbalist to request for protection when they travel and assistance in obtaining a travel visa." Others suggested, "They would also like to know what would be the outcome of that journey, if it would be in their favor." Another reason offered was "for court cases too, so that you can win the case." And finally, "if a person is looking for a plot of land to build a house, one may be asked to bring samples of the land from two possible choices, then the diviner would inquire regarding the two choices. Also in getting a shelter, people consult the diviner."

Pasho added the following as additional motivations, "Assurance that this difficulty they are going through they will overcome. How they can turn back the hands of fate. People don't want to live in obscurity, they want to have a support, they want someone to lean on."

Of all the reasons, however, he singled out the desire to escape obscurity, stating, "That is the key thing in here."

Notwithstanding, these were not the only reasons for engaging the services of diviners. Some people, including pastors, visited them simply to have the diviner inform them of what the future held and to seek intervention to correct whatever may go wrong in the future. The diviner Dili explained,

> You know that the Pentecostal Churches don't believe in sacrifices, however, most of them go back to the Old Testament. And they know that it is we, the traditionalists, who perform sacrifices to God. Yet they do come to us, some even when they have no problems, they just come. They will say, "Check for us. We have to know in advance, the near future, what is going to happen to us." . . . So that if there is any problem we can eliminate it now, we can find a solution to it, and do whatever is necessary.

Pastor Poja related a unique account from his earlier years of another reason why people visited the diviner:

> There was a *babalawo* who used to bring up the dead so that loved ones could speak to them through a curtain. Zorro's mother went there to see this *baba*, even though she was Adventist. The *Baba* first would demand the reason for coming, "I am here because of my son who died, Zorro, call him let me see him." The baba responded, "You can't see him but you will hear his voice." And he charged them heavily. Every five days Zorro's mother went back there. When I came from ASWA I tried to talk her out of it, telling her that this was sorcery, it was evil. She said, "You won't understand, my son is dead, you are alive. This is the only place I can go and hear his voice and it is so comforting to me. If not for this I would have died."

Another reason for going to the diviner was for him to explain mysteries, such as the identity of thieves or the location of missing items. Pastor Pajja recollected incidents like these from his ministry years:

> In Igbobini, Ondo State. They said if they prayed, prayers took a long time to act or to be effective but Aiyelala seems to act with immediate effect. For instance if one stole another person's object, you can't go to the church to conjure or divine, to see or

know who has done it. But if you swore by Ogun something would happen to the guilty one, with Aiyelala it was the same.

Poja's story supports this view:

> This man confided in me, he was a very good elder who loved the Lord and we were friends. He bought a car for his wife. The wife used the car for only two days and the car was gone. They now advised him that he can go to *baba*, which is *babalawo*, [who served also as] the pastor in a spiritual church; he was combining the two roles in Ibadan. [He was informed], "If you go there you can get this car back."

Although the fear of sorcery and witchcraft is prevalent in Yorubaland, curiously none of the four diviners hailing from different towns, and having diverse backgrounds, admitted to ever assisting a client to hurt or do harm to another person. They all responded that they would counsel clients who made requests like this against such a course of action. However, it was the Ilishan diviner Dili who provided insight to another aspect of the functions of the diviner. He said, "If anyone wants to harm you, the person's evil plans can be redirected back to him; we call that 'back to sender.'"

Ironically, presently, some Christians can often be heard praying for whatever evil that was looming to "return to sender." This kind of prayer is common among Pentecostals. Nevertheless, pastor Pida, when asked if he ever had been attacked or harassed by evil spirits, responded,

> Yes, about 3 years ago. My wife and I were on the same bed when a figure came in through the entrance of the room. I made a motion with my hand thinking it was my wife who had gone to the bathroom, but when my hand met my wife's body by my side we realized it must be an evil spirit. Also, I was shot in my dream while sleeping. In both incidents I prayed, and even applied anointing oil around the house in the former case, and in the latter case I prayed that the intention would return to the sender.

A major distinction between Christianity and the magic of traditional religion is its emphasis on the surrender of one's will to God. When people visit the diviner it is often with the aim of having their will or desire emerge supreme. Pastor Pad differentiated between the two phenomena,

> I believe the difference between magic (black power) and miracle is that with miracles it is a matter of waiting on the will of God to be done. But with magic it involves doing the right thing, the right procedure, saying the right words, in the form of incantation, so that the right formula gives the right answer immediately. In the case of magic the right formula gives the right result.

However, it was obvious that a principal reason the diviner was patronized was because as a person of power he could control natural phenomena, such as the rain, and even the decisions of people in favor of his client. During the interview with Diro, he received a call on his cell phone from a client. The researcher heard him informing his client in the Yoruba language how he could be of assistance in controlling the weather. When asked how this could be done, he replied, "We use incantations. We use leaves and incantations, we plant the roots in the ground, sometimes set it on fire to make this happen. For instance the leaves you call tobacco are used in controlling the rain."

Asked if he could also make the rain fall, he confidently remarked,

> Yes, we can make the rain to fall also! You see the one I was speaking with just won a contract and is about to begin work on Monday. I suggested to him that if he would like it we could hold back the rain for a week so that it doesn't disturb his work. But we have to beg God to make it happen because it is God who controls everything.

The Orile focus group shed light on the diviner's power to control people. "Some people are looking for power to control others so that they will obey precisely what you desire—'Do as I say.'"

At the Ilishan focus group, one of the elders shared an experience from his secondary school days of how a classmate demonstrated before everyone present the supernatural power he possessed, "He just did something and incanted some words and before you knew what was happening the leaves began to drop one after the other. That is the power we are talking about."

Other accounts which serve to illustrate this craving for power in the society irrespective of position and religious affiliation included the following: "Some contractors, they do this so that immediately they arrive at an office they can say, 'Sir, I want this job, just sign so that I can have it,' and that's exactly how it would happen, it would get signed for them."

Moreover, "some [church] treasurers will like to do some charms to make people write big checks. Some people go to the diviner to obtain power to bring people under their control."

In addition, "in order to secure high patronage some pastors go to the diviner to do something for their church so that the church will enlarge, so that people will come, so that they will have many members." Another respondent stated, "Some people might have embezzled money in the office, so they will go to the diviner so that he can do something to cover them up, so that accusing fingers will not be pointed at them."

Some even bragged about their powers:

> When two people fight, they do not fight alone but you will hear someone threaten another person, "You dare me, and you will see what will happen to you!" Sometimes people will say, "Who is that person you talked to, don't you know him? He is a very powerful man." When they say he is powerful, they are not talking about his physical strength but spiritual power.

This is in marked contrast with some people's perception about the church: "Some do not believe that the church has the spiritual power needed to respond to the issues they are facing; the church only gathers for worship." Others added, "People believe that with the *babalawo* it is not just talk, but that they possess supernatural power to help people out of their situations." In contrast, "the church is perceived as a religious club."

Another notable observation from the study was the outright audacity of the diviners juxtaposed against the perceived faltering stance of the church, "The people who practice these things manifest boldness/audacity in what they are doing. And they believe that what they are doing will work." The narrator then recounted an incident in which a diviner, who was riding on his motorcycle taxi, boasted that he could hold back the impending rainstorm.

In light of the preceding quest for supernatural power, an appropriate missiological response would be an emphasis on the power of the gospel encountered in the life of believers. As Mashe reiterated at the Ilishan focus group regarding the difficulty for those who have tasted and proven the potency and efficacy of the diviner to leave their old ways, it would require a more formidable encounter to witness to them.

> So imagine such a person coming into the church and needing protection. If you want to take my *juju* from me, the one I have tested and has been very, very, effective, which the church condemns, then there should be a replacement. One that is more potent than what I have been carrying, isn't it? So if there's no replacement, there's no way I will drop it.

Earlier a respondent had also declared, "In all sincerity these charms are highly potent, and highly effective."

Experience

Several of the subjects interviewed along with various persons at the focus groups underscored the importance of finding better alternatives in order to wean people away from the diviners. A hopeful note was struck by Mashe at the Ilishan focus group when he stridently proclaimed:

> Let me just tell you one thing sir, people are fed up of carrying *juju* always if you don't know. Because it takes time for them to dress up, with inserting certain things on your head, to recite some incantations, it takes time. That is why when religious campaigns are organized, if people are sure that they would have lasting solutions, they are ready to drop this thing. That is why the church has to be on its toes.

Spiritual Leadership

Repeatedly, pastors and members expressed the need for an experiential relationship with Christ as a vital element for enabling people to disengage from the diviners. The experience of Christ in the life of a minister was considered by pastor Pad as the most significant in the spiritual experience of the members. "If a minister does not have a personal growing relationship with Christ, he may not have much to offer his church and so the members may wind up going to look for help elsewhere." Then he added the following:

> I think it begins with the pastor himself because you cannot give what you don't have. Leadership is critical. Some may be working for Jesus without knowing Him. If I don't have a living relationship with Jesus then all I will be doing will just be pretending or faking it. A situation will arise that will eventually reveal the true nature of one's faith. When they see that power of God demonstrated in your life people will come to you to pray for them.

At the Orile focus group a similar sentiment was expressed. "The church only gathers for worship but its leaders need to be spiritually strong to meet the spiritual needs of the members." At the same venue another person added, "The pastors need to become more spiritual and focus less on material things of the world and design programs to help their members."

The role of a truly spiritual minister with a deep experiential relationship with Christ can be a big help to people facing the temptation to turn to a diviner for solutions. This was again stressed by Moshe, "If someone comes to me and says that I have this problem that prayer can't solve, I will say let us pray, and will invite a pastor, not some of these fake pastors, but a truly spiritual person and pray."

Trusting God

Responsibility for overcoming the lure of divination and sorcery did not lie solely with the pastors. It was generally believed that members needed to grow in their Christian experience so that they can trust God rather than take their affairs into their own hands. Pastor Pad believed that although leadership was critical, a personal relationship with God would preclude members from involvement in the evil of divination. "Members need to know who God is and the power He has given to us."

Almost every subject interviewed agreed that for members to resist the temptation to resort to the diviner, the church would need to teach them to have trust or faith in God. In spite of the pervasiveness of the practice, Pam observed, "Some of our members are not immune. But others are strong as the Rock of Gibraltar; they will not be moved. They would rather die, than bow."

He observed that their unflinching faithfulness to God, no matter their external circumstances, was the product of their relationship with God and their understanding of Scripture. When Mose was asked why he did not think he could relapse to consult a diviner again, his unruffled response was,

> That can never happen since I have now known Christ. Yes, I know in the world we shall have problems and challenges, but like the Scripture says in John 16:33, "In the world we shall have tribulations, but be not afraid, I have overcome the world." Tribulations may come but in Christ we have overcome the world. My faith is not in *babalawos* who are fellow human beings as I am, but in Christ. No one has come close to what Job has suffered so whether trials, troubles, problems, I will never go back to the diviner!

Mami also forcefully stated, "Some go to the *babalawo* for protection because they are afraid of death. I do not fear death, I fear Christ!"

In summary what the respondents emphatically declared was that their experiential knowledge of the goodness of Christ had led to explicit faith in Christ, rather than the diviner. At the Ilishan focus group pastor Pid espoused the need to emphasize holiness. "Members need to be encouraged to live a life of holiness, because the archenemy uses sin to entrap us. So we need to encourage people, and tell them, 'You cannot live in sin and ask grace to be multiplied.'"

A growing experience with Christ changes the focus of a person's life from the existential, to the eternal, from worldliness to holiness. Perhaps that is why Mose also urged, "Maybe the church should go back to our Bible and practice the simple ways of old, of being fair, and just. I remember when the most luxurious car around was a Peugeot 504 but now people want to ride Jeeps, and they do all kinds of things to make sure they get it, and they believe that the *babalawo* can help them get these."

Personal Testimonies

As a means for extricating people from the practice of divination and helping them on the pathway to transformation, another strategy that emerged from the interviews and discussions were personal testimonies. One person who found this strategy to be effective in leading people to transformed lives over a period of time was Pasho:

> The first thing I tried to do was to tell my background and live in friendship with them; not being afraid of eating in their homes for fear of being charmed. When we talk about these things though we need to know that they are real. But when we have an effective prayer life then we are safe. Then I bring people who have been in similar experiences to share about it, including people who have practiced witchcraft, so people may know there is a way of escape. Rather than simply decreeing that this practice is wrong.

Another person who found this strategy necessary was Pida. The way he was convinced he could help was "by telling the testimonies of my experience, how I have tried the diviners, and their power failed, [and] how Christ has set me free."

Poja also used his personal testimonies as a strategy for extricating people from the grip of the diviners. In evangelistic campaigns he shared his encounters with the diviners, and his estimates of those who repented were "over 200 that I know of. Many others I may not know."

It was also observed that all the diviners interviewed remarked that they constantly benefitted from the referrals or testimonies of satisfied clients to enlarge their client base. Doge was the only one observed to have recently ordered a large canvass banner to publicize his business. (This banner was like an ego trip for him, along with his two American utility vans, with which he proudly posed for photographs.)

The findings that emerged from the data collected presented three cardinal elements, and other core elements that I believe would be required in order to effect worldview transformation. These core elements include: context, community, crisis, conflict, causation, curriculum, and the role of the change agent.

In chapter 5 this new theory is appraised against other missiological models for worldview transformation. The chapter also outlines in detail the role of Scripture in transforming a person's worldview from dependence on divination and sorcery to unshakeable trust in God. Prominent in this model will be the Great Controversy doctrine and its function in enabling the process of worldview transformation in the Yoruba context.

CHAPTER V

TOWARDS A MISSIOLOGICAL TRANSFORMATIONAL MODEL

Introduction

Findings from the qualitative grounded theory research reported in the previous chapter gave rise to a theory of worldview transformation by explanation, encounter, and experience. Its cardinal elements were fresh biblical explanations to respond to unscriptural worldview assumptions, power encounters to deal with the unbridled quest for supernatural power, and an experiential relationship with Christ. Other discoveries revealed that for some the lure of divination and sorcery was attributable to ignorance. This underscored the crucial role of education for worldview transformation. Such education will require a holistic approach to resolving the challenge of divination and sorcery, which is the objective of this chapter.

In this chapter a worldview transformational model shall be presented which develops the cardinal elements from the research findings—explanation, encounter, and experience—into a holistic set of core components to achieve the objective. These components are derived from Scripture and scholarly literature that corroborate the validity of the findings. The core components discussed in this chapter include: context, causation, curriculum, community, conflict, crisis, and the change agent.

Context

Adekunle Alalade, in his book *Limiting Factors to the Success of the Seventh-day Adventist Church in Africa: The Nigeria Case Study*, examined the reasons why almost a century after the Adventist message entered the country the church's growth seemed overshadowed by other denominations. In his comparison of the Adventist Church with other mission churches—Anglican, Methodist, and Catholic—and indigenous Pentecostal churches—Cherubim and Seraphim, the Redeemed Christian Church, and Winners Chapel—he concluded that Adventists have a lot to learn from these churches.[1] In a case of gross hyperbole he posited that the rate of growth of the Adventist Church in the country was at such a pace that it would take another 303 years to reach a million members, and that "we cannot afford to remain in this doomed world for another 303 years before the Lord will come."[2] While his mathematics is inaccurate his study is beneficial to the church, and it draws attention to the methodology of indigenous churches that have triggered explosive, albeit, syncretistic growth.[3]

A primary reason why the Aladura churches, and other local Pentecostal churches that evolved from them, have attained such tremendous acceptance and success within a short period of existence is mainly attributable to their keen perception of the indigenous worldview. Hence, this development lends credence to the urgency of Hiebert's appeal

---

[1]Alalade, *Limiting Factors*, 92.

[2]Ibid., 93.

[3]See the author's study, which examines the growth and spread of Pentecostalism in Nigeria. *Pentecostalism in Nigeria: Phenomenon, Prospects and Problems to Mainline Churches* (Ilishan Remo, Nigeria: Babcock Consulting, Babcock University, 2011).

regarding worldview transformation, when he stated, if the worldview is not transformed, in the long run the gospel is subverted and becomes captive to the local culture. The result is syncretistic Christo-paganism, which has the form but not the essence of Christianity. Christianity becomes a new magic and a new, more subtle form of idolatry.[4]

In order to more effectively communicate the gospel in a manner so as to preclude the snare of syncretism, mission theologians have recognized the need for the contextualization of the gospel—that is, "relating the never-changing truths of Scripture to ever-changing human contexts so that the truths are clear and compelling."[5] To Hiebert this entails double exegesis: of the context, or culture, and the text of Scripture.[6] This approach is premised upon the recognition that all truth is God's truth, and that Scripture and creation offer two valid sources of God's truth. That means, theology (which provides insight to Scripture) and the theories of social sciences (which provide insight to the understanding of God's creation) are "dual revelatory sources of truth."[7]

A literature review about the local culture from the social sciences in addition to the findings from the field research provided the framework for exegeting the Yoruba context. This has facilitated valuable understanding in applying scriptural explanations in

---

[4]Hiebert, *Transforming Worldviews*, 315.

[5]Ott, Strauss, and Tienou, *Encountering Theology of Mission*, 266.

[6]Paul Hiebert, "Syncretism and Social Paradigms," in *Contextualization and Syncretism: Navigating Cultural Currents*, ed. Gailyn Van Rheenen (Pasadena, CA: William Carey Library, 2006), 31-32.

[7]James R. Estep, "Developmental Theories: Foe, Friend, or Folly?" in *Christian Formation: Integrating Theology and Human Development*, ed. James R. Estep and Jonathan H. Kim (Nashville, TN: B & H Academic, 2010), 45-46.

response to the questions and issues in the Yoruba worldview that induce divination and sorcery. The absence of sound hermeneutical principles in the Aladura churches (also evident in many Pentecostal churches) has resulted in the contemporary conundrum where "spirits" of malaria, diabetes, and arthritis are recognized, and sickness is attributed to the working of diverse demonic spirits. The prevalence of this view of sickness and the occurrence of diviners who double as prophets in some Yoruba indigenous churches can be attributed to the "failure of the gospel to penetrate the inner worldview of the [local] culture."[8] The next section shall explore divination and sorcery from the societal and biblical contexts, and recommend a missiological response aimed at producing worldview transformation.

Divination and Sorcery in ATR

Divination is defined as "the art or science of deducing the future or the unknown through the observation and interpretation of some facet of nature or human life, ordinarily of an unpredictable and trivial character."[9] It is also "the practice of consulting beings (divine, human or departed) or things (by observing objects or actions) in the attempt to gain information about the future and such other matters as are removed from normal knowledge."[10] Divination is an ancient, universal, religious phenomenon, widely

---

[8] Ott, Strauss, and Tienou, *Encountering Theology of Mission*, 275.

[9] D. E. Aune, "Divination," *International Standard Bible Encyclopedia* (*ISBE*), 1979 ed., 1:971-974.

[10] W. L. Liefeld, "Divination," *Zondervan Pictorial Encyclopedia* (*ZPE*), 2009 ed., 1:163-166.

practiced in the Ancient Near East and focused on human schemes for uncovering the divine will, which is in contrast to prophetic insight derived from direct revelation.[11]

Witton Davis defines sorcery as "the use of supernatural powers over others through the assistance of evil spirits, synonymous with witchcraft, wizardry and black magic."[12] Sorcery is often used in connection with witchcraft and also can be regarded as "the mystical ability to manipulate the forces of life to do harm to human beings or their property."[13] It is also "the deliberate and malicious use of magic, through rituals and magical paraphernalia to premeditatively manipulate spiritual powers with the intent of inflicting harm or death on other people."[14]

It is widely known that "almost all African societies believe in witchcraft in one form or another,"[15] and that the witchcraft issue is at the center of the African psyche.[16] Accordingly, the belief and practice of sorcery lies at the root of the African worldview

---

[11]F. Scott Spencer, "Divination," *New Interpreter's Dictionary of the Bible* (*NIDB*), 2:143; Aune, "Divination," *ISBE*, 972.

[12]Witton T. Davis, "Magic, Divination and Demonology among the Semites," *American Journal of Semitic Languages and Literature* 14, no. 4 (1898): 242.

[13]I. W. C. van Wyk, "African Witchcraft in Theological Perspectives," *Hervormde Teologiese Studies* 60, no. 4 (2004): 1201-1228.

[14]David Sitton, "Glossary of Terms and Resources on Tribal Peoples," *International Journal of Frontier Mission* 15, no. 2 (April-June 1998): 107.

[15]Kunhiyop, *African Christian Ethics*, 377.

[16]John S. Pobee and Gabriel Oshitelu, *African Initiatives in Christianity: The Growth, Gift and Diversities of Indigenous African Churches—A Challenge to the Ecumenical Movement* (Geneva, Switzerland: World Council of Churches, 1998), 29.

which has been described as saturated with ubiquitous spirits. This is aptly depicted in the statement that "Africans believe their cosmos to be peopled by myriads of intractable and capricious spirits locked in an internecine battle at the center of which is humankind."[17] This anthropocentric world places God, the deities, and ancestors above; people in the middle; and nature forces like witchcraft in the realms below.[18] Sorcery or witchcraft, therefore, is the ability to access and control these existing forces, employing them for one's own benefit, either for good or evil. It is believed that good magic reinforces life,[19] while bad or illicit magic—also known as sorcery—causes harm.[20]

In African Traditional Religion, like most other religions, divination plays a very important role. Diviners, who may be men or women, deal with the question of finding out what may have gone wrong and what could be done to remedy the ill.[21] Laura Grillo, who studied the role and function of divination among the Dogon people of West Africa, explains that divination could result from one of two sources: intuition or revelation.[22] In the former the diviner, who is not a magician, uses rational analysis of social situations and measures, then comes up with a diagnosis of the client's behavior as viewed against a

---

[17] Okorocha, "Religious Conversion in Africa," 173.

[18] Uka, "Spirituality in African Traditional Religion," 171.

[19] Parrinder, *West African Psychology*, 9.

[20] Awolalu, and Dopamu, *West African Traditional Religion*, 246.

[21] Mbiti, *Introduction to African Religion*, 157.

[22] Grillo, "Dogon Divination," 317.

standard of moral norms,[23] while the latter may involve external powers or deities. Among the purposes that divination serves for its users are (1) it serves as a channel of communication between the divinities and humans,[24] (2) during rites of passage such as birth it is employed to determine the destiny of a child, and in marriage to ascertain affinity of the spouses,[25] (3) it serves to reiterate the values that unite the community upon which the functioning of the cosmos is predicated,[26] (4) it helps to interpret dreams, explain signs, and predict the future,[27] (5) it assists in decision-making,[28] and (6) it is used in determining the causes and offering remedies for misfortune.[29]

In contrast to divination, sorcery in most African societies is viewed in a negative light. This is because sorcerers employ their magical arts to cause harm or misfortune to the persons targeted. Sorcerers, however, tend to be treated with ambivalence. On one hand, they are feared because of the powers they control; on the other hand, they are sought, even courted, in times of need or crisis. Some of the factors that may lead to the need for the services of a sorcerer include, but are not limited to, illness, infertility, fear of bewitchment, suspicion of spousal infidelity, and seeking protection, prosperity, and

---

[23]Ibid.

[24]Thorpe, *African Traditional Religions*, 93; Grillo, "Dogon Divination," 319.

[25]Parrinder, *Africa's Three Religions*, 62.

[26]Grillo, "Dogon Divination," 318.

[27]Parrinder, *West African Psychology*, 190-191.

[28]Grillo, "Dogon Divination," 319.

[29]Ibid.

vengeance. In certain instances the roles of a diviner and sorcerer may be performed by a single individual. Sorcery and divination also act as a check against moral misdemeanors because of the fear they invoke. Affirming this view, Ogbu Kalu states that they act as religious policemen.[30]

In the next section a survey of the practices of divination and sorcery in Scripture will be presented in order to develop an appropriate missiological response from the lessons learned from that period.

Divination in the Old Testament

Ancient historical evidence reveals that divination was a common practice in biblical times. The practice of divination was not unique to any nation since both Israelites and the surrounding nations were known to engage in this practice, although the nature and contexts differed.

Among the Nations

The practice of divination was widespread in ancient times among non-Israelite nations such as Mesopotamia, Egypt, Arabia, Greece, and Rome, who sought to understand the future through the aid of skilled specialists.[31] The Babylonians refined the art of divination into a highly technical and respectable discipline, sometimes

---

[30]Ogbu U. Kalu, "The Gods as Policemen: Religion and Social Control in Igboland," in *Religious Plurality in Africa: Essays in Honour of John S. Mbiti*, ed. Jacob K. Olupona and Sulayman S. Nyang (Berlin: Moulton de Gruyter, 1993), 119.

[31]Aune, "Divination," *ISBE*, 972.

employing hepatoscopy, augury, hydromancy, and necromancy.[32] The underlying presupposition behind divination is that the deities communicate with humans, and this communication may be initiated by either God or from human initiative.[33]

Among the Israelites

The biblical attitude to divination in general was characterized by disapproval and prohibition, although some other forms of guidance were viewed neutrally, and others received tacit approval.[34] Divination methods employed by the neighboring nations were forbidden to the Israelites because they were viewed as subsidiaries to magic.[35] However, dreams and visions, which were also common among these nations, were permitted when the origin was from the Lord or His representatives. Diviners in the days of the prophet Isaiah appear to have been ranked alongside judges, warriors, and prophets as pillars of the state (Isa 3:2, 3).[36]

In the Old Testament, besides dreams and visions, another means by which the will of God could be known was through the Urim and Thummim. Although not much can be said about this practice since it appears to have been discontinued after the time of

---

[32]Karen Randolph Joines, "Magic and Divination," *Mercer Dictionary of the Bible (MDB)* (Macon, GA: Mercer University Press, 1990), 539-540.

[33]G. Michael Hagan, "Divination," *Baker Theological Dictionary of the Bible (BTD)* (Grand Rapids, MI: Baker Books, 1996); 182-183.

[34]Aune, "Divination," *ISBE*, 972.

[35]Mark W. Chavalas, "Magic," *BTD*, 502.

[36]Joines, "Magic and Divination," *MDB*, 540; Aune, "Divination," *ISBE*, 972.

King David,[37] it may have been in the form of small pebbles, dice, or short sticks that were used to secure "yes" or "no" answers in various matters (Num 27:21; 1 Sam 23:12; Lev 16:7-10).[38]

The casting of lots is another example of a practice which, while not unique to the Israelite community, seemed to receive the tacit approval of God in the Old and New Testaments. Aune supplies four main purposes for casting lots in OT Scripture:[39] (1) to identify the guilty individual (Josh 7; Jonah 1:7), (2) for selection into a particular office or task (1 Chr 24:31; 25:8; 26:13, 14; Neh 10:31; 11:4; Acts 1:26), (3) the division of land among the tribes (Josh 18:6-10; Num 26:55, 56; 33:54; 34:13; 36:2, 3), and (4) for the selection of the goats, for Azazel and Yahweh, during the Day of Atonement (Lev 16:8-10).

In the New Testament

The Acts of the Apostles records a solitary encounter with a diviner as the gospel advanced into the Greco-Roman world (Acts 16:16-18). This is the only occurrence of the term, *soothsaying*, in the New Testament.[40] There are a few notable insights from this account: the slave-girl diviner was described as possessed, "she was an instrument of demons who used her as a mouthpiece; and was a lucrative source of income for her

---

[37]Aune, "Divination," *ISBE*, 972.

[38]Ibid., 973.

[39]Ibid.

[40]Darrell L. Bock, "Acts," *Baker Exegetical Commentary on the New Testament* (Grand Rapids, MI: Baker Academic, 2007), 536.

owners."[41] Also, the spirit of divination (*pneuma python*)[42] with which she was possessed was regarded as connected with the Delphic oracle (Acts 16:16). Her trade, which produced a good profit to her owners, attested to the fact that something supernatural may have been involved.

Although the Scriptures reveal that God communicated His will through His servants the prophets, another agency engaged in prognostication is Satan—the source of the *pneuma python*. Just as Paul found the presence of the diviner irritating and distracting, so also pagan divination stands in opposition to the mission of God. Regarding the Apostle's reaction to the diviner, a commentator explains, "Paul's concern was that she was saying these things under the influence of an evil spirit. . . . Bystanders could have imagined that Paul and Silas were possessed by similar spirits from the underworld."[43]

Other practices that could be construed as prognostication in the Gospels include the casting of lots for the garments of Christ (Matt 27:35; Mark 15:24; Luke 23:34; John 19:24), and the use of lots to select the priest to offer incense in the temple such as fell on Zacharias, father of John the Baptist (Luke 1:9). The use of lots, although employed by non-Christians, also played a role in the selection of the replacement for Judas, the betrayer (Acts 1:26). This crucial decision, which confronted the Apostles immediately

---

[41]Simon J. Kistemaker, *New Testament Commentary: Acts* (Grand Rapids, MI: Baker, 1990), 592-593.

[42]Chavalas, "Magic," *BTD*, 503.

[43]David G. Peterson, *The Acts of the Apostles* (Grand Rapids, MI: William B. Eerdmans, 2009), 464.

after the resurrection, demands closer examination. It is interesting that the Apostles were not given a dream, vision, theophany, or revelation by which the Apostles were to discern the will of God on this important subject. Rather, after setting biblical parameters, praying, and suggesting their own criteria, the Apostles employed this seemingly innocuous method when they had two acceptable candidates to arrive at the will of God.[44]

While not many incidents of divination may be cited from the Scriptures involving non-Christians, it is evident, however, that the closing events of earth's history will be preceded by a great deal of spiritualistic phenomena involving pseudo-prophetic activities (Matt 7:15; 24:11, 24; Mark 13:22; Luke 16:26; 2 Cor 11:13, 14; 2 Pet 2:1, 2; 1 John 4:1).

The following conclusions may be drawn from the biblical text regarding the phenomenon of divination: (1) the separation between God and the people caused by sin and the consequent loss of direct communication with God provided a rationale for divination (Gen 3:1-7; Isa 59:1), (2) divination arose from the human need to discern the will or desires of God (Isa 8:19; Num 12:6),[45] (3) God does speak through His own servants, the prophets (Deut 18:15-18; Amos 3:7),[46] (4) God encouraged His people to seek to know His will (Isa 8:19-20; 55:6; 2 Chr 20:20; 1 Thess 5:20), (5) the continuing

---

[44]Caution is however needed in employing the practice of lots due to the hermeneutical issue it poses; only in this instance was it employed in the NT, and this was before the coming of the Holy Spirit.

[45]Hagan, "Divination," *BTD*, 183.

[46]Liefeld, "Divination," *ZPE*, 166.

gifts of the Holy Spirit suggest that God is still ready today to reveal His will to His people (1 Cor 12:10-12; 1 Cor 14:1-3; Joel 2:28-30), (6) one of the major functions of the prophetic ministry involved discerning the will of God for His people (Num 12:6; Eph 4:8-13), (7) in God's self-revelation to non-Christian cultures God has always used modes that were translatable, such as God-given dreams and visions (Gen 41:1-42; Dan 2; 5), (8) the apparent endorsement of the use of lots in determining the will of God in both Old and New Testaments seems to indicate God's approbation of the desire to know His will and the future (Josh 7; Jonah 1:7; 1 Chr 24:31; Acts 1:26), and (9) divination is the counterfeit form of the legitimate need for guidance which God often honors (Isa 8:19-20; Isa 45:11).

Sorcery in the Old Testament

The Old Testament records several accounts of the practice of sorcery. Although some scholars generally group sorcery and divination under the generic term *magic*,[47] magic also has been described as "sorcery technically developed."[48] The expression, magic, is derived from *magi* or *magoi*, a priestly caste in Media or Persia[49] who claimed to mediate between the gods and humans.[50]

---

[47]T. J. Kleinhans, "Magic," *The Dictionary of Bible and Religion* (Nashville, TN: Abingdon, 1986), 645-656; B. F. Harris, "Magic and Sorcery," *ZPE*, 4:42-44; Joanne K. Kuemmerlin-McLean, "Magic," *Anchor Bible Dictionary (ABD)* (New York: Double Day, 1992), 4:468-471.

[48]C. von Orelli, "Sorcery and Soothsaying," *The New Schaff-Herzod Encyclopedia of Religious Knowledge*, 1911 ed., 11:6-9.

[49]Harris, "Magic and Sorcery," *ZPE*, 42; Kleinhans, "Magic," *ABD*, 645.

[50] Harris, "Magic and Sorcery," *ZPE*, 42.

Sorcery and magical practices were regarded in those days in a very negative light[51] and were prohibited among the Israelites at the penalty of death[52] (Lev 19:26, 31; Deut 18:9-14; 1 Sam 28:9; Isa 8:16-20; 44:24-28; Jer 14:13-16; 27:8-11; Ezek 13:6-9, 23; Mic 5:12; Nah 3:4; Mal 3:5). The multiplicity of terms used to describe magic suggests that it was a pervasive problem in the Israelite world.[53] The Hebrew word *kischef* in 2 Chr 33:6 (translated in the NRSV as sorcery) is elsewhere translated as witchcraft.[54] Sorcery and magic were eschewed in biblical times because they were regarded as human rebellion seeking to unlock divine secrets, thereby making humanity equal with God.[55]

Some interpreters and translators used the negative and antisocial term, sorcery, to describe female practitioners, while employing the neutral term, magic, to refer to male practitioners.[56] In Exod 22:18 the community was required to put the *mehassepah* (female practitioner) to death, while in texts such as Deut 18:10, which refer to the *mehassep* (male practitioner), no precise punishment is given or the judgment and punishment are left to God (Jer 27:9; Mal 3:5).[57]

In the Old Testament, magic and sorcery played prominent functions in the nation

---

[51]Liefeld, "Divination," *ZPE,* 166; Kuemmerlin-McLean, "Magic," *ABD,* 469.

[52]Mark W. Chavalas, "Magic," *BTD,* 502.

[53]Ibid.

[54]Kimberly B. Stratton, "Magic, Magician," *NIDB,* 3:768.

[55]Chavalas, "Magic," *BTD,* 502.

[56]Kuemmerlin-McLean, "Magic," *ABD,* 468.

[57]Ibid.

of Egypt, where it was learned in temple schools whose patron gods were Thoth and Isis.[58] For this reason, the Exodus narrative has crucial import in the history and experience of the Israelites, primarily because it represented a confrontation between Moses and Aaron, representing the Most High God, and the magicians and sorcerers of Egypt.[59] Archeological records also indicate that Babylonia was another home of magic—charms have been discovered on ancient tablets originating from that region.[60] Jezebel is, however, the most notable character in the Old Testament who engaged in the practice of sorcery (1 Kgs 21:25).

Sorcery in the New Testament

The Greek word *pharmakeia*, translated as sorcery, appears twice (Gal 5:20; Rev 18:23) in the New Testament.[61] In his epistle to the Galatians, the Apostle Paul lists sorcery (or witchcraft) among the works of the flesh, for which a person shall be disinherited from the kingdom of God (Gal 5:20). Mystical Babylon in the book of Revelation is accused of the practice of sorcery by which it enchanted and deceived all the nations of the earth (Rev 18:23). The family word *pharmak* is found four times in Revelation, and each time with negative connotations—the destiny of those who practice

---

[58]Harris, "Magic and Sorcery," *ZPE*, 42.

[59]Ibid., 43.

[60]S. F. Hunter, "Bar-Jesus," *ISBE*, 1:431.

[61]Stratton, "Magic, Magician," *NIDB*, 768.

sorcery is the lake of fire, or second death, for they are the enemies of God.[62]

As the gospel frontiers expanded into Samaria, Philip the evangelist encountered Simon, a man who practiced sorcery (*mageuo*). In this account, Simon and the people discovered the superiority of the power of God in the signs and wonders wrought through Philip, which eventually led to mass conversions, including the former sorcerer (Acts 8:9-13).[63]

Ephesus, however, holds the title as the center of magical activity in the Greco-Roman world.[64] In that center of heathen sorcery, amulets with ambiguous inscriptions and representations of Diana were sold for magical purposes.[65]

Another significant episode between the apostles and a sorcerer is found in Acts 13. The sorcerer Bar-Jesus, also known as Elymas, was described in Scripture as a false prophet even though he was a Jew. He had achieved great status with the Roman proconsul, Sergius Paulus, and the people of Paphos, Cyprus, whom he sought to protect. When he opposed the message of Paul and Barnabas, he was struck with blindness leading the proconsul to realize that the power behind Paul was divine[66] and superior.

---

[62]Ekkehardt Mueller, "Evil Powers and Occult Practices in the Apocalypse," in *The Church, Culture and Spirits: Adventism in Africa*, ed. Kwabena Donkor (Silver Spring, MD: Biblical Research Institute, General Conference of Seventh-day Adventists, 2011), 122-123.

[63]It is noteworthy that although the sorcerer got baptized, his heart was still unconverted and he sought power for pecuniary purposes.

[64]E. Ferguson, "Religions, Greco-Roman," *The IVP Dictionary of the New Testament* (Downers Grove, IL: InterVarsity Press, 2004), 894.

[65]von Orelli, "Sorcery and Soothsaying," 8.

[66]Hunter, "Bar-Jesus," *ISBE*, 1:431.

From this cursory survey of sorcery in the Scriptures, it is evident that although magic, sorcery, and witchcraft are consistently forbidden, the reality of occult powers is acknowledged.[67] Mark Chavalas agrees that the biblical writers attribute a reality to magical power that is not ascribed to the gods;[68] that is, while the practice of idolatry and the gods was disdained, the reality of magic was acknowledged. This realization is crucial in the quest for a missiological solution to this persistent problem plaguing African Christianity. Another prominent point to note is the fact that the Bible designates magic as demonic[69] in contrast to miracles, which are divine.[70] Sorcery is therefore considered a gross sin against God because Christians should trust solely in God.[71]

Another important text dealing with divination and sorcery is the encounter between the Israelites and the prophet Balaam (Num 22-23). Invited by Balak, the Moabite king, to place a curse upon the nascent nation of Israel that was emerging from Egyptian captivity, Balaam's testimony provides insight into the issue of blessings and curses. The first thing worthy of note is the fact that fear was the motive that led Balak to seek the assistance of Balaam in placing a curse on the people of God (vv. 3, 4). Second, the desire for profit caused Balaam to attempt to execute what God had not sanctioned.

---

[67]Harris, "Magic and Sorcery," *ZPE*, 43.

[68]Chavalas, "Magic," *BTD*, 502.

[69]Brempong Owusu-Antwi, "Demons and Demonic Activities in the Bible," in *The Church, Culture and Spirits: Adventism in Africa*, ed. Kwabena Donkor (Silver Spring, MD: Biblical Research Institute, General Conference of Seventh-day Adventists, 2011), 63.

[70]Stratton, "Magic, Magician," *NIDB*, 767.

[71]von Orelli, "Sorcery and Soothsaying," 6.

Third, the perceived power of the spoken word is here displayed. Balak believed that a curse uttered by the prophet would weaken or cast a spell on his enemies, thereby enabling him to have victory over them in battle (Num 22:6, 11). Fourth, the prophet himself affirmed emphatically that no curse or charm would succeed against the people of God (Num 23:23) because Israel was "an accomplished act of Yahweh" (the apple of His eye)[72] (Deut 23:4, 5). Dale Brueggeman explains that "in spite of his fondest wishes to succeed as a highly paid curse specialist, 'no misfortune' was headed Israel's way. Why? The Lord their God is with them."[73]

Balaam's frustrating experience is instructive for God's people today who are confronted with the fear of sorcery: "He had come to bring a curse, but he found them blessed. He had come to bring a divination and an augury, but he found such ineffective. God is in control, and Balaam is His puppet."[74]

The following points can be summed up emanating from this survey of sorcery and magic in Scripture: (1) the Scriptures acknowledge the reality of the dark world of sorcery, magic, witchcraft, or the occult realm (Deut 18:10-12; 2 Kgs 17:17-20; 21:6-16; Rev 16:14), (2) the penalty for engaging in sorcery was death or eternal separation from the people of God (Deut 18:10; Rev 21:8; 22:15), (3) sorcerers and those who sought

---

[72]Timothy R. Ashley, *The Book of Numbers,* The New International Commentary on the Old Testament (Grand Rapids, MI: William B. Eerdmans, 1993), 3:481.

[73]Dale A. Brueggemann, *Numbers: Cornerstone Critical Commentary* (Carol Stream, IL: Tyndale, 2008), 2:363.

[74]Ronald B. Allen, "Numbers," *The Expositor's Bible Commentary* (Grand Rapids, MI: Zondervan, 1990), 1:902.

their services operate in opposition to the will of God (Exod 7:11-13; Jer 27:9, 10; 2 Tim 3:8), (4) magic and sorcery were counterfeits to the miracles of the Bible, and were done to deceive, defraud, harm, or hurt the people of God (Exod 7:9-13; 1 Kgs 18:19-40; Matt 24:24-26; 2 Cor 11:13, 14), and (5) the worldview of people in biblical times included the realm of the supernatural—comprising spirits, angels, demons—thus acknowledging the possibility of the belief in sorcery and the magical.

A missiological response to the worldview assumptions undergirding divination and sorcery is needed to provide the Yoruba people with a clearer understanding of the role of Scripture in discerning the divine will and providing guidance for their everyday lives. The Scriptures reveal God as being firmly in control of earth's history and the lives of those living in obedience to His will. Bible prophecies reveal His sovereignty over human affairs, and the Scriptures reveal His willingness to direct those who enter into covenant relationship with Him. Rather than seeking after diviners and sorcerers, God desires that His people should seek after Him to find peace and assurance (Isa 8:19-20).

Causation

Sorcery and witchcraft appear to serve major functions in the belief system of the Yoruba people; as with all Africans, they help to explain the problem of evil. Affirming this view Samuel Kunyihop, a Nigerian scholar of religion, observes, "Belief in witchcraft serves a very practical purpose in explaining events and the causes behind them."[75] A Yoruba syllogism that captures this logic states:

| The witch shrieked out yesterday | *ájè kè l'ánà* |
| The child died today | *ọmọ kú l'òí yí* |

---

[75]Kunyihop, *African Christian* Ethics, 378.

> Who does not know that yesterday's witch *tani kò mò pé ájè ánà*
> Devoured today's child. *l'ó pa ọmọ òní jẹ.*[76]

Kunhiyop opines that the belief in sorcery and witchcraft can be reckoned as a worldview explanation for negative experiences or seemingly inexplicable reverses in life, such as an untimely death, infertility, conflict, and failure.[77] Another contributory aspect to the practice of sorcery is the belief in mystical causality—an element inherent to the African worldview. To the African nothing just happens;[78] it is, therefore, always necessary to investigate possible spiritual/metaphysical causes in order to determine their spiritual etiology.[79] While belief in sorcery or witchcraft may seem irrational, it really is "a serious philosophical attempt to deal with the question of evil."[80] To Hiebert "the use of magic is essentially pragmatic—if something seems to work, then keep on doing it until it no longer does."[81]

Undergirding this causal belief is the search for coherence. If worldview change is needed, it is imperative to provide coherent explanations, which are more logical and authoritative for evil, illness, and misfortune. Hiebert avers, stating, "At the core of

---

[76]Marc Schiltz, "A Yoruba Tale of Marriage, Magic, Misogyny and Love," *Journal of Religion in Africa* 32, no. 2 (2002): 337.

[77]Kunyihop, "Witchcraft," *Africa Bible Commentary*, ed. Tokunboh Adeyemo (Nairobi, Kenya: Zondervan, 2006), 374.

[78]K. Asamoah-Gyadu, "Health/Healing," *Dictionary of Mission Theology Evangelical Foundations*, ed. John Currie (Nottingham, England: Inter-Varsity Press, 2007), 145.

[79]Imasogie, *Guidelines for Christian Theology in Africa*, 60.

[80]Kunyihop, *African Christian Ethics*, 377.

[81]Hiebert, *Transforming Worldviews*, 118.

worldview transformation is the human search for coherence between the world as we see it and the world as we experience it. Humans seek meaning by looking for order, pattern, symmetry, coherence, unity and noncontradiction."[82]

Although this may seem to be a problem peculiar to those with limited educational opportunities, it would appear that the belief in supernatural causation, which to a scientific mind may appear irrational, is not impacted by education or literacy. African religion scholar, Cyril Okorocha, demonstrates this with a professor of physics who without demur solicited the assistance of a shaman to obtain a job promotion, and a professor of obstetrics and gynecology who took his wife to a prayer house or to his illiterate grandmother to seek the help of a herbalist to aid his wife's conception—even when he was aware that she had lost both fallopian tubes.[83]

On the religious front, several of the popular Pentecostal churches reveal a similar disturbing view of reality. For instance, Bishop David Oyedepo, founder of one of the largest Pentecostal congregations in West Africa, a former architect and proprietor of one of the leading private universities in Nigeria, believes that sickness is caused by spirits. "Every sickness, every disease, is a curse. It is not a product of the weather or any such thing."[84] He further declared, "Malaria is a curse. It is not caused by a mosquito bite. The parasite is not from the mosquito, it's a curse of the law."[85]

---

[82]Ibid., 315.

[83]Okorocha, "Religious Conversion in Africa," 169.

[84]David O. Oyedepo, *The Healing Balm* (Lagos, Nigeria: Dominion, 1996), 40-41.

[85]Ibid., 87.

At the core of mystical causality and witchcraft beliefs—believed to be responsible for illness, suffering, misfortune, evil, and death in African and Yoruba beliefs—is a magical worldview.[86] In order to achieve transformation from a magical to a biblical worldview, better explanations for the origin and nature of evil, suffering, and pain will be required. Peel submits that it was superior explanations to the question of meaning during the Age of Confusion early in Yoruba history that contributed largely to their later acceptance of Christianity.[87] Unfortunately, in the past, missionaries and others who have witnessed in Yorubaland did not thoroughly engage the beliefs in magic, witchcraft, divination, or sorcery, but simply labeled these as superstitions.

Divination is employed in general to provide answers to problems such as (1) sickness, (2) public calamity—such as epidemics, famines, and drought, (3) social actions—such as who to marry, appointing leaders, agriculture, and (4) to identify an offender.[88] David Westerlund in his book on the etiology of sickness among five African tribes, including the Yoruba, observed that there are three main causes of diseases: religious (supra-human), social (human), and natural (mainly physical).[89] The diviner may trace the source of a malady to envy or grudges among parties in a family, hostility

---

[86]Jim Harries, *Vulnerable Mission: Insights into Christian Mission to Africa from a Position of Vulnerability* (Pasadena, CA: William Carey Library, 2011), 210.

[87]Peel, *Religious Encounter*, 230.

[88]David Burnett, *Unearthly Powers* (London: MARC, 1988), 108-111.

[89]David Westerlund, *African Indigenous Religions and Disease Causation: From Spiritual Beings to Living Humans* (Leiden, Netherlands: BRILL, 2006), 6.

of enemies, disturbed communal relationships, witchcraft, or sorcery.[90] In the Yoruba traditional religion, the nature of an illness is indicative of its origin. For instance, physical and psychiatric disorders, barrenness, and death are attributable to the deities.[91] Ancestors, who are guardians of morality, may also inflict illness due to failure to sacrifice or the lack of proper burials on the part of their descendants.[92]

The tenacity of these magical beliefs and belief in supernatural causality imply that the power of God is not sufficiently recognized in these contexts.[93] It would appear that in Yorubaland, as in many other African contexts, dread of the demonic and evil spiritual forces is greater than the fear of God. Consequently, a missiological response to this predicament aimed at transforming the present worldview must include an emphasis on the eternal presence of God, the important ministry of angels, a theocentric focus, and replacement of the magical with a miraculous biblical worldview.

Ever-Presence of God

Among the recommendations given by Hiebert, Shaw, and Tienou in response to the questions raised by folk religions is the need for a theology of the invisible. Part of what this theology should do is to underscore the providence, presence, and power of the

---

[90]Klaus Nurnberger, *The Living Dead and the Living God: Christ and the Ancestors in Changing Africa* (Pretoria, South Africa: Cluster Publications, 2006), 130.

[91]Westerlund, *African Indigenous Religions*, 127.

[92]Ibid., 144.

[93]Harries, *Vulnerable Mission*, 211.

Trinitarian God.[94] It is significant that when God appeared to Moses with a message for the Hebrew nation that He was about to deliver them from Egyptian captivity, He chose to reveal Himself as the I AM (Exod 3:14). In essence, Moses was to inform the people that God had seen their condition, heard their petition, and was going to act for their vindication. Commenting on this passage Walter Brueggemann states,

> God acknowledges and engages the troubles of Israel: affliction, cries, and sufferings. God not only knows, but God is now physically (!) mobilized to be present in the midst of trouble. . . . The verb [come down] not only articulates what is crucial for Israel's understanding of God, which for Christians culminates in the incarnation—God has come down into human history in bodily form.[95]

It is vital to keep in mind that the God of the Exodus is also the incarnate God, who is ever-present with His people and is mighty to save. Perhaps a part of the causes why Christians visit diviners is because the immanence and omnipotence of God have not received enough emphasis so as to instill an immovable faith in the God of the Exodus. Peradventure, like the Israelites, the Yoruba

> are not interested in great philosophical speculations about God's essence. They don't want theological discussion. They are not consumed with splitting hairs over law and gospel or justification and sanctification. What they want is help, deliverance, and salvation. They want God to be there for them.[96]

Unfortunately, the Adventist Church may not have done an adequate job of demonstrating and validating the supremacy of the power of Yahweh over the divinities, powers, and principalities in the Yoruba context. Consequently, the diminutive faith of

---

[94]Hiebert, Shaw, and Tienou, *Understanding Folk Religion*, 371.

[95]Walter Brueggemann, "The Book of Exodus," *NIB*, 2:712.

[96]John L. Dybdahl, *The Abundant Life Bible Amplifier: A Practical Guide to Abundant Christian Living in the Book of Exodus* (Boise, ID: Pacific Press, 1994), 57.

the converts may not have been strong enough to withstand the onslaught of pre-Christian worldview presuppositions and pressures. If the objective of worldview transformation is to be attained, it would therefore be vital to teach and convict the believers in Yorubaland that God is ever present with them. Such promises and assurances are found repeatedly throughout the Old Testament and are an effective means of encouraging faith in Yahweh (Gen 31:3; Deut 21:23; Judg 6:16; Ps 46:7; Jer 1:8).[97]

The Ministry of Angels

Hiebert, Shaw, and Tienou also mention that in response to the questions raised by traditional religious beliefs and practices, the teaching about angels and demons will have to be taken seriously. While there is wisdom in applying caution lest demons are found behind every bush, nevertheless, the Scriptures give clear indication that the invisible realm impacts human affairs on earth.[98] As Kraft observed, the world of angels and demons was more real to Jesus than even the physical world, and so should it be with Christians today.[99] Sadly, as Rick Love depicts, the situation with many converts, such as the Yorubas, is one in which

> they [the people] are more impressed with the devil than they are in awe of Jesus. They focus more on the powers and principalities than they do on the one who has been raised far above every power and principality (Eph 1:21-22). They walk in fear instead of faith. They reflect anxiety instead of confidence.

---

[97] John L. Mackay, *Exodus: A Mentor Commentary* (Ross-shire, UK: Christian Focus Publications, 2001), 74.

[98] Rick Love, *Muslims, Magic, and the Kingdom of God* (Pasadena, CA: William Carey Library, 2000), 89.

[99] Charles H. Kraft, *Christianity with Power: Your Worldview and Your Experience of the Supernatural* (Ann Arbor, MI: Vine Books, 1989), 109.

The obvious need is for a better alternative that will spur trust and faith and replace the need for the mediation of diviners and ancestors to provide protection and good fortune. Teaching regarding the existence and functions of angels can in this context serve a relevant and powerful faith-building purpose. In both the Old and New Testaments, angels play significant roles in the lives of God's people. Patriarchs and prophets experienced the ministry of angels just as did Jesus and the Apostles (Job 1:6; Gen 21:17-19; Judg 13; Dan 10:13, 21; Zech 1; Luke 1:11-20; Matt 2:19-21; Acts 5:18-20; Heb 1:3, 13).

The expression translated angels (Hebrew—*malakh*, Greek—*angelos*) is used to designate messengers—human and heavenly with over 200 occurrences in Scripture—half of which refer to humans, and the other half to spiritual beings.[100] In the life and ministry of Christ, angels announced His birth (Luke 2:9-15), ministered to Him after His temptation (Matt 4:11), and rolled away the stone at His resurrection (Matt 28:2-7). To the believers angels are appointed as ministers to the heirs of salvation (Heb 1:13).

It was two angels who executed God's judgments upon the twin cities of sin, Sodom and Gomorrah (Gen 19), while a single angel exterminated 185,000 Assyrian elite troops overnight. Angels also protect and deliver God's people in times of trouble (Ps 34:7; Dan 6; Acts 5). Thus a knowledge of the presence, power, and ministry of angels can be comforting and reassuring to those from animistic backgrounds who customarily turn to diviners for protection in times of crisis.

Although some have taught the existence of guardian angels for every believer,

---

[100]Maxwell John Davidson, "Angel," *NIDB,* 1:149.

caution needs to exercised on this point. Scholars do not find any clear basis from Scripture for such a doctrine.¹⁰¹ Nevertheless, there are sufficient angels created to care for every single person who ever lived upon the earth (Dan 7:9-10; Heb 12:22).

Clinton Arnold, a New Testament scholar who has written extensively on the subject of spiritual powers, has traced the syncretistic practice of angelogy—the worship or reverence of angels—from within Judaism down to the period of Paul's ministry in Colossae.¹⁰² On account of the temptation to fall into the snare of giving reverence to angels, such as the Colossians did, care will be needed to focus the attention of converts from traditional religions away from angels, who are ministering spirits, to Christ, the Commander of heaven's host. They must turn from the intermediaries to the only Mediator between people and God—Jesus Christ (1 Tim 2:5).¹⁰³

New Focus

Androcentrism is a fundamental quality inherent in all traditional religions and is characterized by efforts to placate, coerce, or bribe the gods, spirits, or divinities to bless or heal.¹⁰⁴ This worldview theme leads people to seek the satisfaction of personal needs

---

¹⁰¹R. T. France, *The Gospel of Matthew,* The New International Commentary of the New Testament (Grand Rapids, MI: William B. Eerdmans, 2007), 1:686; Donald A. Hagner, *Matt 14-28,* Word Biblical Commentary 33b (Waco, TX: Word Books, 1995), 527; Stephen F. Noll, *Angels of Light and Darkness: Thinking Biblically about Angels, Satan, and Principalities* (Downers Grove, IL: IVP, 1998), 172.

¹⁰²Clinton E. Arnold, *The Colossian Syncretism: The Interface between Christianity and Folk Belief at Colossae* (Tubingen, Germany: J.C.B. Mohr, 1995), 8-101.

¹⁰³Ibid., 286.

¹⁰⁴Hiebert, Shaw, and Tienou, *Understanding Folk Religion,* 379.

over and above the demands of God. For worldview transformation to occur in Yorubaland, people will need to be moved from androcentrism to theocentrism—a situation where God becomes the center and focus of all that the believer does.

Such an orientation will prompt a shift in focus from the dominating question, "who is responsible?" that is normally asked in such group contexts. For instance, in the incident recorded in John 9 the question of the disciples to Jesus is stereotypical of those asked by people from animistic backgrounds: "Who sinned, this man or his parents, that he was born blind?" (John 9:2). It is noteworthy that Christ, rather than answering this question on theodicy, shifts the focus from "who" to how God would use the incident for His glory (John 9:3-5). Accordingly, instead of an inordinate focus on any human agent as being responsible for every human predicament, believers are to be led to contemplate the greatness of the God they serve and to believe that He is able to use even the workings of angels and demons for His glory.

> Satan and all his demonic forces are not only subject to God, but God even uses the work of demons to accomplish His purposes (Judg 9:23-24; 1 Sam 16:14; 2 Sam 24:1; 1 Chron 21:1; 1 Kgs 22:19-23). Even Satan's most savage attacks are within God's sovereign control and permissive will for our lives ((Job 1:12; 2:6; 2 Cor 12:7-10). No believer can be touched by Satan's attacks unless God allows it (1 John 5:18-19). Believers who are walking in obedience to God need not fear curses, objects and places dedicated to Satan, or people controlled by the demonic.[105]

This radical reorientation away from human causative agents will encourage "new conceptions, new paradigms and definitions of reality, new understandings of what is possible and what is not, of what is vitally important and what in the end is of little

---

[105]Ott, Strauss, and Tennent, *Encountering Theology of Mission*, 245-246.

importance at all."[106] In place of an obsessive preoccupation with fear for personal safety and a relentless need for protection, there will result a calm, unshakeable trust in God and His sovereign will for those with former androcentric presuppositions.

Supernaturalistic Worldview

The magical worldview prevalent among people from traditional religious and animistic backgrounds was also prevalent in Bible times. Magical presuppositions were the reason why the Israelites persistently turned to the gods of the surrounding nations and to the diviners and sorcerers of their age (Deut 18:14; Isa 44:24; Jer 27:9; 29:8; Mic 3:7).

In his study on the subject of magic, Rick Love describes four types of magic practiced by folk religionists: (1) productive magic—used to facilitate prosperity or success in life, (2) protective magic—employed to overcome fears, (3) destructive magic—for controlling or harming people, and (4) divination—to learn about the future and things that are hidden.[107] The underlying principle in magic can be described simply as, "my will be done." Magic is usually performed by religious specialists and seemingly operates upon similar premises like a simultaneous equation, that is, *Right Ritual + Right Action = Right Result.*

In contradistinction to the magical worldview, the Bible reveals a supernatural worldview that includes the belief in a literal six-day creation week (Gen 1-2), the Exodus experience and the crossing of the Red Sea (Exod 14), the incarnation of Christ

---

[106]Kraft, *Worldview for Christian Witness*, 475.

[107]Love, *Muslims, Magic and the Kingdom of God*, 24-25.

(Luke 1:26-56; 2:1-20), and His resurrection (Matt 28:1-9; Luke 24:1-12). These are in addition to the diverse miracles performed by various prophets and those found throughout the life and ministry of Christ and the Apostles.

Unfortunately, in recent epochs of human history, Christianity seems to have deemphasized its supernaturalistic underpinnings in order to be accepted as a worthy discipline in academia. The attempt to reconcile science and theology resulted in the emergence of the philosophy of deism.[108] Describing the influence of the modern worldview on missionaries who took Christianity to Africa and other continents, Hiebert states that modern dualism "led many missionaries to deny the reality of spirits, magic, witchcraft, divination, and [the] evil eye, which were important in the everyday life of the people they served."[109]

> Modern neoplatonism has left many Western Christians with a spiritual schizophrenia. They believe in God and the cosmic history of creation, fall, redemption, final judgment, and new creation. This provides them with ultimate meaning and purpose in life. Yet they live in an ordinary world that they explain in naturalistic terms—one in which there is little room for God.[110]

In order to accomplish worldview transformation among Yoruba people it would be necessary to restate the fact that God is not opposed to His people knowing about the future or seeking blessings and healing, but the way they accomplish this goal is extremely important (Isa 8:19-20). An appropriate missiological response would therefore be the explanation and understanding of a biblical, miraculous worldview that

---

[108]Burnett, *Unearthly Powers*, 15.

[109]Hiebert, *Transforming Worldviews*, 155.

[110]Ibid., 154.

would contrast with the prevailing magical worldview. This would include advocating: *Right Relationship (with the Lord) + Right Timing (according to divine will) = Right Result (subject to Providence)* (Matt 7:7-11; Rom 8:26-27, 32; Jas 5:13-18; 1 John 5:14-15).

A biblical, miraculous worldview is an affirmation that the God of the Bible is the same as the One who is worshipped today, and He is still present and active in the affairs of this world. He can interrupt the cause of human history as He has done in the past; He remains the same yesterday, today, and forever (Dan 3:16-19; Heb 13:8).

Curriculum

Education was a prominent tool used by missionaries for making converts in Nigeria. However, as Kalu observed, deep level faith development was lacking—evidenced in the tendency of locals to exit from mission churches in preference to the charismatic churches they more easily identified with.[111] One of the greatest agencies responsible for the massive conversion of the African continent to Christianity can be found in the translation of the Scriptures into vernacular languages.[112] Nevertheless, important elements of the supernatural worldview of the people were not engaged and important questions were left unanswered.[113] Mission historian Andrew Walls explains one of the basic differences between Western theology and an African model.

---

[111]Kalu, *Christian Missions in Africa*, 118-119.

[112]Lammin Sanneh, *West African Christianity: The Religious Impact* (Maryknoll, NY: Orbis Books, 1983), 106.

[113]Ott, Strauss, and Tennent, *Encountering Theology of Mission*, 254.

The Western theological process starts from the fact that the northern and western barbarians abandoned their old pantheons and took in God from the outside, envisaged in terms of Yahweh of Hosts, the God of Israel, merged with the highest good of the Greek philosophical tradition. African theology starts at a different point, God has a vernacular name.

Following from this fact it is extremely important that new methods of instruction be developed that are contextually relevant for effective communication to occur. Also, new curricula of instruction must be designed to stem syncretism and dual allegiance, while providing better explanations to pre-Christian worldview presuppositions. Such curricula should address issues of theodicy, suffering, the state of the dead, the issue of the excluded middle, and the question of natural healing therapies. Important modes of teaching will incorporate elements such as orality, storytelling, critical contextualization, functional substitutes, and discipleship.

Orality

The oral nature of the Yoruba context must never be lost sight of if worldview transformation is to be accomplished. Oral cultures, like the Yoruba, have a rich supply of stories, proverbs, riddles, and drama, which can serve as vehicles for more effective transmission of the gospel.[114] Intriguingly, African Traditional Religions have flourished for millennia without scripture, creed, founder, or any other apparatus associated with other religions, largely because of the tenacity and import of oral communication in these communities.

---

[114]M. David Sills, "Mission and Discipleship," in *Theology and Practice of Mission: God, the Church, and the Nations*, ed. Bruce Riley Ashford (Nashville, TN: B & H Academic, 2011), 192-193.

Peel observes that a turning point in Yorubaland was attained when local missionaries began to employ indigenous methods such as a "dialogic format" and local proverbs in their evangelization.[115] Strong Yoruba affinity for their culture and language make orality a noteworthy means to be employed for the purpose of worldview transformation. Christ recognized and utilized the potency of this form, and millennia later His messages continue to be retold with life-changing effect.

Storytelling

Yoruba folklore and oral tradition abound with numerous stories of the cunning and wisdom of certain animals, such as the tortoise and the monkey. Storytelling is an often-overlooked heuristic instrument that can play a vital role in the goal of worldview transformation. In oral cultures, people learn from each other through stories, not from books, because they are living in relational cultures and stories confront the hearer's worldview without being confrontational.[116] In oral cultures, storytelling is crucial because the continuity of the culture relies on memorization and internalization of the habits and mores of tradition by mimicry and rote.[117]

Jesus recognized the power of storytelling, and millennia after His death His deep theological lessons couched in the form of parables have endured and continue to

---

[115]Peel, *Religious Encounter*, 157.

[116]LaNette W. Thompson, "Tell His Story So That All Might Worship," in *Discovering the Mission of God: Best Missional Practices for the 21st Century*, ed. Mike Barnett (Downers Grove, IL: IVP Academic, 2012), 395.

[117]Andrew Walker, *Telling the Story: Gospel, Mission and Culture* (London: SPCK, 1996), 23.

transform lives. Jesus' teaching and discipleship paradigm, which included parables, metaphors, and other literary devices, will resonate perfectly with Yoruba oral traditions (Matt 5; Luke 13:1-5).[118] It is also important to remember that "God is not concept; God is story. God is not idea; God is presence. God is not hypothesis; God is experience. God is not principle; God is life."[119]

Because Yoruba culture, like most African societies, is similar to biblical communities, storytelling and other narrative modes would be more effective teaching devices than the Greek logical and rhetorical patterns that have been employed in the past.[120] The practice of Chronological Bible Storying that entails using story, drama, and songs from Scripture, especially the Old Testament, could be powerful pedagogical tools in this context.[121]

At the moment, movies in the Yoruba language, following the trail of early local drama theatres, and the growing influence of the Nigerian movie industry, popularly referred to as Nollywood, have served to reinforce local beliefs about the influence of diviners in society. Annette Simmons in her book, *Whoever Tells the Best Story Wins*,

---

[118]Austin B. Tucker, *The Preacher as Storyteller: The Power of Narrative in the Pulpit* (Nashville, TN: B & H Academic, 2008), 74-75.

[119]C. S. Song, *In the Beginning Were Stories Not Texts: Story Theology* (Eugene, OR: Cascade Books, 2011), 58-59, 74.

[120]Tucker, *The Preacher as Storyteller*, 74.

[121]Thompson, "Tell His Story So That All Might Worship," 392-397; Ott, Strauss, and Tennent, *Encountering Theology of Mission*, 281.

explains that stories have the power to change reality.[122] Therefore, in order to counteract the influence of the movie industry, which is reinforcing the reality of the spirit world, the church will need to retell with greater effectiveness the biblical stories. The personal and communal stories of the people will need to be connected with the metanarratives of Scripture—the Fall—which led to a fallout of suffering and decay, and the incarnation and resurrection—that resulted in a fallout of joy.[123] The grandest of these metanarratives, however, which is perhaps the single greatest contribution of Adventism to Christianity, is the Great Controversy doctrine. This will be discussed in more detail in the next section.

Another important type of narrative that can be instrumental in worldview transformation, which has heretofore been underutilized by the church in the Yoruba context, is testimonies. Testimonies may be defined as stories depicting God in action in contemporary lives. These stories not only validate the active presence of God in Christian lives, but also demonstrate His power to free from the shackles of unChristian beliefs and habits. People who have experienced the power of God to deliver from dependence on diviners or sorcerers are more effective in planting churches and establishing the faith of others because their own personal lives tell the stories of their transformation.[124] The personal testimonies of Paul and Peter retold to different audiences had a profound influence on the decisions of many and upon the growth of the New

---

[122]Annette Simmons, *Whoever Tells the Best Story Wins: How to Use Your Own Stories to Communicate with Power and Impact* (New York: Amacom Books, 2007), 3.

[123]Walker, *Telling the Story*, 93.

[124]Thompson, "Tell His Story So That All Might Worship," 398.

Testament Church (Acts 9, 22, 26; 10:1-11:8; 15:7-11). It is apparent that a faith crisis is responsible for people visiting the diviners. For faith to be strengthened, gospel workers in the Yoruba context must remember, "Faith cometh by hearing" (Rom 10:17).

Contextualization

It is axiomatic that effective ministry models must take seriously the context in which they operate. Until recently, little effort has been made to develop unique program objectives for ministerial formation in African contexts. Previous models employed and a major part of the church's current leadership were trained with Western-originated models. John Parratt explains that the inadequacy of the Western approach lies chiefly in the fact that it does not deal with issues or questions that are relevant to the African—while it sometimes provides splendid answers to questions nobody is asking.[125]

A contextually developed curriculum will recognize the ecological worldview of the African who regards the cosmos as a sacred egg in which humans weave covenants with the munificent and the malevolent gods who are often at loggerheads in this world.[126] A contextualized curriculum will provide a deeper understanding of local worldviews and lead to more earnest study of hermeneutics, Christian history, and systematic theology, which will form the framework for more contextually relevant solutions. At the center of this enterprise to transform local worldviews must be the Scriptures, which are "mighty in God for pulling down strongholds, casting down

---

[125] John Parratt, *Reinventing Christianity: African Theology Today* (Grand Rapids, MI: William B. Eerdmans, 1995), 194.

[126] Kalu, *Power, Poverty and Prayer*, 91-92.

arguments and every high thing that exalts itself against the knowledge of God, bringing every thought into captivity to the obedience of Christ" (2 Cor 10:4-5 NKJV). Urgent attention must be given to contextually relevant training and curricula especially in the light of the growing resurgence of traditional religions throughout the world, "because, in the eyes of the people, they seem to relate better to ordinary life and spirituality."[127]

The need for complementarity in applying insights gained from systematic theology, biblical theology, and mission theology for worldview transformation in the African context is underscored by Hiebert. Table 1 illustrates the deficiencies of each model and underscores the need for complementarity.

Another vital issue that needs to be incorporated into the curriculum for training of ministers and laity in the Yoruba context is how to conduct critical contextualization. This need is urgent, for it will bring to the fore key questions regarding old unChristian practices, will engage the practices biblically rather than pushing them underground to form a kind of syncretistic dualism.[128] The process, according to Ott, Strauss, and Tennent, should entail the following steps: (1) exegesis of culture, (2), exegesis of Scripture, (3) critical response of the people regarding old practices, and (4) implementation of a contextualized practice.[129]

---

[127]Tite Tienou, "The Training of Missiologists for an African Context," in *Missiological Education for the 21st Century: The Book, the Circle and the Sandals*, ed. J. Dudley Woodberry, Charles van Engen, and Edgar J. Elliston (Maryknoll, NY: Orbis Books, 1996), 97.

[128]Ott, Strauss, and Tennent, *Encountering Theology of Mission*, 283.

[129]Ibid., 282-283. The authors list five possible outcomes of this process: adoption, rejection, modification, substitution, and toleration of old practices.

Table 1. A comparison of evangelical systematic, biblical, and missiological theologies

	Systematic Theology	Biblical Theology	Missiological Theology
Source	The Bible is divine revelation	The Bible is divine revelation	The Bible is divine revelation
Key Question	What are the eternal unchanging realities?	What is the cosmic story?	What does Scripture say to this human situation?
Method	Abstract analogical logic	Historiography	Precedent teachings and cases
Results	Helps develop the synchronic understandings of a biblical worldview	Helps develop the diachronic understandings of a biblical worldview	Helps develop missional vision and motivation based on a biblical worldview
Limitations	Difficulty in bridging from: --structure to story --universal to particular --explanation to mystery Not missiological in nature	Difficulty in bridging from: --story to structure --universal to particular Not missiological in nature	Difficulty in bridging from: --today to cosmic structure --now to cosmic time and story

Source: Paul Hiebert, "Spiritual Warfare and Worldview," in *Global Missiology for the 21st Century: The Iguassu Dialogue*, ed. William D. Taylor (Grand Rapids, MI: Baker Academic, 2000), 165.

Functional Substitutes

The need for developing Christian functional substitutes arises from, and is sequel to, the process of critical contextualization in order to forestall syncretism and the practice of dual allegiance.[130] Because a void will be created by those practices condemned by Scripture, new rituals or customs will be required to fill the vacuum that emerges from the cessation of old forms. While the search for functional substitutes is

---

[130]Marvin K. Mayers, *Christianity Confronts Culture: A Strategy for Crosscultural Evangelism* (Grand Rapids, MI: Zondervan, 1987), 372-373; Bruce L. Bauer, "A Response to Dual Allegiance," *Evangelical Missions Quarterly* 44 (July 2008): 345-346.

imperative, great caution is needed in this endeavor. Michael Cooper, while warning on the resurgence of paganism in Western countries, counsels that Paul's admonition to the Corinthians will need to be heeded in certain circumstances; for the sake of the weak, pre-Christian forms may have to be discontinued altogether where necessary (1 Cor 8:1-3). The experience of the Israelites regarding the worship of Nehushtan, the bronze serpent set up by Moses in the wilderness when they were bitten by fiery snakes, further buttresses this exhortation (2 Kgs 18:4; Num 21:4-9).

Discipleship

Worldview transformation, like conversion, is a process that will take a period of time. Ordinarily the practice of the church in many regions has placed an inordinate focus on the quantity of persons baptized rather than on the quality of their faith experience. The Great Commission calls for a teaching methodology that will produce disciples, rather than mere members (Matt 28:18-20; Rom 12:1-2). This process of discipleship will definitely demand worldview transformation. This subject will be discussed more under the section on the responsibility of the change agent.

Disciple formation will occur in the context of conflicts, both internal and external. The next section will discuss the external world of conflict that needs to be conquered for worldview transformation to happen.

Conflict

Acknowledgment of the existence of an ongoing spiritual war of cosmic proportions has grown in acceptance among many scholars in recent times.[131] Gregory Boyd observes that in the Old Testament a warfare worldview on a cosmic level is evident. However, God has absolute supremacy and never can be threatened by His enemies.[132] New Testament theologian Clinton Arnold has written a trilogy that depicts the spiritual conflicts in the Gospels and Epistles.[133]

The Great Controversy

The Adventist doctrine of the Great Controversy traces the origin of a cosmic conflict to the war that began in heaven (Rev 12:7-12; Isa 14:12-14; Ezek 28:12-17), and reveals how humanity got caught up in this rebellion resulting in the Fall (Gen 3). This metanarrative spans the scope of earth's history, from creation and the Fall, to the earth renewed. It covers all the major events in earth's salvation history (Rev 12; 20-22). In the Yoruba context this doctrine is invaluable for not only explaining the source and originator of evil, but it also demonstrates the presence and workings of demons (evil angels) against believers. It also unveils spiritism as the devil's strategy for ensnaring unwary people into believing that the dead are still present and active in the affairs of the

---

[131]Ott, Strauss, and Tennent, *Encountering Theology of Mission*, 243.

[132]Gregory Boyd, "God at War," in *Perspectives on the Worldwide Christian Movement: A Reader*, 4th ed., ed. Ralph D. Winter and Stephen C. Hawthorne (Pasadena, CA: William Carey Library, 2009), 100.

[133]Clinton Arnold, *The Colossian Syncretism: The Interface between Folk Christianity and Folk Belief at Colossae* (Tubingen, Germany: JCB Mohr, 1995); idem, *Power of Darkness: Principalities and Powers in Paul's Letters* (Downers Grove, IL: InterVarsity Press, 1992); idem, *Ephesians: Power and Magic; The Concept of Power in Ephesians in the Light of Its Historical Setting* (Grand Rapids, MI: Baker 1992).

living (Gen 3:3, 4; 1 Sam 28; Job 14:7-15; Pss 115:17; 143:3; Eccl 9:5-6; John 11; 1 Cor 15:51-57).

The Great Controversy doctrine provides coherent and comprehensive biblical responses to some of the significant questions and fears that plague Yoruba Christians—witchcraft, and ancestor reverence—but most significantly, at its crux it reveals a loving God who came down to suffer with His own and redeem them. On one hand the doctrine answers questions on the subject of theodicy (Job 1-2; Matt 13:24-30; Jas 1:2-4; 1 Pet 4:12-19; Rom 8:18-39), while on the other hand it powerfully demonstrates God's supremacy over evil powers in every encounter of biblical history (Exod 7-15; 1 Sam 5; 1 Kgs 18; Rev 12:7-9; Col 2:15; Rev 20).

Power Encounter

At the heart of the teaching and preaching of Jesus was the coming of the kingdom of God, ably demonstrated by the mighty works He performed to attest that the kingdom was already here (Matt 4:17, 23-25; 13; Mark 1:21-28; Luke 4:31-44; Luke 22:24-30).[134] The history of Christianity and the testimony of missionaries suggest that "whenever the gospel first breaks into a people group or geographic area, the miraculous is frequently present."[135] It is this superior demonstration of power that first catches the attention of people in power-oriented cultures, such as in Africa, and leads them to a

---

[134]George Eldon Ladd, "The Gospel of the Kingdom," in *Perspectives on the World Christian Movement: A Reader,* 4th ed., ed. Ralph D. Winter and Stephen C. Hawthorne (Pasadena, CA: William Carey Library, 2009), 83; Clinton E. Arnold, *3 Crucial Questions about Spiritual Warfare* (Grand Rapids, MI: Baker Books, 1997), 20.

[135]Ott, Strauss, and Tennent, *Encountering Theology of Mission,* 252.

relationship with the Almighty Sovereign of the universe.

> Before people from power-oriented cultures will come to Christ, they often must be convinced that he has the power to address these concerns more effectively than their old religious system. Power-oriented people require power proof, not simple reasoning, if they are to be convinced. A power encounter is a confrontation demonstrating that Jesus' power is superior to that of the old gods.[136]

In her study among power-oriented cultures, Marguerite Kraft discovered concepts that are applicable in similar contexts such as among the Yoruba people. She observed that spiritual power was sought to meet felt needs, which she grouped in six categories: (1) perpetuity needs—fertility for offspring, land, and crops, (2) prosperity needs—good health and orderly progression in life, (3) health needs—to overcome sickness, (4) security needs—protection against capricious spirits, (5) restitution needs—to restore order in the society, and (6) power needs—in order to be in control.[137]

It would appear that from the reports of dual allegiance in Africa the power of the gospel to meet the power needs of its people has not been demonstrated.[138] A closer reading of Scripture confutes the perception that the gospel is vacuous or sterile. Beginning from the book of Genesis, the Word of God is depicted as powerful and creative—ten times in the creation epic the expression "and God said" is presented as culminating in glorious, animated, marvels (Gen 1:3- Gen 2:18). The prophets in the Old Testament similarly depict the Word of God as "an effective, powerful, creative, dynamic

---

[136]Ibid., 254.

[137]Marguerite G. Kraft, *Understanding Spiritual Power: A Forgotten Dimension of Cross-Cultural Mission and Ministry* (Maryknoll, NY: Orbis Books, 1995), 14-19.

[138]Yusufu Turaki, "Evangelical Missiology from Africa: Strengths and Weaknesses," in *Global Missiology for the 21st Century*, ed. William D. Taylor (Grand Rapids, MI: Baker Academic, 2000), 281.

force" (Isa 55:10-11; Jer 23:29).[139] The New Testament likewise presents the Word as powerful (Rom 1:16; Rom 15:19; 1 Thess 1:5; 2 Tim 1:8; Heb 1:1-3).

What clearly is needed in the African context is better elucidation of a theology of power and the cross.[140] Christ needs to be presented as the Victor who routed satanic hosts at the cross. Arnold stresses the three colorful images used in Col 2:9-15 to portray the nature of this victory: (1) Christ disarmed the powers by His death, (2) He exposed the powers—exposure leading to disgrace, and (3) He led the powers in triumphal procession—a vivid imagery of a Roman triumph.[141] As Love avers, there is still a valid need for healing and deliverance through the power of the Holy Spirit and in the name of Christ in power-oriented contexts.[142] These however will need to be submersed in prayer, be led by persons saturated in the Holy Spirit, submitted to the will of God, and subject to scriptural counsel. While tact, caution, and prayer are greatly needed in this ministry due to the excesses and controversies that have arisen in the last two decades, it needs to be remembered that even in the days of the Apostles genuine power encounters elicited syncretistic responses (Acts 19:11-20).[143] This did not mean that they stopped demonstrating the power of God as superior over the forces of evil.

---

[139]Robert L. Plummer, "The Power of the Gospel," in *Global Missiology for the 21st Century*, ed. William D. Taylor (Grand Rapids, MI: Baker Academic, 2000), 160.

[140]Hiebert, Shaw, and Tienou, *Understanding Folk Religion*, 373-375.

[141]Arnold, *The Colossian Syncretism*, 277-283.

[142]Love, *Muslims, Magic, and the Kingdom of God*, 135-136.

[143]Ibid., 132.

Ultimately, it must never be forgotten that the goal of power encounters is to bring transformation of life and allegiance.[144] Hiebert calls for balance as Christians strive to display God's power in transformed lives and through Christlike confrontations of evil. The two extreme positions are (1) the avoidance of bold demonstrations of God's power for fear that it would be labeled magic, and (2) the temptation of sensationalism and the desire to use power for personal glory.[145] Remembering that Christ's greatest victory over satanic principalities and powers occurred at His moment of greatest suffering should give balance to the practice and teaching of power encounters (Col 2:14-15). Also, "the most balanced conclusion is that any theology of mission must put God's power at the center of effective mission and must emphasize that prayer and dependence on God are foundational to the missionary task."[146] The Great Controversy doctrine therefore deconstructs deistic theologies, which on one hand acknowledge the existence of God, yet on the other hand deny the reality of the demonic world and the cosmic dimensions and potency of prayer.

Prayer and Boldness

In his epistles the Apostle Paul declares that Christians are engaged in an unseen spiritual conflict with eternal consequences (2 Cor 10:3-4; Eph 6:10-19; 1 Tim 1:18; 2 Tim 2:3-4). In this conflict the only offensive weapons in the Christian's arsenal are

---

[144]Stephen J. Pettis, "The Fourth Pentecost: Paul and the Power of the Holy Spirit," in *Mission in Acts: Ancient Narratives in Contemporary Context*, ed. Robert L. Gallagher and Paul Hertig (Maryknoll, NY: Orbis Books, 2004), 254.

[145]Hiebert, "Spiritual Warfare and Worldview," 176.

[146]Ott, Strauss, and Tennent, *Encountering Theology of Mission*, 252.

Scripture and prayer, and they are mighty in demolishing the strongholds of the enemy, which include propositional strongholds (worldviews), or spiritual strongholds (Eph 6:10-19; 2 Cor 10:4).

Unfortunately, there appears to be ignorance regarding the power at the disposal of gospel workers, a condition reflected in their approach to ministry. Appropriately applied, prayer can become an instrument for facilitating worldview transformation by moving people from divination to faith and confidence in the living God. In contrast to the audacity manifested by diviners and sorcerers in the discharge of their tasks, the research project discovered that boldness to be deficient among some ministers in Yorubaland. The Scriptures nevertheless reveal that audacity or boldness was a vital element among the disciples of Christ; they prayed for boldness (Acts 4: 29), spoke with boldness (2 Cor 3:12; 7:4), recognized the boldness of their faith (Eph 3:12), and approached the throne of God with boldness (Heb 10:19).

Teaching His disciples how to pray, Christ employed a parable to demonstrate the need for His servants to pray with audacity (Luke 11:8). In that story of a man who goes knocking at his neighbor's door at midnight, Christ sought to convey the lesson that audacity in prayer is always rewarded.[147] God is willing to grant the transforming power of His Holy Spirit to all who ask.

The first quarter of that chapter in the Gospel of Luke is devoted to prayer; it begins with the Lord's prayer, continues with the parable teaching the need for shameless audacity, and concludes by demonstrating how willing God is to grant His children

---

[147] The Greek word *anaidean* is rendered in the New International Version as "shameless audacity."

gifts—even the Holy Spirit. For power-oriented societies like Yorubaland, such confidence in the power of God to protect, heal, save, and deliver will definitely be a catalyst for worldview transformation, moving disciples to a better method for dealing with life's challenges—prayer and trust in God (1 John 5:14-15; Jas 5:13-18). Prayers of intercession can help people cope with life's crises and could give rise to circumstances that open people up to life or worldview transformation.

Crisis

Disequilibrium is a necessary condition for change or transformation to occur in any aspect of human existence. In affirmation Stan May observes,

> Significant worldview change comes about through invention from within, instability from within, intervention from without, and instability from above. When the worldview no longer answers the questions the culture asks for any of the above reasons, the fissures in the old worldview prepare the people group to hear and embrace change.[148]

It would appear then that individuals and communities are often open to change only after periods of crises, for if life progressed without pain, problem, or privation, some would never seek after God. The Scriptures reveal divine intervention in critical moments of individual and national history that changed the natural course of events (Gen 32:24-30; Gen 41; Exod 2-3; Jer 27; Dan 2; Jonah 1-2; Mark 3; Acts 3-4; 8; 10-12; 19).

Crisis situations precipitate confusion and perplexity that interfere with the ordered lives of individuals and communities. Crises trigger a search for meaning,

---

[148]Stan May, "Cultures and Worldviews," in *Discovering the Mission of God: Best Missional Practices for the 21st Century*, ed. Mike Barnett (Downers Grove, IL: InterVarsity Press, 2012), 389.

coherence, and resolution. Consequently, opportunity is provided to teach and introduce alternative, biblical worldview explanations superior to the old assumptions that reveal the sovereignty of God and His eternal presence in individual and cosmic affairs. Furthermore, in such moments of need, effort should be made by gospel workers to be present to provide comfort, succor, and hope to the grieving and suffering (1 Pet 4:12-16).

Crisis may involve natural or supernatural factors. In whatever form they occur, they should be recognized as indicators or opportunities for discovering where the God of comfort and hope may be working (1 Cor 10:13; 2 Cor 1:1-3). For the Ijebu people of Yorubaland, as Peel explained, their loss in battle led to their total abandonment of the old gods and the embrace of Christianity.[149] Gospel workers may therefore pray for crises, which may come in diverse ways, directed by God for opening the door for worldview transformation (Gen 32:22-30; 50:15-21; Dan 4; 2 Cor 4:16-17). In Islamic cultures, dreams and visions have proven effective in leading people to conversion and worldview transformation. In the Yoruba contexts where dreams and spiritual phenomena have vital import, this strategy may also have some value. The experience of the Apostles when confronted by restrictions and bombarded by opposition could serve as a model of intervention—they prayed for signs and wonders from the Lord and the response was instantaneous and earthshaking (Acts 4:23-31).

---

[149]Peel, *Religious Encounter*, 149.

Community

The communal nature of African society has several implications on how the gospel is communicated and received in a setting such as this. Both receptor and communicator must establish cordial relations if transformation is to result. Robert Strauss and Tom Steffen in their article on how worldview change can be attained affirm this point when they state: "Reality itself is not comprehensible outside of human organic relationships. In close relationships worldviews are formed, and then reinforced through experience. It will also be in close relationships and by experiences that worldviews will be transformed."[150]

In communal societies such as Africa, salvation may be personal but not individual. Affirming this view Mbiti notes, "In the traditional African setting, the individual cannot meaningfully embrace the Christian faith while others in the family, or community, do not do the same."[151] Among the elements that could contribute to worldview transformation in Yorubaland are: creating genuine fellowship, establishing communities of joy, and facilitating reconciliation.

Fellowship

In order to help establish new members in new lifestyle practices or to accept new belief paradigms, it is necessary that a new community be created. The church should serve as that new community, which will help the members find love, acceptance,

---

[150]Robert Strauss and Tom Steppen, "Change the Worldview . . . Change the World," *Evangelical Missions Quarterly* 45, no. 4 (October 2009): 463.

[151]Mbiti, *Bible and Theology*, 129.

belonging, and joy. Much more energy needs to be spent in transforming the present church environment into a true community in the African context.

Mbiti condemns the practice of individual conversions, which were a pattern with the early mission churches, and instead recommended that emphasis be made on the "kingdom of God motif."[152] Until the churches in Africa become communities close to what is reflected in the early chapters of the book of Acts, wherein a new community was established, the ethnic, cultural, and social ties of converts will always supersede their affiliations and allegiance to the church and Christ (Acts 2:42-47; 4:32-37; Gal 3:26-29; Eph 2:14-18). The New Testament church did not break bread once a quarter, rather, it seemed to be a daily affair. The church in Yorubaland would become a contagious and influential community if the kind of fellowship that existed in the early church was recreated today.

The English word *fellowship* implies a community of partners, of persons of similar positions, or persuasion. Establishing true fellowship in the Yoruba context, known to be strongly hierarchical by nature, will require a new paradigm of authority, one that is derived from the self-giving Servant, Christ, and shared by His leaders with the followers.[153] In such communities, openness must be nurtured and concern for the members emphasized. The gospel must not only be preached, but lived out in community where members feel free to share their problems in a non-judgmental environment, rather than feeling the need to secretly visit a diviner.[154] Such a community will have

---

[152]Ibid., 192.

[153]Nurnberger, *The Living Dead and the Living God*, 106.

[154]Ibid., 130.

transformational influence in group-centered Yoruba communities where values like shame and honor have pivotal functions.

Joy

One aspect of the African worldview that has often been ignored in mission and ministry in the African context is the overtly affective dimension of their cultures and religion. Suffused with loud and colorful ceremonies, rituals, and sacrifices, African culture and religion is a celebration of life and death. Unfortunately, the historic mission churches did not provide much room for any of this exuberance to be released. It is precisely for this reason that the African Independent Churches found such a powerful footing and strong following in society. Presently, it is among their ranks and the Pentecostal churches where Christianity is experiencing the fastest growth on the continent.

Rites of passage and various individual and community celebrations offer additional opportunity for communal gathering, witnessing, and prayer. Where these celebrations do not conflict with Christian principles they should be exploited to demonstrate the incarnational ministry of the God who rejoices with those who rejoice, and mourns with those who mourn (Rom 12:15). Rather than seeking to bridle the affective dimension of the African worldview, a theology of joy should be developed modeled after Paul's epistle to the Philippian church (Phil 4:4-10). Affirming the need for a joyful Christian experience Smith states,

> Christianity is supremely a religion of joy. In Christ we find that our joy is made complete and that this joy is nurtured by all the gifts of God, most notably through worship and within worship specifically by the joyous celebration of the Lord's Supper. In worship the joy that is given us is the capacity to know even more that the deepest longings of our souls are met in Christ Jesus. Christ is always

sufficient for us. Always! In a very real sense, our capacity for joy is not limited by the circumstances of our lives, for Christ's presence to us is not limited by them.[155]

This joy results from the celebration of the blessings of the Lord. It erupts from lips of those who have experienced deliverance from evil. It emanates from the heart at rest, secure in the assurance of having an abiding relationship with the King of kings. It exudes from those who have a peace that the world cannot give or take away and that is irrespective of present material status. Worship in the African context, which provides occasions for joyful expression and celebration, can be instrumental in leading to worldview transformation among a people who are familiar with emotions such as fear, anxiety, and evil apprehension.

Reconciliation

One of the functions of diviners is their role as mediators who seek to restore harmony in estranged relationships, whether between the living and the living dead, or among members of communities that are closely-knit, or between humans and the divinities.

> When working with people who are functioning with a magical worldview the Christian missionary may have much to learn from diviners before he or she begins to suggest changes to their practices, Hence, also Kirwen tells us, "The more a Christian Priest takes on the role of the diviner . . . the more effective and meaningful he becomes in the life of the Africans."[156]

In Yorubaland, as in most of Africa, misfortune is construed to be the result of

---

[155]Smith, *Transforming Conversion*, 105-106.

[156]Harries is a missiologist and missionary who lived and worked for many years in sub-Saharan Africa. *Vulnerable Mission*, 217.

sin, and sin is caused by a "violation of a relationship between an individual or community and the gods, ancestors, spirits, humans, animals and plants, or the earth."[157] Sin in the African context, just as in biblical thought, brought severe and immediate consequences on every aspect of life—disease, drought, barrenness, defeat in war, and everything shameful.[158] The role of the diviner therefore was to repair these violated relationships and restore order and balance in the community.[159] The chain reaction of evil activated by transgressions in African religions could be offset only by the appropriate ritual, sacrifice, cleansing, pilgrimage, or ascetic processes administered by a ritual specialist, a diviner.[160]

In closely-knit societies as Yorubaland where emotions such as jealousy, anger, envy, and hatred are suppressed in order to maintain communal harmony, these hidden emotions often eventually erupt in witchcraft accusations and explode in pent-up anger on hapless victims.[161] Klaus Nunberger posits,

> If a worldview as a whole does not change, the assumptions that form part of the package can also not be dislodged. The reason for their tenacity is that they are externalized symbols of subjectively experienced forces such as hatred, anger, jealousy, failure or shame. They are not normally recognized as such by the preachers of the gospel, and thus the suffering, forgiving, reconciling, healing, restoring, transforming, power of the gospel of Christ is not brought to bear.[162]

---

[157]Hiebert, Shaw, and Tienou, *Understanding Folk Religion*, 145.

[158]Nurnberger, *The Living Dead and the Living God*, 44.

[159]Hiebert, Shaw, and Tienou, *Understanding Folk Religion*, 145.

[160]Ott, Strauss, and Tennent, *Encountering Theology of Mission*, 97; Nurnberger, *The Living Dead and the Living God*, 45.

[161]Hiebert, Shaw, and Tienou, *Understanding Folk Religion*, 174.

[162]Nurnbereger, *The Living Dead and the Living God*, 45-46.

Christianity can contribute greatly to the African quest for cosmic harmony and reconciliation because it recognizes that indeed "the whole creation groaneth" (Rom 8:22) as a result of humanity's brokenness and sin. The work of Christ's redemption was not solely for the purpose of human redemption, but through humans was to extend to the entire cosmos and culminate in the creation of new heavens and a new earth.[163] Genuine reconciliation occurs as a fruit of the gospel and reveals the power of the gospel in a broken world splintered by divisions and isms, to bring glory to God.[164]

In "Christianity the language of reconciliation is not grounded in a historical or sociological reality, but in a theological one."[165] For it is in Christ that the two elements of reconciliation—horizontal, between individuals and people, and vertical, with God—find their resolution, culminating in the creation of a new community, a new humanity with a common identity—the family of God.[166]

In this community discipleship training is crucial to lead people to resolve and discontinue pre-Christian practices. Training of this nature should encompass the fruit and gifts of the Holy Spirit (Gal 5:22-25; 1 Cor 12:4-11, 28-31; Rom 12:4-8; Eph 4:4-16), teaching people to experience the power of the gospel in a fellowship of love.

---

[163] Bruce Riley Ashford, "The Story of Mission: The Grand Biblical Narrative," in *Theology and the Practice of Mission: God, the Church, and the Nations*, ed. Bruce Riley Ashford (Nashville, TN: B & H Academic, 2011), 14-15.

[164] Ott, Strauss, and Tennent, *Encountering Theology of Mission*, 95.

[165] Emmanuel Katongole and Chris Rice, *Reconciling All Things: A Christian Vision for Justice, Peace and Healing* (Downers Grove, IL: InterVarsity Press, 2008), 29.

[166] Ott, Strauss, and Tennent, *Encountering Theology of Mission*, 97.

Through the empowerment of the Holy Spirit such discipleship training that emphasizes how to live reconciled lives will lead to transformation.

An important missiological response to the brokenness of society will be the creation of an authentic community. This community should be one where concern and compassion lead to openness and trust. Above all, it must be a community of love, for love is the most powerful transformational agency in the world (1 John 4:8; 1 Cor 13:4-8, 13).

Change Agent

Societies would remain largely unchanged were no event, crisis, or person to invade their space or time. While it is without argument that crisis occasions are precursors for worldview change, the role of change agents in the process is of even greater significance. New Testament scholar James Packer underscores the importance of the change agent, the preacher in this case, in the experience of conversion:

> We think of conversion as a work of God and so from one standpoint it is, but it is striking to observe that in the three New Testament passages where *epistrepho* is used transitively, of "converting" someone to God; the subject of the verb is not God, as we might have expected, but the preacher (Lk 1:16; Jas 5:19f; Acts 26: 17f).' . . . The task of the preacher is not simply to inform the hearers but to invite them to respond.[167]

In support of this position, examination of the conversion encounters in Acts, referred to in a previous chapter, reveal that although people may have theophanic experiences and be blessed by personal inspiration by studying Scriptures, the role of the

---

[167] James Parker, quoted in Eddie Gibbs, "Conversion in Evangelistic Practice," in *Handbook of Religious Conversion*, ed. Newton Malony and Samuel Southard (Birmingham, AL: Religious Education Press, 1992), 278.

change agent is important (Rom 10:14-15).

Self-Examination

A prerequisite for effective ministry in the goal of worldview transformation must however be self-evaluation. It is important to first remove the beam in one's eye that may hinder proper discernment in the community to be witnessed (Matt 7:5). This process of self-examination by the change agent involves an appraisal of one's own knowledge and understanding of God.[168] Fortunately, God uses only broken people, leaders with a limp (Eph 2:1-3; Rom 7:7-25). He begins by first healing the brokenness in them, and then sends them out to be instruments of healing. Mission agents should be those who have experienced the demonstrated power of God in their lives to bring change (Rom 5:8-11; 2 Cor 5:18).

Active participation in church activities does not translate to the personal intimate relationship with God required for a change agent.[169] For gospel workers to be effective change agents they need to be persons possessed and directed by the Holy Spirit. Their lives must be lives in which spiritual formation is occurring and where there is a total exchange of their ideas and images for Christ's.[170] These change agents must themselves

---

[168]Charles E. Van Engen, "Toward a Contextually Appropriate Methodology in Mission Theology," in *Appropriate Christianity*, ed. Charles H. Kraft (Pasadena, CA: William Carey Library, 2005), 205.

[169]Henry Blackaby and Norman Blackaby, *Called and Accountable: Discovering Your Place in God's Eternal Purpose* (Birmingham, AL: New Hope, 2007), 124.

[170]Dallas Willard, "The Gospel of the Kingdom and Spiritual Formation," in *The Kingdom Life: A Practical Theology of Discipleship and Spiritual Formation*, ed. Alan Andrews (Colorado Springs, CO: NavPress, 2010), 49.

be apprentices who have acquired experiential knowledge derived from walking with the Holy Spirit and not mere book knowledge.[171] Such persons will have begun the journey to freedom by relinquishing control of their lives to Christ.[172] For them, ministry is no longer about right technique or methodology, but inclining their ears to listen daily to the voice of the Lord for His directions for His mission (Isa 30:21). Such Spirit-led witnesses will be effective change agents among the Yorubas who place great value on spiritual realities.

Relationships

Another key element that will enhance the success of the change agent in leading a community to worldview transformation is identifying the opinion leaders with whom to build relationships.[173] This is especially crucial in group-oriented societies such as Africa where decisions are better taken communally rather than individually. Elucidating on the importance of relationship building, Katie Rawson expounds from results of interviews she had conducted that "the most common conversion pattern I have encountered . . . has been conversions to community before conversion to Christ."[174]

---

[171]Keith J. Matthews, "The Transformational Process," in *The Kingdom Life: A Practical Theology of Discipleship and Spiritual Formation*, ed. Alan Andrews (Colorado Springs, CO: NavPress, 2010), 95.

[172]Bill Hull, "Spiritual Formation from the Inside Out," in *The Kingdom Life: A Practical Theology of Discipleship and Spiritual Formation*, ed. Alan Andrews (Colorado Springs, CO: NavPress, 2010), 126.

[173]Katie J. Rawson, "Contextualizing the Relationship Dimension of the Christian Life," in *Appropriate Christianity*, ed. Charles H. Kraft (Pasadena, CA: William Carey Library, 2005), 347.

[174]Ibid., 345.

Jesus, in an atmosphere where He forged intimate relationships with His disciples, was able to transform them to become replicas of Himself. Change agents need to recognize the fact that disciple-making is primarily about apprenticeship. Only as they are willing to be vulnerable will God make their efforts enduring and life-transforming. This will mean establishing relationships of interdependence rather than of superiority or independence.

Mentorship

In recent years the concept of mentorship and its transformational value has become a subject of discussion in leadership. Mentorship is recognized in education as a critical factor responsible for student success and satisfaction.[175] The greatest agency that can bring about transformation, apart from the inner working of the Holy Spirit, is a mentor—one who lives out the values and principles that are taught in words. A mentor is a discipler, a person who: (1) gives up personal will for the will of God, (2) lives a daily life of spiritual sacrifice for God's glory, and (3) strives to be consistently obedient to God.[176]

The Scriptures are the greatest handbook on mentoring and Christ was without doubt the greatest mentor who ever lived. Approaching the subject from a biblical perspective, Gunter Krallmann describes a mentor as one who

> in the biblical sense establishes a close relationship with a protégé and on that basis through fellowship, modeling, advice, encouragement, correction, practical assistance

---

[175] W. Brad Johnson, *On Being a Mentor: A Guide for Higher Education Faculty* (Mahwah, NJ: Lawrence Erlbaum, 2006), 4.

[176] Ted Engstrom and Paul Cedar, *Compassionate Leadership* (Venture, CA: Regal Books, 2006), 64.

and prayer support influences his understudy to gain a deeper comprehension of divine truth, lead a godlier life and render more effective service to God.[177]

The great heroes of Scripture each had a mentor who invested time and effort in shaping them to become the life changers they were. A few examples of mentor-protégé relationship in Scriptures include Moses and Joshua (Exod 24; Num 27), Elijah and Elisha (1 Kgs 19:19-21; 2 Kgs 2), Jehoiada and Joash (2 Kgs 11-12), Peter and Mark, Barnabas and Saul (Acts 4:36; 9:27; 12:25).

Similarly in Yorubaland, gospel workers who establish mentorship relationships will be effective agencies for worldview transformation. Through them relationships of trust will be established, and lives of righteousness and holiness will be mirrored. Yorubaland needs mentors who themselves have Jesus as their Discipler.

In the previous chapter the research findings revealed the overpowering influence of traditional religious Yoruba worldview values, which motivate Adventists to engage in pre-Christian practices of divination and sorcery. To respond to this missiological challenge, a set of core components was considered necessary to thoroughly engage these practices holistically in order to achieve worldview transformation. These included the context, causation, curriculum, conflict, crisis, community, and change agent. Better biblical studies are needed that will provide meaningful explanations to previous worldview assumptions. Adventists also need to encounter the power of the gospel and experience Spirit-led relationships with Christ.

These core components outlined will enable believers in Yorubaland to achieve a

---

[177]Gunter Krallmann, *Mentoring for Mission: A Handbook on Leadership Principles Exemplified by Jesus Christ* (Atlanta, GA: Authentic, 2002), 122.

better quality of Christian life and escape lives of dual allegiance and syncretism, which many have hitherto fallen prey to. This model will empower Yoruba Christians to develop a biblically shaped worldview in place of a magical worldview.

In the following chapter, recommendations and conclusions from this qualitative grounded research project will be presented. The chapter will also highlight the implications from this research project for further academic and ecclesiastical undertakings.

CHAPTER VI

SUMMARY, RECOMMENDATIONS, AND CONCLUSION

Introduction

After over a century of Christian evangelization in Yorubaland the influence of traditional religious practices is still compelling. Among the largest churches in Western, Southern, and Eastern Africa are congregations led by Yoruba founders, who portray a fusion of local worldview with the Christian faith—the result is syncretism of a viral nature. Moreover, this new breed of Christianity has gone international with the largest churches in Eastern and Western Europe having Yoruba clergymen as their founders.

At the core of these syncretistic practices are worldview assumptions that have not been thoroughly engaged or resolved biblically. As a result, practices reflecting dual allegiance are common in this region because people are searching for every means to address their existential needs and the fear their folk religious beliefs engender. Pre-Christian practices such as divination and sorcery involving believers are sad depictions of worldview continuity.

This qualitative research project was undertaken with the aim of bringing transformation from a traditional Yoruba worldview to a biblically shaped worldview. The grounded theory research provides the Seventh-day Adventist Church with a biblical transformational model that should curb practices that induce dual allegiance in the Yoruba context.

Summary

A prime reason why Christians in Yorubaland revert to pre-Christian practices such as divination and sorcery was discovered to be the result of a worldview shaped from childhood and influenced by societal pressure. Triggered by personal crises and the desire to satisfy existential needs or to allay their fears, some Christians resort to consulting diviners. The project discovered that years in the church, education, position, and international travel exposure do not have a significant effect on who visits a diviner.

The study suggested a transformational theory that included explanation, encounter, and experience for transforming the worldview of Yoruba believers. The research findings were consistent with other models of conversion and worldview transformation suggested by scholars such as Hiebert, Kraft, and Rambo, whose models were referred to in chapter 3. Cardinal elements that arose from the study—better biblical explanations, powerful encounters with the gospel, and the need for experiential relationships with Christ—were themes derived from the concepts and categories which emerged from the data.

A missiological model to produce holistic worldview transformation was developed in the final chapter of this project from the grounded theory research. This model comprised the following crucial components: context, causation, curriculum, conflict, crisis, community, and change agent.

Yoruba Culture and Religion

Although Yoruba history revealed the fact that migration led to their present habitations in Western Africa, their exact origins cannot be uncontrovertibly determined.

A notable characteristic among the Yorubas is their urban communal living. Ile-Ife is, however, recognized to be the center of Yoruba civilization.

Accommodation is a dominant feature in Yoruba religious and social life. People are known to display strong attachments to their traditions, yet are quick in adopting modern ways and technology.

Ceremonies play important roles in Yoruba society. Nevertheless, religion stands out as a key defining quality of this people group. Yoruba cosmology consists of a supreme deity, his lieutenants, the divinities, innumerable spirits—munificent and malevolent—and, the ancestors. The Ifa oracle and its priest, the *babalawo*, perform vital functions in the religious, societal, and communal lives of Yoruba people. Fear of witches, enemies, and the ancestors, the inverse side of their gregarious and ebullient lifestyles, lead many to seek the protection and mediation of diviners.

Yoruba society has accommodated and adopted beliefs from the two major monotheistic religions, Islam and Christianity, and indigenized them. However, the Yorubas hold first to their cultural identity before any other religious affiliation. As a result, indigenous Christianity is laced with local worldview assumptions that promote syncretism and dual allegiance.

Conversion in Social Science and Scripture

Conversion and worldview transformation was the focus of chapter 2. A contrast was made between conversion and the deeper level of transformation involving the worldview of believers. It was established that when the worldview of believers was not transformed, the result was the prevalence of dual allegiance and syncretism in worship practices. Tracing the history of conversion through the ages of church history, the study examined the various stages of conversion through a multidisciplinary approach, combining insights from Scripture and from the social sciences. It also examined the factors that influenced conversion in early church history.

Special attention was focused on conversion narratives in the book of Acts in order to gain insights useful for the Yoruba people. Likewise, the study examined the history of conversion in the Yoruba context by missionaries and the early indigenous evangelists. This study concluded with suggested missiological implications regarding worldview transformation in the Yoruba context. While the social sciences provided brilliant insights into the nature, process, and features of conversion, the study affirmed that it was only by using this understanding and applying the power of the Scriptures that worldview transformation could be achieved.

Research on Divination and Sorcery

Apart from the literature review, another aspect of the study entailed conducting field-based grounded theory research on the practice of divination and sorcery among Christians in Yorubaland. The grounded theory research entailed face-to-face interviews with five pastors, three members who had at some time in the past consulted a diviner but had long overcome this practice, and five diviners from different sections of Remo Local Government. Focus group discussions were also conducted as part of the project, comprising members with knowledge regarding the subject of divination and sorcery from Ilishan No.1, and Orile-Iganmu Seventh-day Adventist churches.

Significance of Worldview

An analysis of the findings from the field research revealed the overwhelming influence of the Yoruba worldview as the primary cause for the practices of divination and sorcery. Worldview influence was a theme that ran through the findings from the data collected. Yoruba culture and religion, instilled from birth and inculcated by societal pressure, during periods of personal crises induced the practices of divination as people sought the cause and cure for their predicament.

Unresolved needs and fears prompted people to seek the help of diviners on account of the conviction that misfortune generally has a spiritual cause and that the solution for these misfortunes could be procured from a diviner. Group-centered Yoruba cultures, which emphasized values such as shame and honor and the enjoyment of a good life, encourage people to turn to diviners who they regarded as mediators between the living and other spiritual agencies. For these people the diviner holds the answers to their questions and problems.

Missiological Model for Worldview Transformation

The project culminated with the development of a missiological model for worldview transformation that is to move people from dependence on divination and sorcery to a biblically shaped worldview. It developed the themes that emerged from the grounded theory research and suggested holistic biblical responses to the needs and fear that lead people to consult diviners.

To provide better explanations for the causes and sources of misfortune it is expedient to pay closer attention to the cultural context, the prevailing belief in mystical causation, and to examine previous methods of evangelization. Hence the need for contextualization, the promotion of a biblical, miraculous worldview, and relevant discipleship processes.

The power orientation of the Yoruba culture is one of the reasons why divination holds such a powerful fascination for this people group. To respond to that need it is important for Yoruba people to have an encounter with the power of the gospel, to understand the role of the cosmic conflict metanarrative, and to learn how to respond to personal crisis in biblically appropriate ways. The Adventist doctrine of the Great Controversy in part accounts for the existence of evil spirits and also reveals the sovereignty of God whose will is supreme and whose power is superior to any other power.

Crises create the environment for openness to new experiences and circumstances which can induce and be exploited for worldview transformation. The Holy Spirit can turn crisis situations into powerful life transformational encounters.

The study demonstrated the need for an experiential relationship with Christ through the creation of a new community and the influence of a Spirit-led change agent. A new community of compassion, care, and forgiveness, in addition to a demonstration of authentic Christian faith in the life of a change agent, is one requirement for achieving the goal of worldview transformation.

Recommendations

Divination and sorcery are practices rooted in the worldview of the Yoruba people. To achieve transformation from pre-Christian practices to a biblically shaped worldview, the following recommendations will need to be considered and implemented.

1. Open discussions on these subjects need to be conducted in all churches where such practices are prevalent. These discussions should be directed towards raising awareness of this worldview challenge and introducing the church to biblically appropriate responses to the causes that motivate such practices.

2. Bible conferences should be required on a conference-wide basis where the pernicious nature of these practices will be exposed and careful study of the Bible conducted to respond to the problem. At Bible conferences instruction should be shared on how to implement critical contextualization. This instruction is needed to confront the challenge the local culture poses to Christians in everyday life. If every member of the church family was trained in how to apply these principles, members would be better equipped to live authentic Christian lives.

3. Monthly pastors' meetings should be utilized for encouraging ministers to create environments where members can sense trust, compassion, and concern. Such a climate will motivate persons living in fear or in dire need of support to find help among the members of the church.

4. A special focus should be directed at ensuring that instruction on how worldviews are transformed is included in ministerial formation curricula at every level. Understanding the influence of African Traditional Religion will not be sufficient unless practical guidelines are shared on how to lead people from old to new ways. Specialized, contextually relevant Bible studies need to be developed in Yorubaland that respond to practices such as divination and sorcery. Issues pertaining to worldview practices need to be considered of primary importance rather than doctrinal questions about evolution or the existence of God

5. Preaching and teaching methods need to be adapted to the local context for them to be more effective. Oral and other narrative modes of instruction would be more effective in this context than Western logical patterns with which ministers are trained.

6. Local cultural ceremonies should be transformed into Christian programs and Christian functional substitutes found for rituals and rites of passages infusing them with new meanings and significance. The communal celebratory nature of the people should be incorporated into their joyful service to the Lord.

7. Christian drama, skits and stories should be employed to demonstrate the vanity of trusting in charms and other spiritual tokens. The power and security of putting on Christ should be emphasized, as well as the peace and assurance that come from walking with the Lord. Testimonies of those who have stood firm for the Lord, and of those who have renounced old practices such as divination and sorcery should be incorporated and made a part of worship services.

Conclusion

Divination and sorcery are pre-Christian practices that have plagued the quality of Christian lives among many persons in Yorubaland. Worldview assumptions, which motivate these practices, are triggered by fear and insecurity. In order therefore to transform the worldview of Yoruba people and lead them to deeper faith and a more authentic Christian experience, the Scriptures need to be applied to their needs and fears. A missiological model to respond to the faith crisis that induces dual allegiance must consist of the following components: context, causation, curriculum, conflict, crisis, community, and change agent. This model, developed from a clear understanding of local culture and sound insights of Scripture, will definitely bring about worldview transformation in Yorubaland.

BIBLIOGRAPHY

Abass, Lanre, and Bolatito Asiata. "Suicide and Human Dignity: An African Perspective." *Humanity and the Social Science Journal* 5, no. 1 (2010): 50-62.

Abimbola, Wande. "Ifa: A West African Cosmological System." In *Religion in Africa*, edited by Thomas D. Blakely, Walter E. A. van Beek, and Dennis L. Thomson, 100-116. London: James Currey, 1994.

_____. *Ifa Divination Poetry*. New York: NOK Publishers, 1977.

Adegbite, Ademola. "The Drum and Its Role in Yoruba Religion." *Journal of Religion in Africa* 18, no. 1 (1988): 15-26.

Adeyemi, Lere. "Traditional Music." In *Understanding Yoruba Life and Culture*, edited by Nike S. Lawal, Matthew N. O. Sadiku, and P. Ade Dopamu, 589-598. Trenton, NJ: Africa World Press, 2004.

Adogame, Afe. "Building Bridges and Barricades." *Marburg Journal of Religion* 3, no.1 (March 1998): 1-13. http://archiv.ub.uni-marburg.de/mjr/pdf/1998/adogame 1998.pdf (accessed November 5, 2013).

_____. "Reverse Mission: Europe a Prodigal Continent?" http://www.edinburgh2010.org/fileadmin/files/edinburgh2010/files/News/Afe_ Reverse%20mission_ edited.pdf (accessed October 7, 2011).

Afolayan, Michael O. "Epistemology: Defining and Conceptualizing Knowledge among the Yoruba." In *Understanding Yoruba Life and Culture*, edited by Nike S. Lawal, Matthew N. O. Sadiku, and P. Ade Dopamu, 187-200. Trenton, NJ: Africa World Press, 2004.

Agboola, David. *A History of Christianity in Nigeria: The Seventh-day Adventists in Yorubaland—1914-1964*. Ibadan, Nigeria: Daystar Press, 1987.

Ajayi, Bade. "Ifa Divination: Its Structure and Application." In *Understanding Yoruba Life and Culture*, edited by Nike S. Lawal, Matthew N. O. Sadiku, and P. Ade Dopamu, 113-124. Trenton, NJ: Africa World Press, 2004.

_____. "Riddles and the Child." In *Understanding Yoruba Life and Culture*, edited by Nike S. Lawal, Matthew N. O. Sadiku, and P. Ade Dopamu, 501-511. Trenton, NJ: Africa World Press, 2004.

_____. "The Talking Drum." In *Understanding Yoruba Life and Culture*, edited by Nike S. Lawal, Matthew N. O. Sadiku, and P. Ade Dopamu, 575-588. Trenton, NJ: Africa World Press, 2004.

Akintoye, Stephen A. "From Early Times to the 20th Century." In *Understanding Yoruba Life and Culture*, edited by Nike S. Lawal, Mathew Sadiku, and P. Ade Dopamu, 3-30. Trenton, NJ: Africa World Press, 2004.

Alalade, Adekunle A. *Limiting Factors to the Success of the Seventh-day Adventist Church in Africa: The Nigeria Case Study*. Ibadan, Nigeria: Agbo-Areo Publishers, 2008.

Alana, O. E. "Traditional Religion." In *Understanding Yoruba Life and Culture*, edited by Nike S. Lawal, Matthew N. O. Sadiku, and P. Ade Dopamu, 65-80. Trenton, NJ: Africa World Press, 2004.

Allen, Ronald B. "Numbers." *The Expositor's Bible Commentary*. Grand Rapids, MI: Zondervan, 1990. 2:657-1097.

Amanze, Philemon O., and Michael O. Akpa. *Seventh-day Adventist Response to Spiritism: The Nigerian Experience*. Ilishan Remo, Nigeria: Babcock University Press, 2011.

Aremu, P. S. O. "Between Myth and Reality: Yoruba Egungun Costumes as Commemorative Clothes." *Journal of Black Studies* 22, no. 1 (1991): 6-14. http://jbs.sagepub.com/content/22/1/6.full.pdf (accessed November 25, 2011).

Armstrong, Robert G. "The Etymology of the Word '*Ogun*.'" In *Africa's Ogun: Old World and New*, edited by Sandra T. Barnes, 29-38. Bloomington, IN: Indiana University Press, 1989.

Arnold, Clinton E. *3 Crucial Questions about Spiritual Warfare*. Grand Rapids, MI: Baker Books, 1997.

_____. *The Colossian Syncretism: The Interface between Christianity and Folk Belief at Colossae*. Tubingen, Germany: J.C.B. Mohr, 1995.

_____. *Ephesians: Power and Magic. The Concept of Power in Ephesians in the Light of Its Historical Setting*. Grand Rapids, MI: Baker, 1992.

_____. *Power of Darkness: Principalities and Powers in Paul's Letters*. Downers Grove, IL: InterVarsity Press, 1992.

Asamoah-Gyadu, K. "Health/Healing." *Dictionary of Mission Theology Evangelical Foundations*. Edited by John Currie. Nottingham, England: Inter-Varsity Press, 2007. 143-146.

_____. "Spirit Mission and Transnational Influence: Nigerian-led Pentecostalism in Eastern Europe." *PentecoStudies* 9, no. 1 (2010): 74-96.

Ashford, Bruce R., ed. "The Story of Mission: The Grand Biblical Narrative." In *Theology and the Practice of Mission: God, the Church, and the Nations*, 6-16. Nashville, TN: B & H Academic, 2011.

Ashley, Timothy R. *The Book of Numbers*. The New International Commentary on the Old Testament. Edited by R. K. Harrison. Grand Rapids, MI: William B. Eerdmans, 1993. 3:481.

Aune, D. E. "Divination." *International Standard Bible Encyclopedia*. Edited by Geoffrey W. Bromiley. Grand Rapids, MI: William B. Eerdmans, 1979. 1:971-974.

Awolalu, J. O., and P. A. Dopamu. *West African Traditional Religion*. Ibadan, Nigeria: Onibonoje Press, 1979.

Ayorinde, J. A. "Oriki." In *Sources of Yoruba History*, edited by Saburu O. Biobaku, 63-76. Oxford: Clarendon Press, 1973.

Ayuk, Ayuk. "Portrait of a Nigerian Missionary." *Asian Journal of Pentecostal Studies* 8, no. 1 (2005): 117-141.

Babatunde, Emmanuel. "Traditional Marriage and Family." In *Understanding Yoruba Life and Culture*, edited by Nike S. Lawal, Matthew N. O. Sadiku, and P. Ade Dopamu, 217-235. Trenton, NJ: Africa World Press, 2004.

Bainbridge, William S. "The Sociology of Conversion." In *Handbook of Religious Conversion*," edited by H. Newton Malony and Samuel Southard, 178-191. Birmingham, AL: Religious Education Press, 1992.

Bamgbose, Ayo. "Traditional Folk Tales." In *Understanding Yoruba Life and Culture*, edited by Nike S. Lawal, Matthew N. O. Sadiku, and P. Ade Dopamu, 547-560. Trenton, NJ: Africa World Press, 2004.

Barnes, Sandra T., ed. "The Many Faces of Ogun." In *Africa's Ogun: Old World and New*, 1-26. Bloomington, IN: Indiana University Press, 1989.

Barrett, Leonard. "African Religions in the Americas: The Islands in Between." In *African Religions: A Symposium*, edited by Newell S. Booth, 183-216. New York: NOK Publishers, 1977.

Bascom, William. *Ifa Divination: Communication between God's and Men in West Africa*. Bloomington, IN: Indiana University Press, 1969.

_____. "Some Aspects of Yoruba Urbanism." In *Africa: Social Problems of Change and Conflict*, edited by Pierre L. Van Den Berghe, 369-380. San Francisco, CA: Chandler Publishing Co., 1965.

Bauer, Bruce L. "A Response to Dual Allegiance." *Evangelical Missions Quarterly* 44 (July 2008): 345-346.

Bediako, Kwame. *Christianity in Africa: The Renewal of a Non-Western Religion*. Edinburgh: Edinburgh University Press, 1995.

Beier, Ulli. *The Return of the Gods: The Scared Art of Susanne Wenger*. Cambridge: Cambridge University Press, 1975.

_____. *Yoruba Myths*. Cambridge: Cambridge University Press, 1980.

Beit-Hallahmi, Benjamin, and Michael Argyle. *The Psychology of Religious Behaviour, Belief and Experience*. London: Routledge, 1997.

Blackaby, Henry, and Norman Blackaby. *Called and Accountable: Discovering Your Place in God's Eternal Purpose*. Birmingham, AL: New Hope, 2007.

Bock, Darrell L. "Acts." *Baker Exegetical Commentary on the New Testament*. Grand Rapids, MI: Baker Academic, 2007. 5:535-538.

Booth, Newell S. Jr., ed. "God and the Gods in West Africa." In *African Religions: A Symposium*, 159-181. New York: NOK Publishers, 1977.

Boyd, Gregory. "God at War." In *Perspectives on the Worldwide Christian Movement: A Reader*, edited by Ralph D. Winter and Stephen C. Hawthorne, 100-111. 4th ed. Pasadena, CA: William Carey Library, 2009.

Brant, Howard. *Acts: Courageous Witness in a Hostile World: A Guide for Gospel Foot Soldiers*. Eugene, OR: Wipf and Stock, 2013.

Bremborg, Anna Davidson. "Interviewing." In *The Routledge Handbook of Research Methods in the Study of Religion*, edited by Michael Stausberg and Steven Engler, 310-322. New York: Routledge, 2011.

Brown, Warren S., and Carla Caetano. "Conversion, Cognition, and Neuropsychology." In *Handbook of Religious Conversion*, edited by H. Newton Malony and Samuel Southard, 147-158. Birmingham, AL: Religious Education Press, 1992.

Bruce, F. F. *Acts of the Apostles*. Rev. ed. Grand Rapids, MI: Eerdmans, 1988.

Brueggemann, Dale A. *Numbers*. Cornerstone Biblical Commentary. Carol Stream, IL: Tyndale House, 2008. 2:363-367.

Brueggemann, Walter. "The Book of Exodus." *The New Interpreter's Bible: A Commentary in Twelve Volumes.* Nashville, TN: Abingdon Press, 1994. 1:711-713.

Burnett, David. *Unearthly Powers.* London: MARC, 1988.

Bryant, M. D., and Christopher Lamb, eds. "Conversion, Contours of Controversy and Commitment in a Plural World." In *Religious Conversion: Contemporary Practices and Controversies*, 1-19. London: Cassell, 1999.

Celnik, Anne. "Ethics in the Field." In *Research Training for Social Scientists*, edited by Dawn Burton, 97-108. London: Sage, 2000.

Chamaz, Kathy. *Constructing Grounded Theory: A Practical Guide Through Qualitative Analysis.* Thousand Oaks, CA: Sage, 2006.

Chavalas, Mark W. "Magic." *Baker Theological Dictionary of the Bible.* Edited by Walter A. Elwell. Grand Rapids, MI: Baker Books, 1996. 502-503.

Chester, Stephen J. *Conversion at Corinth: Perspectives on Conversion in Paul's Theology and the Corinthian Church.* London: T & T Clark, 2003.

CIA World Fact Book. "Nigeria." www.cia.gov/library/publications/the-world-factbook/geos/ni.html (accessed November 7, 2011).

Corbin, Juliet. "Strauss' Grounded Theory." In *Routledge International Handbook of Qualitative Nursing Research*, edited by Cheryl Tatano Beck, 169-182. New York: Routledge, 2013.

Creswell, John W. *Research Design: Qualitative, Quantitative, and Mixed Methods Approaches.* Thousand Oaks, CA: Sage, 2014.

Crook, Zeba A. *Reconceptualising Conversion: Patronage, Loyalty and Conversion in the Religions of the Ancient Mediterranean.* Berlin: Walter de Gruyter, 2004.

Crumbley, Deidre H. *Spirit, Structure, and Flesh: Gendered Experiences in African Instituted Churches Among the Yoruba of Nigeria.* Madison, WI: The University of Wisconsin Press, 2008.

Curry, Mary C. "The Yoruba Religion in New York." In *New York Glory: Religions in the City*, edited by Tony Carnes and Anna Karpathakis, 74-87. New York: New York University Press, 2001.

Davidson, Maxwell J. "Angel." *The New Interpreter's Dictionary of the Bible.* Edited by Katharine Doob Sakenfeld. Nashville. Abingdon. 2006. 1:148-155.

Davidson, Judith, and Silvana Di Gregorio. "Qualitative Research and Technology: In the Midst of a Revolution." In *The Sage Handbook of Qualitative Research*, edited by Norman K. Denzin and Yvonna S. Lewin, 627-643. 4th ed. Thousand Oaks, CA: Sage, 2011.

Davis, Witton T. "Magic, Divination and Demonology among the Semites." *American Journal of Semitic Languages and Literature* 14, no. 4 (1898): 242.

Dennett, R. E. *Nigerian Studies or the Religious and Political System of the Yoruba*. London: Frank Cass and Company, 1968.

Denzer, LaRay. "Yoruba Women: A Historiographical Study." *International Journal of African Historical Studies* 27, no. 1 (1994): 1-39.

Denzin, Norman K., and Yvonna S. Lincoln, eds. "Entering the Field of Qualitative Research." In *Strategies of Qualitative Inquiry*. Thousand Oaks, CA: Sage Publications, 1998.

Donkor, Kwabena., ed. *The Church, Culture and Spirits: Adventism in Africa*. Silver Spring, MD: Biblical Research Institute, General Conference of Seventh-day Adventists, 2011.

Dopamu, P. A. "System of Discipline." In *Understanding Yoruba Life and Culture*, edited by Nike S. Lawal, Matthew N. O. Sadiku, and P. Ade Dopamu, 175-185. Trenton, NJ: Africa World Press, 2006.

_____. "Traditional Festivals." In *Understanding Yoruba Life and Culture*, edited by Nike S. Lawal, Matthew N. O. Sadiku, and P. Ade Dopamu, 651-668. Trenton, NJ: Africa World Press, 2004.

Dopamu, P. A., and E. O. Alana. "Ethical Systems." In *Understanding Yoruba Life and Culture*, edited by. Nike S. Lawal, Matthew N. O. Sadiku, and P. Ade Dopamu, 155-173. Trenton, NJ: Africa World Press, 2004.

Dosunmu, Paul A. "A Missiological Study of the Phenomenon of Dual Allegiance in the Seventh-day Adventist Church Among the Yoruba People of Nigeria." PhD diss., Andrews University, 2011.

Drewal, Henry J., and Margaret Thompson Drewal. *Gelede: Art and Female Power among the Yoruba*. Bloomington, IN: Indiana University Press, 1990.

Dybdahl, John L. *The Abundant Life Bible Amplifier: A Practical Guide to Abundant Christian Living in the Book of Exodus*. Boise, ID: Pacific Press, 1994.

Elliston, Edgar J. *Introduction to Missiological Research Design*. Pasadena, CA: William Carey Library, 2011.

Engler, Steven. "Grounded Theory." In *The Routledge Handbook of Research Methods in the Study of Religion*, edited by Michael Stausberg and Steven Engler, 256-274. New York: Routledge, 2011.

Engstrom, Ted and Paul Cedar. *Compassionate Leadership*. Venture, CA: Regal Books, 2006.

Estep, James R. "Developmental Theories: Foe, Friend, or Folly?" In *Christian Formation: Integrating Theology and Human Development*, edited by James R. Estep and Jonathan H. Kim, 37-61. Nashville, TN: B & H Academic, 2010.

Euba, Femi. *Archetypes, Imprecators, and Victims of Fate: Origins and Developments of Satire in Black Drama*. New York: Greenwood Press, 1989.

Fadipe, N. A. *Sociology of the Yoruba*. Ibadan, Nigeria: Ibadan University Press, 1970.

Farrow, Steven S. *Faith, Fancies and Fetich*. London: Society for Promoting Christian Knowledge, 1924.

Ferguson, E. "Religions, Greco-Roman." *The IVP Dictionary of the New Testament*. Edited by Daniel G. Reid. Downers Grove, IL: InterVarsity Press, 2004. 894-896.

Fletcher, M. S. "On Conversion." In *Psychological Insight into the Bible: Texts and Readings*, edited by Wayne G. Rollins and D. Andrew Kille, 226-229. Grand Rapids, MI: William B. Eerdmans, 2007.

Flinn, Frank K. "Conversion: Up from Evangelicalism or the Pentecostal and Charismatic Experience." In *Religious Conversion: Contemporary Practices and Controversies*, edited by Christopher Lamb and M. Darrol Bryant, 51-72. London: Cassell, 1999.

Fowler, James. "Faith Development at 30: Naming the Challenges of Faith in a New Millennium." *Religious Education* 99, no. 4 (2004): 409-410.

_____. *Stages of Faith: The Psychology of Human Development and the Quest for Meaning*. New York: HarperCollins, 1981.

France, R. T. *The Gospel of Matthew*. The New International Commentary of the New Testament. Grand Rapids, MI: William B. Eerdmans, 2007. 1:686.

Gaiser, Frederick J. "A Biblical Theology of Conversion." In *Handbook of Religious Conversion*, edited by H. Newton Malony and Samuel Southard, 93-107. Birmingham, AL: Religious Education Press, 1992.

Gaventa, Beverly R. "Conversion in the Bible." In *Handbook of Religious Conversion*, edited by H. Newton Malony and Samuel Southard, 41-54. Birmingham, AL: Religious Education Press, 1992.

Gehman, Richard. "African Religion Lives." *Evangelical Missions Quarterly* 27, no. 4 (1991): 350-353.

General Conference of Seventh-day Adventists. "West Nigeria Conference: 1914-2009." Office of Archives and Statistics. http://www. adventiststatistics.org/view_ Summary.asp?FieldInstID=1696061 (accessed October 5, 2011).

Gillespie, Bailey V. *Religious Conversion and Personal Identity*. Birmingham, AL: Religious Education Press, 1979.

Glaser, Barney G., and Anselm L. Strauss. *The Discovery of Grounded Theory: Strategies for Qualitative Research*. Chicago, IL: Aldine, 1967.

Gonzalez, Justo L. *Acts: The Gospel of the Spirit*. Maryknoll, NY: Orbis Books, 2001.

Gooren, Henri. *Religious Conversion and Disaffiliation: Tracing Patterns of Change in Faith Practices*. New York: Palgrave Macmillan, 2010.

Grbich, Carol. *Qualitative Data Analysis: An Introduction*. Thousand Oaks, CA: Sage, 2013.

Hagan, Michael G. "Divination." *Baker Theological Dictionary of the Bible.* Edited by Walter A. Elwell. Grand Rapids, MI: Baker Books, 1996. 182-183.

Harris, B. F. "Magic and Sorcery." *The Zondervan Pictorial Encyclopedia of the Bible.* Edited by Merrill C. Tenney and Moises Silva. Grand Rapids, MI: Zondervan, 2009. 4:42-44.

Hertig, Paul. "The Magical Mystery Tour: Philip Encounters Magic and Materialism in Samaria: Acts 8:4-25." In *Mission in Acts: Ancient Narratives in Contemporary Context*, edited by Robert L. Gallagher and Paul Hertig, 103-113. Maryknoll, NY: Orbis Books, 2004.

Hiebert, Paul G. "Conversion and Worldview Transformation." *International Journal for Frontier Missions* 14, no. 2 (April-June 1997): 83-86.

_____. "Conversion in Hinduism and Buddhism." In *Handbook of Religious Conversion*, edited by H. Newton Malony and Samuel Southard, 9-21. Birmingham, AL: Religious Education Press, 1992.

_____. "The Flaw of the Excluded Middle." In *Perspectives: On the World Christian Movement*, edited by Ralph D. Winter and Stephen C. Hawthorne, 407-414. 4th ed. Pasadena, CA: William Carey Library, 2009.

_____. "Spiritual Warfare and Worldview." In *Global Missiology for the 21st Century: The Iguassu Dialogue*, edited by William D. Taylor, 163-177. Grand Rapids, MI: Baker Academic, 2000.

_____. *Transforming Worldviews: An Anthropological Understanding of How People Change*. Grand Rapids, MI: Baker Academic, 2008.

Hiebert, Paul, Daniel Shaw, and Tite Tiénou. *Understanding Folk Religion: A Christian Response to Popular Beliefs and Practices*. Grand Rapids, MI: Baker Books, 1999.

Hughes, R. K. *Acts: The Church Afire*. Wheaton, IL: Crossway Books, 1996.

Hull, Bill. "Spiritual Formation from the Inside Out." In *The Kingdom Life: A Practical Theology of Discipleship and Spiritual Formation*, edited by Alan Andrews, 105-136. Colorado Springs, CO: NavPress, 2010.

Hunter, S. F. "Bar-Jesus." *The International Standard Bible Encyclopedia*. Edited by Geoffrey W. Bromiley. Grand Rapids, MI: William B. Eerdmans, 1979. 1:431.

Idowu, Bolaji E. *African Traditional Religion*. London: SCM Press, 1973.

_____. *Olodumare: God in Yoruba Belief*. London: Longmans, 1962.

Ige, Simeon Abiodun. "The Cult of Ancestors in African Traditional Religion." *An Encyclopedia of the Arts* 10, no. 1 (2006): 26-31. http://assets00.grou.ps/0F2E3C/wysiwyg_files/ FilesModule/mtofolives/ 20100927151021-mitrtueogmxwpafbx/ Ancestors_and_African_ Religions.pdf (accessed November 25, 2011).

Ilesanmi, Simeon O. "From Periphery to Center: Pentecostalism Is Transforming the Secular State in Africa." *Harvard Divinity School* 35, no. 4 (2007): 30-36.

Isichei, Elizabeth. *A History of Christianity in Africa: From Antiquity to the Present*. Grand Rapids, MI: Eerdmans, 1995.

Johnson, Obadiah. *The History of the Yorubas*. London: Routledge and Kegan Paul, 1921.

Johnson, W. B. *On Being a Mentor: A Guide for Higher Education Faculty*. Mahwah, NJ: Lawrence Erlbaum, 2006.

Joines, Karen R. "Magic and Divination." *Mercer Dictionary of the Bible*. Edited by Watson E. Mills. Macon, GA: Mercer University Press. 1990. 539-540.

Kalu, Ogbu, U. "The Gods as Policemen: Religion and Social Control in Igboland." In *Religious Plurality in Africa: Essays in Honour of John S. Mbiti*, edited by Jacob K. Olupona and Sulayman S. Nyang. Berlin: Moulton de Gruyter, 1993.

_____. "Osondu: Patterns of Igbo Quest for Jesus Power." In *The Collected Essays of Ogbu Uke Kalu,* Volume 2, *Christian Missions in Africa: Success, Forment and Trauma*, edited by Wilhemina J. Kalu, Nimi Wariboko, and Toyin Falola. Trenton, NJ: Africa World Press, 2010.

_____. *Power, Poverty and Prayer: The Challenges of Poverty and Pluralism in African Christianity, 1960-1996*. Trenton, NJ: Africa World Press, 2006.

Kasdorf, Hans. *Christian Conversion in Context*. Scottdale, PA: Herald Press, 1980.

Katongole, Emmanuel, and Chris Rice. *Reconciling All Things: A Christian Vision for Justice, Peace and Healing*. Downers Grove, IL: InterVarsity Press, 2008.

Keegan, Sheila. *Qualitative Research: Good Decision Making Through Understanding People, Cultures and Markets*. Philadelphia, PA: Kogan Page, 2009.

King, Noel Q. *African Cosmos: An Introduction to Religion in Africa*. Belmont, CA: Wadsworth Publishing Company, 1986.

Kirkpartrick, Lee A. "Attachment Theory and Religious Experience." In *Handbook of Religious Experience*, edited by Ralph W. Hood Jr., 446-475. Birmingham, AL: Religious Education Press, 1995.

Kistemaker, Simon J. *Acts*. New Testament Commentary. Grand Rapids, MI: Baker Books, 1990. 592-593.

Kleinhans, T. J. "Magic." *The Dictionary of Bible and Religion*. Edited by William H. Gentz. Nashville, TN: Abingdon, 1986. 645-646.

Kraft, Charles H. *Anthropology for Christian Witness*. Marknoll, NY: Orbis Books, 1996.

_____. *Christianity with Power: Your Worldview and Your Experience of the Supernatural*. Ann Arbor, MI: Vine Books, 1989.

_____. ed. "Contextualization and Time: Generational Appropriateness." In *Appropriate Christianity*, 255-273. Pasadena, CA: William Carey Library, 2005.

_____. "Conversion in Group Settings." In *Handbook of Religious Conversion*, edited by H. Newton Malony and Samuel Southard, 259-275. Birmingham, AL: 1992.

_____. *Worldview for Christian Witness*. Pasadena, CA: William Carey Library, 2008.

Kraft, Marguerite G. *Understanding Spiritual Power: A Forgotten Dimension of Cross-Cultural Mission and Ministry*. Maryknoll, NY: Orbis Books, 1995.

Krallmann, Gunter. *Mentoring for Mission: A Handbook on Leadership Principles Exemplified by Jesus Christ*. Atlanta, GA: Authentic Publishing, 2002.

Kreider, Alan. *The Change of Conversion and the Origin of Christendom*. Harrisburg, PA: Trinity Press International, 1999.

Kuemmerlin-McLean, Joanne K. "Magic." *Anchor Bible Dictionary*. Edited by David Noel Freedman. New York: Double Day 1992. 4:464-471.

Kunhiyop, Samuel W. *African Christian Ethics*. Grand Rapids, MI: Zondervan, 2008.

Kunyihop, Samuel W. "Witchcraft." In *Africa Bible Commentary*, edited by Tokunboh Adeyemo. Nairobi, Kenya: Zondervan, 2006.

Ladd, George E. "The Gospel of the Kingdom." In *Perspectives on the World Christian Movement: A Reader*, edited by Ralph D. Winter and Stephen C. Hawthorne, 83-95. 4th ed. Pasadena, CA: William Carey Library, 2009.

Law, Robin. *The Oyo Empire: c. 1600-c. 1836—A West African Imperialism in the Era of the Atlantic Slave Trade*. Oxford: Clarendon Press, 1977.

_____. "Traditional History." In *Sources of Yoruba History*, edited by Saburu O. Biobaku, 25-40. Oxford: Clarendon Press, 1973.

Lawson, Thomas E. *Religions of Africa: Traditions in Transformation*. San Francisco: Harper and Row Publishers, 1984.

Lenski, R. C. H. *The Interpretation of the Acts of the Apostles*. Minneapolis, MN: Augsburg Publishing House, 1964.

Liefeld, W. L. "Divination." *Zondervan Encyclopedia of the Bible*. Edited by Merrill C. Tenney and Moises Silva. Grand Rapids, MI: Zondervan, 2009. 2:163-166.

Lloyd, P. C. "Sacred Kingship and Government among the Yoruba." In *Africa and Change*, edited by Colin M. Turnbull, 289-309. New York: Alfred A Knopf, 1973.

Love, Rick. *Muslims, Magic, and the Kingdom of God*. Pasadena, CA: William Carey Library, 2000.

Lucas, Olumide J. *The Religion of the Yorubas*. Lagos, Nigeria: C. M. S. Bookshop, 1948.

Mackay, John L. *Exodus: A Mentor Commentary*. Ross-shire, UK: Christian Focus Publications, 2001.

Marshall, Catherine, and Gretchen B. Rossman. *Designing Qualitative Research*. 2nd ed. Thousand Oaks, CA: Sage, 1995.

Matson, David L. *Household Conversion Narratives in Acts: Patterns and Interpretation*. Sheffield, UK: Sheffield Academic Press, 1996.

Matthews, Keith J. "The Transformational Process." In *The Kingdom Life: A Practical Theology of Discipleship and Spiritual Formation*, edited by Alan Andrews, 83-104. Colorado Springs, CO: NavPress, 2010.

May, Stan. "Cultures and Worldviews." In *Discovering the Mission of God: Best Missional Practices for the 21st Century*, edited by Mike Barnett, 377-390. Downers Grove, IL: InterVarsity Press, 2012.

Mayers, Marvin K. *Christianity Confronts Culture: A Strategy for Crosscultural Evangelism*. Grand Rapids, MI: Zondervan, 1987.

Mbiti, John S. *Bible and Theology in African Christianity*. Nairobi, Kenya: Oxford University Press, 1986.

_____. *Introduction to African Religion*. 2nd ed. Oxford, UK: Heinemann Educational Books, 1991.

McIntosh, Majorie K. *Yoruba Women, Work, and Social Change*. Bloomington, IN: Indiana University Press, 2009.

McKenzie, Peter. *Hail Orisha!: A Phenomenology of a West African Religion in the Mid-Nineteenth Century*. Leiden, Netherlands: Brill, 1997.

Milne, Bruce M. *Acts: Witnesses to Him*. Ross-shire, UK: Christian Focus Publications, 2010.

Moloye, Olugbemi. "Traditional High Fashion in Transition." In *Understanding Yoruba Life and Culture*, edited by Nike S. Lawal, Matthew N. O. Sadiku, and P. Ade Dopamu, 377-387. Trenton, NJ: Africa World Press, 2004.

Moon, Jay W. *African Proverbs Reveal Christianity in Culture: A Narrative Portrayal of Builsa Proverbs—Contextualizing Christianity in Ghana*. Eugene, OR: America Society of Missiology Monograph Series 5, 2009.

Moreau, A. Scott. "Paul Hiebert's Legacy of Worldview." *Trinity Journal* 30, no. 2 (Fall 2009): 223-233.

Morgan, David L. *Focus Group Guidebook*. Thousand Oaks, CA: Sage, 1998.

Morse, Janice M. "Designing Funded Qualitative Research." In *Strategies of Qualitative Inquiry*, edited by Norman K. Denzin and Yvonna S. Lincoln, 56-85. Thousand Oaks, CA: Sage, 1998.

Mueller, Ekkehardt. "Evil Powers and Occult Practices in the Apocalypse." In *The Church, Culture and Spirits: Adventism in Africa*, edited by Kwabena Donkor, 105-129. Silver Spring, MD: Biblical Research Institute, General Conference of Seventh-day Adventists, 2011.

Na'Allah, Abdul R. "Influence of Traditional Oral Poetry on World Religions." In *Understanding Yoruba Life and Culture*, edited by Nike S. Lawal, Matthew N. O. Sadiku, and P. Ade Dopamu, 561-571. Trenton, NJ: Africa World Press, 2004.

Ngong, David Tonghou. "Salvation and Materialism in African Theology." *Studies in World Christianity* 15, no. 1 (2009): 1-21.

Nock, Arthur D. *Conversion: The Old and New in Religion from Alexander the Great to Augustine of Hippo*. London: Oxford University Press, 1933.

Noll, Stephen F. *Angels of Light and Darkness: Thinking Biblically about Angels, Satan, and Principalities*. Downers Grove, IL: IVP, 1998.

Nurnberger, Klaus. *The Living Dead and the Living God: Christ and the Ancestors in Changing Africa*. Pretoria, South Africa: Cluster Publications, 2006.

Ogunba, Oyin. "Ceremonies." In *Sources of Yoruba History*, edited by Saburi O. Biobaku, 87-110. Oxford: Clarendon Press, 1973.

Ojo, Elizabeth. "Women and the Family." In *Understanding Yoruba Life and Culture*, edited by Nike S. Lawal, Matthew N. O. Sadiku, and P. Ade Dopamu, 237-256. Trenton, NJ: Africa World Press, 2004.

Okafor, Gabriel M. *Development of Christianity and Islam in Modern Nigeria*. Wurzburg, Germany: Echter Verlag, 1992.

Okorocha, Cyril C. "Religious Conversion in Africa: Its Missiological Implications." *Mission Studies* 9, no. 2 (1992): 168-181.

Oladipo, Caleb O. *The Development of the Doctrine of the Holy Spirit in the Yoruba (African) Indigenous Christian Movement*. New York: Peter Lang Publishing, 1996.

Olaniyan, Richard A. "Installation of Kings and Chiefs Past and Present." In *Understanding Yoruba Life and Culture*, edited by Nike S. Lawal, Matthew N. O. Sadiku, and P. Ade Dopamu, 271-282. Trenton, NJ: Africa World Press, 2004.

Olomola, Isola. "Contradictions in Yoruba Folk Beliefs Concerning Post-life Existence: Ado Example." *Journal des Africanistes* 58, no. 1 (1988): 107-118. http://www.persee.fr/web/revues/home/prescript/article/jafr_0399-0346_1988_num_58_1_2255 (accessed November 25, 2011).

Olupona, Jacob K. "The Study of Yoruba Religious Tradition in Historical Perspective." *Numen* 40, no. 3 (1993): 240-273. http://www.jstor.org/stable/3270151 (accessed November 25, 2011).

Onadeko, Tunde. "Yoruba Traditional Adjudicatory Systems." *African Study Monographs* 29, no. 1 (March 2008): 15-28. http://repository.kulib.kyoto-u.ac.jp/dspace/bitstream/2433/66225/1/ASM_29_15.pdf (accessed November 25, 2013).

Onongha, Kelvin. *Pentecostalism in Nigeria: Phenomenon, Prospects and Problems to Mainline Churches*. Ilishan Remo, Nigeria: Babcock Consulting, Babcock University, 2011.

Orcher, Lawrence T. *Conducting Research: Social and Behavioral Science Methods*. Glendale, CA: Pyrczak Publishing, 2005.

Ott, Craig, Stephen J. Strauss, and Timothy C. Tennent. *Encountering Theology of Mission: Biblical Foundations, Historical Developments, and Contemporary Issues*. Grand Rapids, MI: Baker Academic, 2010.

Owomoyela, Oyekan. *Yoruba Trickster Tales*. Lincoln, NE: University of Nebraska Press, 1997.

Owusu-Antwi, Brempong. "Demons and Demonic Activities in the Bible." In *The Church, Culture and Spirits: Adventism in Africa*, edited by Kwabena Donkor, 51-67. Silver Spring, MD: Biblical Research Institute, General Conference of Seventh-day Adventists, 2011.

Oyedepo, David O. *The Healing Balm*. Lagos, Nigeria: Dominion Publishing House, 1996.

Oyetade, Akintunde B. "The Enemy in the Belief System." In *Understanding Yoruba Life and Culture*, edited by Nike S. Lawal, Matthew N. O. Sadiku, and P. Ade Dopamu, 81-95. Trenton, NJ: Africa World Press, 2004.

Paloutzian, Raymond F., Steven L. Jackson, and James E. Crandall. "Conversion Experience, and Belief System, and Personal and Ethical Attitudes." In *Psychology and Christianity: Integrative Readings*, edited by J. Raymond Fleck and John D. Carter, 216-227. Nashville, TN: Abingdon, 1981.

Parratt, John. *Reinventing Christianity: African Theology Today*. Grand Rapids, MI: William B. Eerdmans, 1995.

_____. "Religious Change in Yoruba Society: A Test Case." *Journal of Religion in Africa* 2, no. 1 (1969): 113-128.

Parrinder, Geoffrey. *Africa's Three Religions*. London: Sheldon Press, 1969.

_____. *Religion in an African City*. Westport, CT: Negro Universities Press, 1972.

_____. *West African Psychology*. New York: AMS Press, 1976.

Peace, Richard V. *Conversion in the New Testament: Paul and the Twelve*. Grand Rapids, MI: William B. Eerdmans, 1999.

Peel, J. D. Y. *Aladura: A Religious Movement Among the Yoruba*. London: Oxford University Press, 1968.

_____. *Religious Encounter and the Making of the Yoruba*. Bloomington, IN: Indiana University Press, 2000.

_____. "The Christianization of African Societies." In *Christianity in Independent Africa*, edited by Fashole-Luke, Edward, Richard Gray, Adrian Hastings and Godwin Tasie, 443-454. Bloomington: Indiana University Press, 1978.

Peterson, David G. *Acts of the Apostles*. Grand Rapids, MI: William B. Eerdmans, 2009.

Pettis, Stephen J. "The Fourth Pentecost: Paul and the Power of the Holy Spirit." In *Mission in Acts: Ancient Narratives in Contemporary Context*, edited by Robert L. Gallagher and Paul Hertig, 248-256. Maryknoll, NY: Orbis Books, 2004.

Plummer, Robert L. "The Power of the Gospel." In *Discovering the Mission of God: Best Missional Practices for the 21st Century*, edited by Mike Barnett, 158-170. Downers Grove, IL: InterVarsity Press, 2012.

Pobee, John S. and Gabriel Oshitelu. *African Initiatives in Christianity: The Growth, Gift and Diversities of Indigenous African Churches—A Challenge to the Ecumenical Movement*. Geneva, Switzerland: World Council of Churches Publication, 1998.

Prior, Randall. "Orality: The Not-So-Silent Issue in Mission Theology." *International Bulletin of Missionary Research* 35, no. 3 (2011): 143-147.

Raji, A. O., and H. O. Danmole. "Traditional Government." In *Understanding Yoruba Life and Culture*, edited by Nike S. Lawal, Matthew N. O. Sadiku, and P. Ade Dopamu, 259-270. Trenton, NJ: Africa World Press, 2004.

Rambo, Lewis R., and Charles E. Farhadian. "Converting: Stages of Religious Change." In *Religious Conversion: Contemporary Practices and Controversies*, edited by Christopher Lamb and M. Darrol Bryant, 23-34. London: Cassell, 1999.

Rambo, Lewis R. "The Psychology of Conversion." In *Handbook of Religious Experience*, edited by Ralph W. Hood Jr., 159-177. Birmingham, AL: Religious Education Press, 1995.

_____. *Understanding Religious Conversion*. New Haven, CT: Yale University Press, 1993.

Rawson, Katie J. "Contextualizing the Relationship Dimension of the Christian Life." In *Appropriate Christianity*, edited by Charles H. Kraft, 341-359. Pasadena, CA: William Carey Library, 2005.

Ray, Benjamin C. *African Religions: Symbol, Ritual, and Community*. Englewood Cliffs, NJ: Prentice-Hall, 1976.

_____. "Aladura Christianity: A Yoruba Religion," *Journal of Religion in Africa* 23, no. 3 (1993): 266-291.

Reeves, Keith H. "The Ethiopian Eunuch: A Key Transition from Hellenist to Gentile Mission-Acts 8:26-40." In *Mission in Acts: Ancient Narratives in Contemporary Context*, edited by Robert L. Gallagher and Paul Hertig, 114-122. Maryknoll, NY: Orbis Books, 2004.

Renzetti, Claire M., and Raymond M. Lee. *Researching Sensitive Topics*. Newbury Park, CA: Sage, 1993.

Rice, Andrew. "Mission from Africa." *The New York Times*, 8 April 2009.

Roof, Wade C. "Research Design." In *The Routledge Handbook of Research Methods in the Study of Religion*, edited by Michael Stausberg and Steven Engler, 68-80. London: Routledge, 2011.

Rutayisire, Antoine. "The Rwandan Martyrs of Ethnic Ideology." In *Sorrow and Blood: Christian Missions in Contexts of Suffering, Persecution and Martyrdom*, edited by William David Taylor, Antonia Van der Meer, and Reg Reimar, 245-250. Pasadena, CA: William Carey Library, 2012.

Ryan, Patrick S. *Imale: Yoruba Participation in the Muslim Tradition*. Missoula, MT: Scholars Press, 1978.

Sadiku, Matthew N. O. "The Practice of Christianity." In *Understanding Yoruba Life and Culture*, edited by Nike S. Lawal, Matthew N. O. Sadiku, and P. Ade Dopamu, 125-136. Trenton, NJ: Africa World Press, 2004.

Sanneh, Lammin. *West African Christianity: The Religious Impact*. Maryknoll, NY: Orbis Books, 1983.

Sawyerr, Harry. *God: Ancestor or Creator?—Aspects of Traditional Belief in Ghana, Nigeria and Sierra Leone*. London: Longman, 1970.

Schiltz, Marc. "A Yoruba Tale of Marriage, Magic, Misogyny and Love." *Journal of Religion in Africa* 32, no. 2 (2002): 335-365.

Shaw, R. D. "Qualitative Social Science Methods in Research Design." In *Introduction to Missiological Research Design*, edited by Edgar J. Elliston, 141-157. Pasadena, CA: William Carey Library, 2011.

Sheppard, Michael. *Appraising and Using Social Research in the Human Services: An Introduction for Social Work and Health Professionals*. London: Jessica Kingsley Publishers, 2004.

Simmons, Annette. *Whoever Tells the Best Story Wins: How to Use Your Own Stories to Communicate with Power and Impact*. New York: Amacom Books, 2007.

Sills, M. David. "Mission and Discipleship." In *Theology and Practice of Mission: God, the Church, and the Nations*, edited by Bruce Riley Ashford 186-199. Nashville, TN: B & H Academic, 2011.

Silverman, David. *Interpreting Qualitative Data: Methods for Analysing Talk, Text and Interaction*. Thousand Oaks, CA: Sage, 1993.

Sitton, David. "Glossary of Terms and Resources on Tribal Peoples." *International Journal of Frontier Mission* 15, no. 2 (April-June 1998): 107.

Smith, Gordon T. *Transforming Conversion: Rethinking the Language and Contours of Christian Initiation*. Grand Rapids, MI: Baker Academic, 2010.

Smith, Robert. *Kingdoms of the Yoruba*. London: Methuen & Co., 1969.

Sodiq, Yushua. "The Practice of Islam." In *Understanding Yoruba Life and Culture*, edited by Nike S. Lawal, Matthew N. O. Sadiku, and P. Ade Dopamu, 137-151. Trenton, NJ: Africa World Press, 2004.

Song, C. S. *In the Beginning Were Stories Not Texts: Story Theology*. Eugene, OR: Cascade Books, 2011.

Spencer, F. S. *Acts*. Sheffield, UK: Sheffield Academy Press, 1997.

_____. "Divination." *New Interpreter's Dictionary of the Bible*. Edited by Katharine Doob Sakenfeld. Nashville: Abingdon, 2008. 2:143-145.

_____. *The Gospel of Luke and Acts of the Apostles*. Nashville: Abingdon Press, 2008.

Stern, Mark J., Susan C. Seifert, and Domenic Vitiello. "Migrants, Community, and Culture." *Creativity and Change* (2008): 1-12. http://www.plancincinnati.org/documents/working_groups/Arts_Culture/plans/SIAP%20-%20Migrants.pdf (accessed November 25, 2013).

Stott, John R. W. *The Message of Acts: The Spirit the Church and the World*. Leicester, UK: InterVarsity Press, 1990.

Stratton, Kimberly B. "Magic, Magician." *The New Interpreter's Dictionary of the Bible*. Edited by Katharine Doob Sakenfeld. Nashville: Abingdon, 2008. 3:767-769.

Strauss, Anselm, and Juliet Corbin. "Grounded Theory Methodology: An Overview." In *Strategies of Qualitative Inquiry*, edited by Norman K. Denzin and Yvonna S. Lincoln, 158-183. Thousand Oaks, CA: Sage, 1998.

Strauss, Robert, and Tom Steppen. "Change the Worldview . . . Change the World." *Evangelical Missions Quarterly* 45, no. 4 (October 2009): 463.

Swinton, John, and Harriet Mowat. *Practical Theology and Qualitative Research*. London: SCM Press, 2006.

Taiwo, Rotimi. "Discursive Practices in Nigerian Pentecostal Christian Songs." *California Linguistic Notes* 33, no. 2 (2008): 1-20. http://hss.fullerton.edu/liguistics/cln/Sp %2008%20pdf/Taiwo-CDA.pdf (accessed November 2, 2008).

Talbert, Charles H. *Reading Acts: A Literary and Theological Commentary on the Acts of the Apostles*. New York: Crossroad Publishing Company, 1997.

Tamminen, Kalevi, and Kari E. Nurmi. "Developmental Theories and Religious Experience." In *Handbook of Religious Experience*, edited by Ralph W. Hood Jr., 269-311. Birmingham, AL: Religious Education Press, 1995.

Ter Haar, Gerrie. *Imagining Evil: Witchcraft Beliefs and Accusations in Contemporary Africa*. Trenton, NJ: Africa World Press, 2007.

Thompson, LaNette W. "Tell His Story So That All Might Worship." In *Discovering the Mission of God: Best Missional Practices for the 21st Century*, edited by Mike Barnett, 391-405. Downers Grove, IL: IVP Academic, 2012.

Thorpe, S. A. *African Traditional Religions: An Introduction*. Pretoria, South Africa: University of South Africa, 1991.

Tienou, Tite. "The Training of Missiologists for an African Context." In *Missiological Education for the 21st Century: The Book, the Circle and the Sandals*, edited by J. Dudley Woodberry, Charles Van Engen, and Edgar J. Elliston, 93-100. Maryknoll, NY: Orbis Books, 1996.

Tippett, Alan R. "The Cultural Anthropology of Conversion." In *Handbook of Religious Conversion*, edited by H. Newton Malony and Samuel Southard, 192-205. Birmingham, AL: Religious Education Press, 1992.

Tucker, Austin B. *The Preacher as Storyteller: The Power of Narrative in the Pulpit*. Nashville, TN: B & H Academic, 2008.

Turaki, Yusufu. "Evangelical Missiology from Africa: Strengths and Weaknesses." In *Global Missiology for the 21st Century*, edited by William D. Taylor, 271-283. Grand Rapids, MI: Baker Academic, 2000.

Ukah, Asonzeh. "African Christianities: Features, Promises and Problems." www.ifeas.uni-mainz.de/workingpapers/AP79.pdf (accessed November 2, 2008).

Uka, E. M., ed. "Ethics of African Traditional Religion." In *Readings in African Traditional Religion: Structure, Meaning, Relevance and Future*. Bern, Germany: Peter Lang, 1991.

_____, ed. "Spirituality in African Traditional Religion." In *Readings in African Traditional Religion: Structure, Meaning, Relevance, and Future*, 167-179. Bern, Germany: European Academic Publishers, 1991.

Ullman, Chana. *The Transformed Self: The Psychology of Religious Conversion*. New York: Plenum Press, 1989.

UN Habitat. "The State of African Cities, 2010." www.unhabitat.rog/documents/SOAC10/SOAC-PR1-en.pdf (accessed November 7, 2011).

UN Population Fund. "The State of World Population 2011." New York: UNFPA, 2011, 119.

Van Engen, Charles E. "Peter's Conversion: A Culinary Disaster Launches the Gentile Mission—Acts 10:1-11:18." In *Mission in Acts: Ancient Narratives in Contemporary Context*, edited by Robert L. Gallagher and Paul Hertig, 133-143. Maryknoll, NY: Orbis Books, 2004.

Van Engen, Charles E. "Toward a Contextually Appropriate Methodology in Mission Theology." In *Appropriate Christianity*, edited by Charles H. Kraft, 203-226. Pasadena, CA: William Carey Library, 2005.

Van Wyk, I. W. C. "African Witchcraft in Theological Perspectives." *Hervormde Teologiese Studies* 60, no. 4 (2004): 1201-1228.

Villepastour, Amanda. *Ancient Text Messages of the Yoruba Bata Drum: Cracking the Code*. Surrey, UK: Ashgate Publishing, 2010.

Von Orelli, C. "Sorcery and Soothsaying." *The New Schaff-Herzod Encyclopedia of Religious Knowledge*. Edited by Samuel Macauley Jackson. New York: Funk and Wagnalls Company, 1911. 11:6-9.

Walaskay, Paul W. *Acts*. Louisville, KY: Westminster John Knox Press, 1998.

Walls, Andrew F. *The Cross-Cultural Process in Christian History*. Maryknoll, NY: Orbis Books, 2002.

Walker, Andrew. *Telling the Story: Gospel, Mission and Culture*. London: SPCK, 1996.

Webster, James B. *The African Churches Among the Yoruba: 1888-1922*. Oxford: Oxford University Press, 1964.

Westerlund, David. *African Indigenous Religions and Disease Causation: From Spiritual Beings to Living Humans*. Leiden, Netherlands: BRILL, 2006.

Willard, Dallas. "The Gospel of the Kingdom and Spiritual Formation." In *The Kingdom Life: A Practical Theology of Discipleship and Spiritual Formation*, edited by Alan Andrews, 27-57. Colorado Springs, CO: NavPress, 2010.

Witherington III, Ben. *The Acts of the Apostles: A Socio-Rhetorical Commentary*. Grand Rapids, MI: William B. Eerdmans, 1998.

Yount, William R. *Created to Learn*. Nashville, TN: B & H Publishing Group, 2010.

VITA

Personal

Name: Kelvin Okey Onongha

Date of Birth: January 17, 1965

Marital Status: Married to Juliet Onongha, October 12, 1997

Education

1992	B. A. Religion/Biology (Andrews University, ASWA Campus, Nigeria)
2002	M. A. Religion (Andrews University, ASWA Campus, Nigeria)
2010	DMin., Global Mission Leadership (Andrews University, Babcock University Campus, Nigeria)
2014	PhD. Religion, World Mission Emphasis, Andrews University

Professional

1992	District Pastor, Edo-Delta Mission
1995	Mission Evangelist/Communication Director
1999	Lecturer/Preceptor, Babcock University
2000	Ordination to Gospel Ministry
2000	Secretary, South East Mission
2005	Lecturer, Babcock University
2007	Associate Vice-President Student Development
2012	Adjunct Lecturer, World Missions, Andrews University